ALGEBRA SIMPLIFIED

Basic & Intermediate

Kerry Kauffman

Algebra Simplified Basic & Intermediate

Cover art by Delia Latham

ISBN 978-1-105-04681-0

Preface

Have you taken an algebra class where the teacher writes problems on a blackboard with the steps and answers but fails to explain the steps involved in the solution? If so, then perhaps you tried to teach yourself directly from the textbook. After reading the textbook, are you still confused about the topic? If so, you are among the many students I have worked with in my years as a tutor who have had the same problems. This book helps solve both issues.

Algebra Simplified Basic & Intermediate is intended to assist students in basic to intermediate high school algebra, basic college algebra or anyone interested in learning algebra. The material is presented in textbook style format with each concept illustrated through numerous examples. The examples are solved step by step to explain each concept as simply as possible. Important notes and tips for easier learning are presented in bold throughout the book. The goal is provide students sufficient detail in the examples so they can solve similar problems on their own, which are presented at the end of each section.

At the end of each chapter there is a section titled *Key Terms and Concepts to Review*. Students should understand everything in this section before proceeding to the next chapter. Answers to problem sets along with key steps in the solution of each problem are found at the end of each chapter. The book concludes with an appendix featuring a large section of word problems involving real life situations. Students generally have more difficulty solving word problems, so this section should be of great assistance. Finally, there is a glossary containing all the important terms used throughout the book.

About the Author

Kerry Kauffman has a Bachelor of Science Degree in Statistics from Lehigh University. He has tutored students in algebra, geometry, trigonometry, statistics, calculus, number theory and other courses at the high school and college level since 2000. He has worked on tutoring websites tutorsteach.com, tutornation.com and liveperson.com and has assisted students taking online college courses from Kaplan University and University of Phoenix.

Table of Contents

Chapter 6

Rational Expressions and Functions

Chapter 7

Radical Functions and Variation

Appendix

Chapter 1

Algebra Basics

What is Algebra?

Algebra is a type of mathematics where symbols are used to represent amounts that are unknown. These unknown quantities are generally combined with mathematical operations (addition, subtraction, multiplication, division, square root, cube root, exponents, etc) to form statements that describe the relationship of things that change over a period of time. These statements are expressed using equations, expressions and terms. Problems can be solved by translating words into algebraic equations. The description of a problem using an equation and other mathematical concepts is known as a **mathematical model.** A mathematical model can be used to solve numerous types of problems in every day life.

Suppose you are in a store looking for some new shirts. On one rack a brand is selling for $17.95 per shirt and on another rack you see some shirts selling for $20 for one and $15 for each additional shirt. You decide that you need 4 new shirts, all of the first brand or all of the second brand. What is the total cost and which is the better deal?

You can use a mathematical model to figure out the total cost of the shirts. The procedure to solve such a problem can be thought of in terms of mathematical symbols and variables. A **variable** is an unknown quantity and is typically represented by a letter. In word problems, many times the variable is a letter which relates to the unknown quantity. For example, if you want to solve for the number of objects, use n. If you want the length or width of a two dimension figure, use l and w, respectively.

The model used for the shirts on the first rack is "c equals 17.95 times n" ($c = 17.95n$), where c is the total cost of shirts and n is the number of shirts. For the first brand of shirts, you will pay $17.95 times 4 for a total of $71.80.

The model used for the shirts on the second rack is "c equals 20 plus 15 times a" ($c = 20 + 15a$), where c is the total cost of shirts and a is the number of additional shirts purchased. The first shirt on the second rack is $20 plus $15 times 3 additional shirts for a total of $65. Therefore the second brand is the better buy when you want to buy 4 shirts.

An **algebraic expression** is a combination of variables and/or numbers and mathematical operations (addition, subtraction, multiplication, division, raising to a power and finding a root). In the example above example, an **equation** is used to represent each model because they contain an = sign. It's easy to remember the difference between an expression and an equation. The word "equation" contains the word **equate**, which means equals. An equation can be solved for the given variable or variables.

Words and phrases can represent different mathematical operations. It's important to be able to translate words and phrases into equations when solving word problems.

Here are some common words and phrases and their associated mathematical operation.

sum of, added to, increased, plus: **addition**
minus, decreased, less than, reduced by: **subtraction**
twice, product, multiplied by, times, of: **multiplication**
quotient, divided by, ratio, into: **division**

Types of Numbers

In algebra you will be working with a wide variety of types of numbers. The types of numbers are as follows:

- Integers, natural numbers, whole numbers, rational numbers, irrational numbers.
The set of all of these numbers form what is known as the **real numbers**.

Natural numbers are the easiest to understand. When you count, you start at 1 and count up to 2, 3, 4, 5, etc. assuming you are counting by 1. The *natural* way to count is counting by 1. If you think of natural numbers in that sense, it's easy to remember that the natural numbers are the set of numbers {1,2,3,4,5,6,7,....}

When thinking about **whole numbers** think of the word *whole* and what it means. When thinking of a whole, you think of the entire thing.   The statement *I ate the whole pie* means that there is no portion of the pie left over, no fraction of the pie. The set of whole numbers are basically the set of natural numbers with 0 added to the set {0,1,2,3,4,5,6,7,.....}

Integers include all the whole numbers and also the negative of the whole numbers. So the set of integers are {...., -4, -3, -2, -1, 0, 1, 2, 3, 4, ...}. Even integers are integers that are divisible by 2, whereas odd integers are not divisible by 2.

Rational numbers are all numbers that can be represented as a ratio or a fraction. The easiest way to remember this is notice the word "ratio" is the first 5 letters in rational.

Some examples of rational numbers are as follows:

- 4 1/2, $\frac{16}{5}$, $\frac{7}{2}$, 4.35, -12.2, -35

Terminating and **repeating decimals** are also rational because every terminating and repeating decimal can be written as a fraction.

For example 2/3 = .666.....   (repeating)
2/11 = .18181... (repeating)
45% = 0.45   (terminating)
120.5 = 120 1/2 = 241/2 (terminating)

Irrational numbers are decimals that do not terminate and do not repeat. A very common irrational number is **Pi (π)** = 3.1415926...... many square roots are also irrational numbers, although not all of them. Those that can be simplified such as $\sqrt{9}$ = 3, $\sqrt{16}$ = 4, etc are rational.

Fractions and Decimals

Fractions and **decimals** represent the same thing in different ways. If you have half of a pie, you can represent that as the fraction ½ or the decimal 0.50. A quarter is ¼ or 0.25. Converting decimals to fractions can be done simply by moving the decimal point over to the right until you are past the last digit. That number becomes the numerator of the fraction (the number above the bar in a fraction). Then count how many decimal places you moved and that number represents a power of 10 which goes in the denominator of the fraction (the number under the bar in a fraction). For example, take 0.25 and move the decimal point over 2 places to the right to get 25. The 25 becomes the numerator of the fraction. Since you moved the decimal 2 places, that is the 2nd power of 10 or 10^2 = 10 times 10, which is 100. The fraction becomes 25/100, which is simplified to ¼ since 25 divides evenly into both 25 and 100.

Other examples:

0.001 changed to a fraction becomes 1/1000 since the decimal point is moved 3 places to the right and 10^3 = 1000.

0.37 changed to a fraction becomes 37/100 since the decimal point is moved 2 places to the right and 10^2 = 100.

2.426 changed to a fraction becomes 2426/1000, which can be simplified to 1213/500 since 2 divides evenly into both 2426 and 1000.

To change a fraction to a decimal we must divide the numerator by the denominator. For practice, try long division with fractions and check your work on a calculator.

Sometimes quantities will be represented as percentages, which can be converted to decimals by moving the decimal point over 2 places to the left. An easy way to remember to move the decimal 2 places is to think of the word *cent*. That is part of percent. A cent is 1/100 of a dollar. One percent (represented as 1%) is 1/100 and 100 is 10^2. Recall that the power corresponds to the number of decimal places you move.

Example:

Change 35% to a decimal.

Take 35 and move the decimal point over two places to the left to get 0.35.

• **Note that the decimal point is to the right of the last number in a whole number.**

From this point you can change 0.35 into a fraction.

35/100 simplifies to 7/20 since 5 divides evenly into both 35 and 100.

• **Note that all numbers ending in 5 are divisible by 5.**

Example:

Change 524% to a decimal.

Take 524 and move the decimal point over two places to the left to get 5.24.

From this point you can change 5.24 into a fraction.

524/100 = 131/25 since 4 divides evenly into both 524 and 100.

•**Note if you don't know that 4 divides evenly, you can start by dividing the numerator and denominator by 2 since all even numbers are divisible by 2.**

Fractions with a numerator larger than the denominator are known as **improper fractions**. These fractions can be changed into a **mixed number**, which is a combination of a whole number and a **proper fraction** (numerator is smaller than the denominator).

Example:

18, 32, and 9 are improper fractions.
5   7   4

2 ½, 5 ⁷/₈ and 11 2/3 are mixed numbers.

To change 18/5 into a mixed number you divide 5 into 18, which divides into 3 times since 5 times 3 is 15. The remainder is 3, which turns into 3/5 as a fraction (the remainder over the denominator). The mixed number is then 3 3/5. To change a mixed number to an improper fraction, multiply the denominator of the fraction by the whole number then add the numerator. Take that result and put it over the denominator.

Example:

Change 4 3/7 to an improper fraction.

$7 \cdot 4 = 28$ (denominator times whole number)
$28 + 3 = 31$ (add the numerator)
31/7   (result over the denominator)

    You can also think of a fraction as a **ratio** between two numbers. The fraction 1/3 can also be written as 1 to 3 or 1:3. To find an equivalent fraction you can simply multiply the numerator and denominator by the same number.

Example: (1/3)(2/2) = 2/6
             (1/3)(3/3) = 3/9
             (1/3)(4/4) = 4/12
             (1/3)(5/5) = 5/15

    These are all **equivalent fractions**. This technique is used when you find a common denominator when adding or subtracting fractions.

Example: 2/3 + 5/6

    The common denominator is 6, so we have to get 2/3 into an equivalent fraction with a denominator of 6. We have to multiply the denominator by 2 to get 6, so we must multiply the numerator by 2 as well. Therefore,

2/3 + 5/6
(2/3)(2/2) + 5/6
4/6 + 5/6

    Now we can add the fractions. Finding common denominators for adding and subtracting fractions will be discussed in further detail in a later chapter.

A **proportion** is two or more equivalent fractions equal to each other.

Examples of proportions include

2/3 = x/6,   4/9 = 12/27,   -1/3 = 2/6, x/8 = 6/16 and -3/2 = -12/8.

Prime Numbers, Composite Numbers and Absolute Value

    A **prime number** is a natural number that is only divisible by 1 and itself. Note that 1 is not considered a prime number. The first several prime numbers are 2,3,5,7,11,13,17,19,23,29 and 31.

    A **composite number** is a natural number that is not a prime number, therefore it is divisible by more than just itself and 1. The first several composite numbers are 4,6,8,9,10,12,14,15,16,18,20,21,22,24,25,26,27,28 and 30.

    Absolute value is essentially the distance between a number and 0 and since distance is always a positive number, the absolute value of any number is always positive.

For example:

▪ Take two numbers -4 and 4. The distance from -4 to 0 is 4 and the distance from 4 to 0 is also 4, so the absolute value of -4 and 4 are both 4.

Absolute value is noted as follows:
▪ Absolute value of 4... |4| = 4
  Absolute value of -4... |-4| = 4

Numbers with the same absolute value are known as **opposites**. Notice in the following examples that opposites add to 0.

Examples of opposites:

5 and – 5, 5 + (-5) = 0
14 and -14, 14 + (-14) = 0
-4.3 and 4.3, -4.3 + 4.3 = 0

Review Problems: Set 1

1. The cost of a general admission ticket to a baseball game is $8. Groups of 20 or more receive a $20 discount. Write a mathematical model to describe the total cost of the tickets for groups of 20 or more.

2. Determine whether each of the following is an algebraic expression or an equation.

a. $3x + 6 = 14$
b. $\dfrac{14x - 32}{16}$
c. $6a + 14b - 9c + 1$
d. $y = 13x - 14$
e. $F = 1.8C + 32$

3. Use variables to create a formula for the following scenarios:

a. The perimeter of a rectangle is two times the length plus two times the width.
b. The area of a triangle is one half the length of the base times the height.
c. The sales price is the difference between the regular price and the amount of the discount.

Classify each as rational or irrational

4. 1/3
5. $\sqrt{14}$
6. 3 2/9
7. -14.8
8. 2π
9. 15%

Change each fraction to a decimal and determine whether the decimal is terminating or repeating.

10. 8/9
11. 10/4
12. -4/22
13. 24/40

Change each percent to a decimal.

14. 14%
15. 435%
16. 2.7%

Change each decimal to a fraction.

17. 0.85
18. 0.096
19. 0.146

Change each improper fraction to a mixed number.

   20. 23/4
   21. 42/5
   22. 19/6

Change each mixed number to an improper fraction.

   23. 4 4/7
   24. 10 1/8
   25. 7 2/9

Real Numbers: Operations and Properties

Order of Operations

   A **mathematical operation** is a calculation by mathematical methods which include addition, subtraction, multiplication, division, raising a number to an exponent and taking absolute value. Oftentimes there is more than one operation in an expression. When this occurs there is a specific order in which the expression must be evaluated. First you perform all calculations inside parentheses, then evaluate exponents and roots, multiplication and division from left to right, then addition and subtraction from left to right.
The order of operations is often difficult to remember, but I like to use a system I learned when I was in school. Remember the simple sentence "Please excuse my dear aunt Sally". The first letter in each word is the first letter in each operation in the correct order (PEMDAS).

   Here's a few examples on how evaluating the expression ignoring the order of operations will give a different and wrong answer than using the order of operations.

Example: Evaluate $4+ 3[-1 + 6(5-3)^2 +2]$

   Ignoring the order of operations you could take 4+3 to get 7, then multiply by -1 to get -7. From there add 6 to get -1. Next you would multiply by 5 to get -5, subtract 3 to get --8 then square it to get 64. Finally add 2 to get 66.

Using the correct order of operations you get the following

$4 + 3[-1 + 6(2)^2 +2]$ (evaluate the 5-3 inside the parentheses)
$4 + 3[-1 + 6(4) +2]$ (evaluate 2^2)
$4+ 3[-1 + 24 + 2]$ (multiply 6 and 4)
$4+ 3(25)$ (add the numbers inside the brackets)
$4 + 75$ (multiply 3 and 25)
79 (add 4 and 75)

Example: Evaluate $5(6 + 4)^2 - 3(2 - 3^2) + 4$

   Ignoring the order of operations, you would take 5 times 6 to get 30, then add 4^2 to get 30 + 16 = 46. From there subtract 3 to get 43 then multiply by 2 to get 86. Next, subtract 3^2 which would be 86 – 9 = 77. Finally add 4 to get 81.

Using the correct order of operations you get the following

$5(10)^2 - 3(2- 3^2) + 4$ (evaluate the 6 + 4 inside the parentheses)
$5(10)^2 - 3(2 - 9) + 4$ (evaluate 3^2 inside the parentheses)
$5(10)^2 -3(-7) + 4$ (evaluate 2 – 9 inside the parentheses)
$5(100) - 3(-7) + 4$ (evaluate 10^2)
$500 - 3(-7) + 4$ (multiply 5 and 100)
$500 + 21 + 4$ (multiply -3 and -7)
525 (add 500, 21 and 4)

• Note if you have absolute value symbols in the problem, perform them with the parentheses and other grouping symbols first.

Properties

There are many different properties of real numbers.

The **commutative property of addition** states that changing the order when adding doesn't affect the sum. Think of the word *commute* and how one might commute to work or to school. This means that a person travels to and from work or school. The distance is the same both directions, assuming the same route is taken to and from. So for any two numbers, *a* and *b*, $a + b = b + a$ demonstrates the commutative property.

The **commutative property of multiplication** states that changing the order when multiplying doesn't affect the outcome. For any two numbers *a* and *b*, $a \cdot b = b \cdot a$.

•Note that $a \cdot b$ is often written as *ab*.

The **associative property of addition** states that changing the grouping does not affect the outcome when adding. Think of the meaning of the word *associate*. When one associates with someone, he or she is grouped with that person. Same can be applied here. For any numbers *a,b* and *c*, $a + (b + c) = (a + b) + c$.

The **associative property of multiplication** follows the same principle and states that changing the grouping does not affect the outcome when multiplying. Therefore, $(ab)c = a(bc)$.

The **distributive property of multiplication** shows how multiplication distributes over addition. For numbers *a,b* and *c*, $a \cdot (b + c) = ab + ac$.

The identity properties show how when you add 0 to a number or multiply 1 to a number you still get that number. **Identity property of addition** is $(a + 0 = a)$ and the **Identity property of multiplication** is $(a \cdot 1 = a)$.

The **inverse property of addition** shows how when you add a number to its inverse (or opposite), the result is 0. For example $-4 + 4 = 0$.

The **inverse property of multiplication** shows how when you multiply a number by its inverse, the result is 1. For example $2 \cdot (\frac{1}{2}) = 1$.

Division properties:
$0/a = 0$ for all numbers of *a*, except when *a* is 0
$0/a$ is undefined if $a = 0$
$0/0$ is indeterminate

• Note that for all practical purposes, it's important to understand how to use the property more than knowing the name of the property.

Examples:

Commutative property of addition

$1 + 2 = 2 + 1$
$\quad 3 = 3$

Commutative property of multiplication

$2 \cdot 3 = 3 \cdot 2$
$\quad 6 = 6$

It doesn't matter what order we add or multiply numbers together, the result will be the same.

Associative property of addition

1 + (2 + 3) = (1 + 2) + 3
    1 + 5 = 3 + 3 (from the order of operations, we add what's inside the parentheses first)
      6 = 6

Associative property of multiplication

$2 \cdot (3 \cdot 4) = (2 \cdot 3) \cdot 4$
    $2 \cdot 12 = 6 \cdot 4$ (from the order of operations, we multiply what's inside the parentheses first)
      24 = 24

Grouping the numbers differently does not affect the answer when adding or multiplying numbers.

Distributive property of multiplication

2(4 + 5) = 2(4) + 2(5) (multiplied the 2 by 4 and then 2 by 5)
   2(9) = 2(4) + 2(5) (added numbers inside the parentheses on left side of the = sign)
     18 = 8 + 10   (multiplied on both sides of the equation)
     18 = 18

Identity property of addition and identity property of multiplication

2 + 0 = 2,   2(1) = 2

When you add 0 to a number, the result is that number. When you multiply 1 to a number, the result is that number.

Inverse property of addition and inverse property of multiplication

2 + (-2) = 0,   2(1/2) = 1

    When you add a number to its opposite (the negative of that number), the result is 0. When you multiply a number by its inverse (switch numerator and denominator, ex: 1/3 is inverse of 3/1), the result is 1.

Using Operations With Real Numbers

    When adding two positive numbers, the result is a positive number. When adding two negative numbers, the result is a negative number.

Examples:

4 + 9 = 13, -4 + -9 = -13.

    When subtracting two positive numbers the result will be positive if the smaller number is being subtracted from the larger number and negative if the larger number is being subtracted from the smaller number. The result will be zero is both numbers have the same value.

Examples:

10 - 15 = -5, 15 - 10 = 5, 10 - 10 = 0.

• **If you have trouble with this concept consider a real life situation involving money. If you have $15 and give someone $10, you still have $5 left. If you have $10 and owe someone $15, you can pay $10 and still owe $5, this having a $5 deficit or -$5.**

    When subtracting a negative number, you add the second number to the first. The double negative turns into a positive, or an addition. For example, -4 - (-6) turns into -4 + 6, which is 2. Think of a number line and this might make more sense. Typically when subtracting you move to the left on the number line, the the double negative makes you move right on the number line. It's as if you have two magnets with the negatives against each other, it repels, pushing the magnets in opposite directions.

Examples:

-3 - (-13) = -3 + 13 = 10,   -15 - (-7) = -15 + 7 = -8

Multiplying and dividing numbers with like signs results in a positive number, whereas multiplying and dividing numbers of opposite signs yields a negative number.

Examples:

24/6 = 4, -24/6 = -4, (-2)(-7) = 14, (-2)(7) = -14

If you have a number raised to a positive integer exponent, you multiply that number by itself the number of times indicated in the exponent. If you have a fraction raised to a positive integer exponent, you multiply the fraction by itself the number of times indicated in the exponent.

Examples:

$5^3 = 5 \cdot 5 \cdot 5$

$2^4 = 2 \cdot 2 \cdot 2 \cdot 2$

$(1/3)^3 = (1/3)(1/3)(1/3)$.

$(3/5)^3 = (3/5) \cdot (3/5) \cdot (3/5)$

When multiplying fractions, multiply the numerators and the denominators separately.

Examples:

(4/7)(2/5) = (4 · 2)/(7 · 5) = 28/10

(2/9)(5/6) = (2 · 5)/(9 · 6) = 10/54

When dividing fractions, multiply the first fraction by the **reciprocal** of the second.

Example:

(4/7) / (2/5) = (4/7) · (5/2) = 20/14

(2/9) / (5/6) = (2/9) · (6/5) = 12/45

Evaluating Expressions

Sometimes you will encounter problems where you have to evaluate an expression given the values of the variables in the expression.

Example: Evaluate the expression for x = 4, y = 2 and z = -1

$(2xy - 3)^2 + 5z - 14$

In a problem like this, you substitute the values for the variables into the expression. Sometimes people get confused and put the numbers in the expression but fail to remove the variable. If you think of a *substitute*, it's a replacement. A substitute teacher is in for the regular teacher. Both teachers are not present at the same time. In a sporting event, when a player is put in as a substitute, the other player leaves the game. So in the previous problem, evaluating would be as follows:

$[2(\textbf{4})(\textbf{2}) - 3]^2 + 5(\textbf{-1}) - 14$

Following the order of operations, you get

$(16-3)^2 + 5(-1) - 14$	(parentheses)
$13^2 + 5(-1) - 14$	(parentheses)
$169 + 5(-1) - 14$	(exponent)
$169 - 5 - 14$	(multiplication)
150	(subtraction)

     Learning how to evaluate expressions is important when dealing with formulas involving the **area** of two dimensional geometric figures and the **volume** of three dimensional geometric solids.

<u>Areas of common two dimensional geometric figures</u>

Square Area = s^2 (side squared)

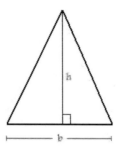

Triangle Area = $(1/2)bh$ (1/2 base times height)
Rectangle Area = LW (length times width)

Trapezoid Area = $(1/2)(b_1 + b_2)h$ (½ times the sum of the bases times the height)

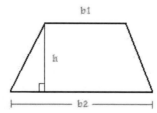

Circle Area = πr^2 (π times radius squared)

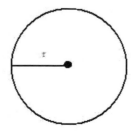

Parallelogram Area = *bh* (base times height)

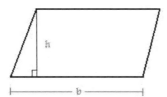

Volumes of common three dimensional geometric solids

Cube Volume = s^3 (side cubed)

Sphere Volume = $(4/3)\pi r^3$ (4/3 times π times radius cubed)

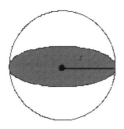

Cylinder Volume = $\pi r^2 h$ (π times radius squared times height)

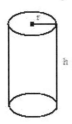

Cone Volume = $(1/3)\pi r^2 h$ (1/3 times π times radius squared times height)

Rectangular Solid Volume = *LWH* (length times width times height)

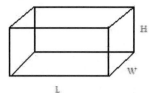

Example: Find the area of a parallelogram with base 4 inches and height 9 inches.

A = bh, where *b* is the base and *h* is the height

$A = (\mathbf{4})(\mathbf{9})$

$A = 36$ inches^2

Example: Find the area of a trapezoid with base lengths 10 and 7 and height 6.

Let $b_1 = 10$, $b_2 = 7$, $h = 6$

Now evaluate the expression

$A = (1/2)(b_1 + b_2)h$

$A = (1/2)(\mathbf{10+7})(\mathbf{6})$

$A = (1/2)(17)(6)$

$A = 3(17)$

$A = 51$ units^2

Example: Find the volume of a cone with radius 4 and height 8

Let $r = 4$, $h = 8$

$V = (1/3)\pi r^2 h$

$V = (1/3)\pi(\mathbf{4})^2(\mathbf{8})$

$V = (1/3)\pi(16)(8)$

$V = (1/3)\pi(128)$

$V = 42\ 2/3\ \pi$ units^3

Example: Find the volume of a cylinder with radius 6 cm and height 11 cm.

$V = \pi r^2 h$

$V = \pi(\mathbf{6})^2(\mathbf{11})$

$V = \pi(36)(11)$

$V = 396\pi$ cm^3

• Note that the units for area are squared and the units for volume are cubed. An easy way to remember this is that when calculating area, you are dealing with two dimensions and dealing with volume you are dealing with three dimensions.

Review Problems: Set 2

Match the expression with the property of real numbers it represents.

1. $a + b = b + a$ a. associative property of addition
2. $a(1) = 1$ b. commutative property of multiplication
3. $a(b+c) = ab + bc$ c. inverse property of multiplication
4. $a + 0 = a$ d. distributive property of multiplication
5. $a(1/a) = 1$ e. commutative property of addition
6. $a + (b + c) = (a + b) + c$ f. identity property of multiplication
7. $ab = ba$ g. inverse property of addition
8. $a + (-a) = 0$ h. identity property of addition

Perform the operations indicated.

9. $-4(12)$
10. $-15 - (-10)$
11. $-10 + 17$
12. $-3(-5)(8)$
13. $48 / (-4)$
14. $(1/2) + (1/3)$
15. $(1/4)(-2/9)$

Evaluate each expression.

16. $10 - 5(6)$
17. $(5 + 2 \cdot 3)^2$
18. $6^2 - 3^3$
19. $4 + 3(6-2) + 5^2$
20. $-6 + 3|4-8|$
21. $-3[14 + 3(6-9) - 4^2]$
22. $\dfrac{3[11 - (7 - 4)^2 + 9]}{2^3 + 5}$

Evaluate each expression for the given variables

23. $x=100y$, solve for x when y is... 4, 8, 10
24. $y=(1/3)x + 10$, solve for y when x is... 6, 12, 36
25. $a = \dfrac{144}{b}$, solve for a when b is... 12, 36, 72
26. $ab + 14$ for $a = 4$, $b = -3$
27. $\dfrac{y_2 - y_1}{x_2 - x_1}$ for $y_2 = 5$, $y_1 = 6$, $x_2 = 11$, $x_1 = 6$
28. $x + xy + xyz$ for $x = 5$, $y = -3$, $z = 7$
29. $p(1 - p) + r(1 - r)$ for $p = 0.4$, $r = -1.6$

Find the area and the volume of the geometric figures described

30. The area of a triangle with base length 10 inches and height 5.2 inches.
31. The volume of a rectangular solid with length 4.2 cm, width 4.5 cm and height 8 cm.
32. The area of a circle with radius 10 inches.
33. The volume of a sphere with radius 6.9 cm.
34. The area of a trapezoid with base lengths 5 inches and 7 inches and height 12 inches.

Simplifying Algebraic Expressions and Combining Like Terms

Many times algebraic expressions are not in the simplest form. We use the properties of real numbers mentioned in a previous section in order to rewrite an expression in a less complex form. For example, suppose we want to simplify the expression $5(20x)$.

Using the associative property of multiplication, we can regroup the 5 with the 20 to get $(5 \cdot 20) \cdot x$. Remember the order of operations and combine what is inside the parentheses to get 100x.

- **Note that $5(20x)$ and $100x$ are the same thing, but $100x$ is the simplest form of the expression.**

We can use the same property when dealing with expressions involving fractions. For example, suppose we want to simplify the expression $(9/2)x(4/3)$.

Using the associative property of multiplication, we can regroup 9/2 with 4/3 to get $(9/2)x(4/3)$. Using the commutative property of multiplication, we get $(9/2)(4/3)x$.

- **Note that the expression is easier to simplify when the fractions are next to each other.**

From here you can multiply first or you can simplify first. I always find it easier to simplify the fractions first then multiply. The way to simplify is to look to see if the numerators divide evenly into the denominators or the denominators divide evenly into the numerators. If not, see if there are any **common factors** between the numerators and denominators. Remember that the **numerator** is the top number in a fraction and the **denominator** is the bottom number in a fraction. A common factor is a number that divides evenly into both numbers.

Notice that the 2 divides evenly into 4 and 3 divides evenly into 9.

$(9/2)(4/3)x = (3/2)(4/1)x$ (when dividing the 3 into the 9)

$\qquad = (3/1)(2/1)x$ (when dividing the 2 into the 4)

$\qquad = (6/1)x$

$\qquad = 6x$

In a problem such as this with small numbers, simplifying is easily done if you multiply first, but with larger numbers, I suggest simplifying the fractions first before multiplying.

Now let's consider problems that combine multiplication and addition. A problem such as $10(2 + 9)$ can be solved in two ways. We can use the order of operations and add the 2 and 9 first to get $10(11) = 110$. We can also use the distributive property. Recall the distributive property states that for real numbers a, b and c, $a(b + c) = ab + bc$.

Using the distributive property, we distribute the 10 across the 2 and the 9 to get

$10(2 + 9) = 10(2) + 10(9)$
$\qquad = 20 + 90$
$\qquad = 110$

We can basically think of the distributive property as the number or term outside of the parentheses being multiplied by each term inside the parenthesis and adding the products. What if there is a problem with a fraction that needs to be distributed? You might be able to simplify first before multiplying. For example, in the problem $(1/4)(8x + 24)$, notice that the 4 divides evenly into both 8 and 24. Simplifying first eliminated the fraction completely and we are left with $2x + 6$.

• Note that you must be able to simplify the 4 with BOTH terms inside the parentheses or you cannot simplify.

What happens in the case where a negative sign (-) is in front of the parentheses in a problem? We can think of it in two ways. Treat it as if it was a -1 and then distribute, or change the sign of every term inside the parentheses.

Example: Simplify - (-4x - 14y + 10).

The negative sign out in front of the parentheses changes the signs of all terms inside the parentheses and the result is 4x + 14y – 10.

By distributing a -1 with every term you will see the same result

(-1)(-4x) + (-1)(-14y) + (-1)(10) = 4x + 14y – 10.

Combining Like Terms

Before knowing how to combine like terms, we need to define that a term is. A **term** is a number, variable, a product of variables or a product of numbers and variables. Examples of terms are 4, 12, -15, x, y, 2x, 5y, 16xy, x^2y^6z, 2/3. In an algebraic expression, terms are separated by an addition sign. (Note you often see subtraction signs in algebraic expressions, but technically it's addition of a negative term) Terms are considered **like terms** if they have the same variables raised to the same power.

Example: 2x and 3x are like terms, 5 and -8 are like terms, x^6y and 4x^6y are like terms but 4x and y, xy and xz and x^2y and y^2x are not like terms.

To combine like terms we add or subtract the terms, keeping the variables and the exponents the same.

Example: Simplify 2x + 6 - 5x + 16 + 4x by combining like terms.

2x, -5x and 4x are like terms
6 and 16 are like terms

Therefore, (2x - 5x + 4x) + (6 + 16) = x + 22

Example: Simplify x^2y + 2yx + 4xy + 5x^2y – 14

(x^2y + 5x^2y) + (2xy + 4xy) – 14

6x^2y + 6xy -14

•**Note that 2yx and 4xy are like terms so the order or the variables can be changed before combining. The order in which the variables appear in these terms does not matter due to the commutative property of multiplication.**

Example: Simplify 5(3y - 2) + 9(y + 4)

In this type of problem, apply the distributive property of multiplication and then combine like terms.

5(3y) + 5(-2) + 9(y) + 9(4)

15y - 10 + 9y + 36

(15y + 9y) + (-10 + 36)

24y + 26

Review Problems: Set 3

Simplify each of the following expressions.

    1. $4(y + 7) - 10y$
    2. $12(3m - 6) + 5m$
    3. $(-6a)(-4b)$
    4. $9(z + 4) - 3(z - 5)$
    5. $-(x - 4y + 12)$
    6. $5(a + b) + 4(3a - 4b) - (a - 7b)$
    7. $3x + 14x - 5x - 2x + 40x$
    8. $(2/3)ab - (-1/2)ab$
    9. $(-3)(4a)(2b)$

Use the distributive property to remove the parentheses.

    10. $-5(a + 4)$
    11. $(2/3)(6p + 12)$
    12. $3.5(8t + 16)$
    13. $12(-6a - 9b + 3c)$
    14. $(2/5)(10x - 15y + 20)$
    15. $(-9x - z)(-11)$
    16. $-(-x - 5)$

Tell whether or not the terms are like terms and if so, combine them.

    17. $5x, -9x$
    18. $6ty, 14tz$
    19. $10xyz, -34xyz$
    20. $-2x^2y, 19x^2y$
    21. $-100x, -9x$
    22. $0.02yz, 1.44yz^2$

Linear Equations and Their Solutions

An equation is a simple mathematical statement showing that two quantities are the same. In a linear equation, the variable will have an exponent of one. The solutions to linear equation are those values for the variable which makes the statement true. All other values for the variable are not part of the solution.

For example, take a simple equation such as $2 + x = 6$. You can use trial and error to find a solution to the equation. If you use 3, you find that $2 + 3 = 6$ is a false statement, therefore 3 is not a value for x which makes the statement true. It's obvious that $x = 4$ is the only value which makes the statement true, so 4 is said to be a solution of the equation.

Example: Is 8 a solution to the equation $2x - 14 = 7$?

To solve, substitute 8 in for x.
      $2(\mathbf{8}) - 14 = 7$
        $16 - 14 = 7$
          $2 \neq 7$, therefore 8 is not a solution of the equation.

Generally speaking, the solutions to the equation will not be known and we'll have to find them. The key to solving linear equations is to isolate the variable to one side of the equation. That means to have only the variable on the one side of the = and numbers on the other side.

Example: Solve $2x + 6 = 10$

The first step is to remove the 6 from the left side of the equation since we want to isolate the variable. To do that, subtract 6 from both sides of the equals sign. Why do we subtract 6 from both sides when we are only concerned about removing the 6 from the left side of the equals sign? We do so to maintain equality.

Suppose there are 2 people playing a card game and at the end of each turn, the players must have the same number of cards. All players start a hand with an equal number of cards. If the first player gets rid of one card on his turn, the other players must each get rid of one card on their turn to maintain an equal number of cards at the end of the turn.

That's the same idea when solving the equation. We must maintain equality on both sides of the equals sign, therefore

$2x + 6 = 10$
$2x + 6 - 6 = 10 - 6$ (subtract 6 to both sides of the equation)
$2x = 4$ (simplify both sides of the equation)
$x = 2$ (divide both sides of the equation by 2)

• **Note that whatever mathematical operation is performed to one side of the = sign must be performed to the other side to maintain equality.**

An easy way to check the answer is to substitute the answer back into the original equation.

$2(2) + 6 = 10$, therefore $4 + 6 = 10$ and $10 = 10$ is a true statement, which confirms the answer.

Example: Solve $(2/3)x = -24$

To isolate the x, divide the equation by 2/3, which is the same as multiplying by the reciprocal of 3/2.

$(3/2)(2/3)x = -24(3/2)$
$x = -72/2$
$x = -36$

Remember to check by substituting -36 into the original equation for x.

We could solve the equation by multiplying by 3 first to remove the fraction and then divide by 2.

$3(2/3)x = -24(3)$ (multiply both sides by 3)
$2x = -72$
$x = -36$ (divide both sides by 2)

• **Note that when isolating the variable, the last step will generally be dividing the entire equation by the number in front of the variable (coefficient).**

Many times we will have to use the distributive property and then combine like terms before solving.
Example: Solve $8(x - 4) = 3(x + 6)$

$8(x) + 8(-4) = 3(x) + 3(6)$ (apply the distributive property on both sides of the =)
$8x - 32 = 3x + 18$
$8x - 32 + 32 = 3x + 18 + 32$ (add 32 to both sides of the = to get all numbers on the right)
$8x = 3x + 50$ (combine like terms on both sides)
$8x - 3x = 3x - 3x + 50$ (subtract 3x from both sides of the = to isolate the x)
$5x = 50$ (combine like terms on both sides)
$x = 10$ (divide both sides by 5)

In problems with more than one fraction with different denominators, you should multiply by a **common denominator**, preferably the **lowest common denominator (LCD)** first.

Example: $(1/3)(9x - 21) = (5/2)(x + 4) + 2$

The problem contains the fractions 1/3 and 5/2. The LCD of these fractions is 6 (an easy way to get a common denominator is simply multiply the denominators of the fractions). The LCD can be found by taking the highest power of each factor and multiplying them together. The factors in the denominators of this problem are 1, 3 and 2. Multiplying these numbers together gives us the LCD of 6. Finding common denominators will be dealt in greater depth in an upcoming chapter.

$6(1/3)(9x - 21) = 6(5/2)(x + 4) + 6(2)$ (multiply both sides of the equation by LCD of 6)
$\qquad 2(9x - 21) = 15(x+4) + 12$
$\qquad\quad 18x - 42 = 15x + 60 + 12$ $\qquad$ (apply the distributive property to both sides of the =)
$\quad 18x - 42 + 42 = 15x + 60 + 12 + 42$ (add 42 to both sides of the = to get all numbers to the right side)
$\qquad\qquad 18x = 15x + 114$ $\qquad\qquad$ (combine like terms on the right side)
$\qquad 18x - 15x = 114$ $\qquad\qquad$ (subtract 15x from both sides to isolate the x on the left side)
$\qquad\qquad\quad 3x = 114$ $\qquad\qquad$ (combine like terms on the left side)
$\qquad\qquad\qquad x = 38$ $\qquad\qquad$ (divide both sides by 3)

Some problems involve manipulating the formula to solve for a particular variable in the formula. The techniques used to solve for a particular variable are the same as used above. The key is isolate the variable to be solved for and have all other quantities on the other side.

Example: Solve $A= (1/2)(b_1 + b_2)h$ for h.

First multiply the equation by 2 to remove the fraction.
$2(A) = 2(1/2)(b_1 + b_2)h$
$2A = (b_1 + b_2)h$
$h = 2A/(b_1 + b_2)$ (divide the equation by $(b_1 + b_2)$)

Example: Solve $F = 1.8(C) + 32$ for C.

$\qquad F - 32 = 1.8(C) + 32 - 32$ (subtract 32 from both sides to isolate C)
$\qquad F - 32 = 1.8(C)$
$(F - 32)/1.8 = C$ (divide both sides by 1.8)

Example: Solve $y = mx + b$ for x.

$y - b + mx$ (subtract b from both sides)
$\dfrac{y - b}{m} = x$ (divide both sides by m to isolate x)

Changing Words to Form an Equation

Many problems in algebra are in the form of words. In order to solve them, we must know how to translate the words into an equation. The key steps in solving a problem are analyzing the problem, forming the equation, solving the equation and checking the result.

Example: John and Steve have been collecting baseball cards since 2003. They now have accumulated a total of 40,000 cards. If John has 7,500 more cards than Steve, how many cards do each of them have?

First, assign a variable for the number of cards that either John or Steve has.

Let x = number of cards that Steve has
Since John has 7,500 more cards than Steve, he has 7,500 + x cards

Number of cards that Steve has   + Number of cards that John has = total number of cards

$\qquad\qquad x \qquad\qquad\qquad + \qquad 7,500 + x \qquad\qquad\qquad = \qquad 40,000$

Solving the equation

$\qquad x + 7,500 + x = 40,000$
$\qquad\quad 2x + 7,500 = 40,000$ $\qquad\qquad$ (combine like terms on the left side)
$\quad 2x + 7,500 - 7,500 = 40,000 - 7,500$ (subtract 7,500 from both sides to isolate the x)
$\qquad\qquad\quad 2x = 32,500$ $\qquad\qquad$ (combine like terms on both sides)

$x = 16{,}250$ (divide both sides by 2)

Steve has 16,250 cards
John has 23,750 cards

Example: Suppose you wish to decide between two long distance phone plans. The first plan is $0.20 for the first minute, $0.07 for each additional minute. The second plan is $0.15 for the first minute and $0.10 for each additional minute. How many minutes must you talk for the first plan to be cheaper than the second plan?

First plan

Let m = total minutes

Cost for first minute plus cost for each additional minute

     0.20   + $0.07(m - 1)$

Second plan

Cost for first minute plus cost for each additional minute

     0.15   + $0.10(m - 1)$

•Note we use m-1 because it's not the total minutes at the second rate, it's all the minutes except the first.

Solving the problem

          $0.20 + 0.07(m - 1) = 0.15 + 0.10(m - 1)$ (set the equations equal to find at how many minutes the cost will be the same)

          $0.20 + 0.07m - 0.07 = 0.15 + 0.10m - 0.10$ (use distributive property on both sides)

          $0.13 + 0.07m = 0.05 + 0.10m$ (combine like terms on both sides)

          $0.13 - 0.13 + 0.07m = 0.05 - 0.13 + 0.10m$ (subtract 0.13 from both sides)

          $0.07m = -0.08 + 0.10m$ (combine like terms on both sides)

          $0.07m - 0.10m = -0.08 + 0.10m - 0.10m$ (subtract $0.10m$ from both sides to isolate m)

          $-0.03m = -0.08$ (combine like terms on both sides)

          $m = 2\ 2/3$ (divide both sides by -0.03)

    Once the phone call reaches 3 minutes, it's cheaper to use the first plan. You can check this by substituting 3 in for m in both equations. When doing so, you get 0.34 for the first plan and 0.35 for the second plan after 3 minutes.

Example: The angles of a triangle are in the ratio of 2 to 4 to 9. Find the measure of each angle.

First, we must know that the sum of the measures of the angles of a triangle is 180.
If each angle was the same measure, we could let x = measure of each angle. Since they aren't the same length we take x and multiply by the numbers in the ratio and assign each to an angle.

    First angle = $2x$

Second angle = 4x
   Third angle = 9x

2x + 4x + 9x = 180 (the sum of the angles of the triangle is 180)
         15x = 180 (combine like terms)
           x = 12   (divide both sides by 15)

To find the measures of each angle substitute 12 into x for each angle.

First angle = 2(12) = 24
Second angle = 4(12) = 48
Third angle = 9(12) = 108

Check by making sure the measures of the angles add up to 180.

24 + 48 + 108 = 180

Example: A school wants to have an enclosed rectangular playground and has enough money in the budget to afford 550 feet of fencing. If the length is to be 125 feet longer than the width, what are the dimensions of the fence that encloses the playground?

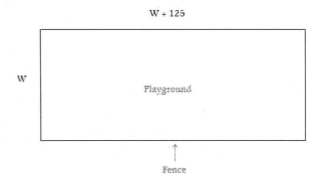

Let W = width of the fence.
The length is W + 125.

2 times the length + 2 times the width = 550

      2(W + 125)   +   2W = 550

     2(W + 125) + 2W = 550
       2W + 250 + 2W = 550   (apply the distributive property)
             4W + 250 = 550   (combine like terms on the left side)
                  4W = 300   (subtract 250 from both sides)
                  W = 75   (divide both sides by 4)
The width of the playground is 75 feet. To find the length, substitute 75 into W in the equation W + 125. Therefore, the length of the playground is 200 feet.
Example: Shawn is 8 years older than Mary. Amanda is 4 years younger than Shawn and Scott is twice as old as Amanda. Their ages combined are 60. How old is each of them?

Since Shawn's age is based off of Mary's and everyone else is based off of that, we set Mary's age = x.

Mary   = x
Shawn = x + 8 (eight more than Mary)
Amanda = (x + 8) - 4 = x + 4 (four younger than Shawn)
Scott = 2(x + 4) (twice Amanda)

Mary's age plus Shawn's age plus Amanda's age plus Scott's age equals 60

$$x \quad + \quad x + 8 \quad + \quad x + 4 \quad + \quad 2(x + 4) \quad = 60$$

Solving the problem.

$$x + x + 8 + x + 4 + 2(x + 4) = 60$$
$$3x + 12 + 2(x + 4) = 60 \quad \text{(combine like terms on the left side)}$$
$$3x + 12 + 2x + 8 = 60 \quad \text{(distributive property)}$$
$$5x + 20 = 60 \quad \text{(combine like terms on the left side)}$$
$$5x + 20 - 20 = 60 - 20 \quad \text{(subtract 20 from both sides to isolate } x)$$
$$5x = 40 \quad \text{(combine like terms on both sides)}$$
$$x = 8 \quad \text{(divide both sides by 5)}$$

Therefore, Mary is 8 years old. We can find the ages of Shawn, Amanda and Scott by substituting 8 into the other equations.

Shawn = 8 + 8 = 16
Amanda = 8 + 4 = 12
Scott = 2(8 + 4) = 24

Check by adding all the ages together to make sure they equal 60.

8 + 16 + 12 + 24 = 60.

Solving Equations With Absolute Value

Recall that the absolute value of x, (noted at $|x|$) is the distance between x and 0. Therefore, the absolute value is always a positive number. When solving equations with absolute value, we have to set up two equations, a positive case and a negative case. For example, $|x| = 5$ means that the positive case is $x = 5$ and the negative case is $x = -5$. The same idea holds true for more complex problems with absolute value.

Example: Solve $|x + 5| = 9$.

The first equation (positive case) is $x + 5 = 9$
$$x = 4$$
The second equation (negative case) is $x + 5 = -9$
$$x = -14$$

Therefore, $x = -14$ or 4

Example: Solve $|2x + 7| = 4x + 2$.

Positive case is $2x + 7 = 4x + 2$
$$2x = 4x + 2 - 7 \quad \text{(subtract 7 from each side)}$$
$$2x = 4x - 5$$
$$2x - 4x = -5 \quad \text{(subtract } 4x \text{ from each side to isolate } x)$$
$$-2x = -5$$
$$x = 5/2 \quad \text{(divide both sides by -2)}$$

Negative case is $2x + 7 = -(4x + 2)$
$$2x + 7 = -4x - 2 \quad \text{(apply the } - \text{ in front of the parentheses on the right side)}$$
$$2x = -4x - 2 - 7 \quad \text{(subtract 7 from both sides)}$$
$$2x = -4x - 9$$
$$2x + 4x = -9 \quad \text{(add } 4x \text{ to both sides)}$$
$$6x = -9$$
$$x = -9/6 \quad \text{(divide both sides by 6)}$$
$$x = -3/2 \quad \text{(simplify -9/6 to -3/2)}$$

Substitute each value for x into the original equation to see which satisfy the equation. There is no need for this substitution on equations without a variable on both sides of the equation.

Check, for $x = 5/2$

$|2(5/2) + 7| = 4(5/2) + 2$
$|(10/2) + 7| = 20/2 + 2$
$|5 + 7| = 10 + 2$
$|12| = 12$, therefore $12 = 12$. So 5/2 is a solution to the equation.
Check for $x = -3/2$

$|2(-3/2) + 7| = 4(-3/2) + 2$
$|(-6/2) + 7| = -12/2 + 2$
$|-3 + 7| = -6 + 2$
$|4| \ne -4$, therefore -3/2 is not a solution to the equation.

•Note that the equation for the positive case is written by simply dropping the absolute value sign. The equation for the negative case is written by dropping the absolute value and taking the negative of the other side of the equation.

Example: Solve $3|4x - 5| = 6x$.

Positive case is $3(4x - 5) = 6x$
$\quad\quad\quad 12x - 15 = 6x$ (apply the distributive property)
$\quad\quad\quad 12x = 6x + 15$ (add 15 to both sides)
$\quad\quad\quad 12x - 6x = 15$ (subtract 6x from both sides)
$\quad\quad\quad 6x = 15$ (combine like terms on left side)
$\quad\quad\quad x = 15/6$ (divide both sides by 6)
$\quad\quad\quad x = 5/2$ (simplify 15/6 to 5/2)

Negative case is $3(4x - 5) = -6x$
$\quad\quad\quad 12x - 15 = -6x$
$\quad\quad\quad 12x = -6x + 15$
$\quad\quad\quad 12x + 6x = 15$
$\quad\quad\quad 18x = 15$
$\quad\quad\quad x = 15/18$
$\quad\quad\quad x = 5/6$

Check the possible solutions to make sure they satisfy the original equation.

For $x = 5/2$, $3|4(5/2) - 5| = 6(5/2)$
$\quad\quad\quad 3|(20/2) - 5| = 30/2$
$\quad\quad\quad 3|10 - 5| = 15$
$\quad\quad\quad 3|5| = 15$
$\quad\quad\quad |5| = (15/3)$
$\quad\quad\quad |5| = 5$
$\quad\quad\quad 5 = 5$, therefore 5/2 is a solution to the equation.

For $x = 5/6$, $3|4(5/6) - 5| = 6(5/6)$
$\quad\quad\quad 3|(20/6) - 5| = 30/6$
$\quad\quad\quad 3|(20/6) - 5| = 5$
$\quad\quad\quad |(20/6) - (30/6)| = 5/3$
$\quad\quad\quad |-10/6| = 5/3$
$\quad\quad\quad |-5/3| = 5/3$
$\quad\quad\quad 5/3 = 5/3$, therefore 5/6 is a solution to the equation.

•Note that when there is a number in front of the absolute value sign, you can drop the absolute value sign and use the distributive property of multiplication.

Example: Solve $5|x + 7| = 3(x - 3)$

Positive case is $5(x + 7) = 3(x - 3)$

$$5x + 35 = 3x - 9 \qquad \text{(apply distributive property to both sides)}$$
$$5x = 3x - 9 - 35 \qquad \text{(subtract 35 from both sides)}$$
$$5x = 3x - 44 \qquad \text{(combine like terms on the right side)}$$
$$5x - 3x = -44 \qquad \text{(subtract 3x from both sides)}$$
$$2x = -44 \qquad \text{(combine like terms on the left side)}$$
$$x = -22 \qquad \text{(divide both sides by 2)}$$

Negative case is $5(x + 7) = -3(x - 3)$

$$5x + 35 = -3x + 9$$
$$5x = -3x + 9 - 35$$
$$5x = -3x - 26$$
$$5x + 3x = -26$$
$$8x = -26$$
$$x = -26/8$$
$$x = -13/4$$

Check both answers to see if they satisfy the original equation.

For $x = -22$, $\quad 5|-22 + 7| = 3(-22 - 3)$
$$5|-15| = 3(-25)$$
$$|-15| = 3(-25)/5$$
$$|-15| = -75/5$$
$$15 \neq -15, \text{ therefore -22 is not a solution to the equation.}$$

For $x = -13/4$, $\quad 5|(-13/4) + 7| = 3[(-13/4) - 3]$
$$5|(-13/4) + (28/4)| = 3[(-13/4) - (12/4)]$$
$$5|15/4| = 3(-25/4)$$
$$|15/4| = (-75/4)/5$$
$$|15/4| = -15/4$$
$$15/4 \neq -15/4, \text{ therefore -13/4 is not a solution to the equation.}$$

Neither are solutions, so there is no solution to this problem.

•Note that for problems with an absolute value on both sides of the equation, solve using the same method. Set up the positive case and the negative case and solve both equations. For example $|x - 3| = |x|$. The positive case is $x - 3 = x$ and the negative case is $x - 3 = -x$.

Review Problems: Set 4

Solve each equation.

1. $6x + 10 = 0$
2. $-5y + 14 = 0$
3. $(3/4)x - 12 = 0$
4. $12 = (-x/9)$
5. $9 - x = 25$
6. $a + 14 = 3a - 10 + a$
7. $3(x + 2) - 2 = -(4 + x) + x$
8. $5(x + 10) = 150$
9. $(1/2)x + 3 = (2/3)x + 14$
10. $b + 25 = 4(b + 12)$

Determine whether the given value is a solution of the equation.

11. $x = 5$ for $3(x + 4) = 35$
12. $x = -2$ for $2x - 10 = -6$
13. $x = 10$ for $(4/5)x - 20 = -12$
14. $x = -8$ for $16 - 2x = 0$
15. $x = \frac{1}{2}$ for $22x + 19 = 30$

Solve each formula for the given variable.

16. $A = (1/2)bh$ for b
17. $P = 2L + 2W$ for W
18. $E = mc^2$ for m
19. $I = Prt$ for r
20. $y = mx + b$ for m

Solve each word problem.

21. Tom and Jack are golfers. Each one hits one shot on the first hole. Jack hit the ball 35 yards longer than Tom. Their combined distance was 625 yards. How far did each hit his shot?
22. The area of a triangle is 30 cm² and the base of the triangle is 6 cm. What is the height of the triangle?
23. Monica paid $51 for 3 shirts. The second shirt was $4 more than the first shirt and the third shirt was $1 more than the second shirt. How much did each shirt cost?
24. A rectangular fence has a perimeter of 400 meters. If the length is 80 meters longer than the width, what are the dimensions of the fence?

Solve each equation.

25. $|x + 4| = 10$
26. $|5x - 6| = 24$
27. $|-2x + 3| = 3x$
28. $6|3x - 1| = 12 (x - 5)$

Key Terms and Concepts to Review

• Mathematical model
• Variable
• Algebraic expression
• Equation
• Real numbers, natural numbers, whole numbers, integers, composite numbers, absolute value, rational numbers, irrational numbers, prime numbers, terminating and repeating decimals
• Properties of real numbers: associative property of addition, associative property of multiplication, commutative property of addition, commutative property of multiplication, distributive property of multiplication, identity property of addition, identity property of multiplication, inverse property of addition, inverse property of multiplication
• Addition, subtraction, multiplication and division of real numbers
• Order of Operations
• Simplifying expressions, evaluating expressions, common denominator
• Translating words into equations
• Solving basic linear equations
•Equivalent fractions, proportions, cross multiplication

Answers To Problem Sets

Problem Set 1
Answers and key steps in solution.

1. $8n - 20$ for $n \geq 20$ (8 dollars times n minus 20 dollar discount, n is the number of people in the group)
2. a. Equation, b. Expression, c. Expression, d. Equation, e. Equation (Equations have = and expressions do not)
3. a. $P = 2L + 2W$ (L = length, W = width) b. $A = (1/2)bh$ (b = base, h = height), c. $s = r - d$ (s = sales price, r = regular price, d = discount)
4. Rational because 1/3 is a fraction.
5. Irrational because $\sqrt{14}$ is non-repeating and non-terminating.
6. Rational because 3 2/9 can be expressed as a fraction (3 2/9 or 29/9).
7. Rational because -14.8 can be expressed as a fraction (-148/10 or -74/5).
8. Irrational because π is irrational, therefore any multiple of π is irrational.
9. Rational because 15% can be expressed as a fraction (15/100 = 3/20).
10. 0.888.... repeating
11. 2.5 terminating
12. -.1818... repeating
13. 0.6 terminating
14. 0.14 (14% = 14/100 = 0.14)
15. 4.35 (435/100 = 4.35)
16. 0.027 (27/100 = .027)
17. 17/20 (85/100 = 17/20 since both 85 and 100 are divisible by 5)
18. 12/125 (0.096 = 96/1000, then divide everything by 8 to get 12/125)
19. 73/500 (0.146 = 146/1000 = 73/500 since both 146 and 100 are divisible by 5)
20. 5 ¾ divide 23 by 4 to get 5 with a remainder of 3. The remainder of 3 is put over the denominator.
21. 8 2/5 divide 42 by 5 to get 8 with a remainder of 2. The remainder of 2 is put over the denominator.
22. 3 1/6 divide 19 by 6 to get 3 with a remainder of 1. The remainder of 1 is put over the denominator.
23. 32/7, $(7 \cdot 4 + 4)/7 = 32/7$
24. 81/8, $(8 \cdot 10 + 1)/8 = 81/8$
25. 65/9, $(9 \cdot 7 + 2)/9 = 65/9$

Problem Set 2
Answers and key steps in solution.

1. e (commutative property of addition)
2. f (identity property of multiplication)
3. d (distributive property of multiplication)
4. h (identity property of addition)
5. c (inverse property of multiplication)
6. a (associative property of addition)
7. b (commutative property of multiplication)
8. g (inverse property of addition)
   (for answers 1 – 8 refer to the properties of real numbers for explanations)
9. -48
10. -5, -15 + 10 = -5
11. 7 -10 + 17 = 17 - 10 = 7
12. 120, (-3)(-5)(8) = 15 · 8 = 120
13. -12
14. 5/6, ½ + 1/3 = 3/6 + 2/6 = 5/6
15. -2/36 or -1/18, (1 · -2)/(4 · 9) = -2/36
16. -20, 10 - 30 = -20
17. 121, $(5 + 6)^2 = 11^2 = 121$

18. 9, $6^2 - 3^3 = 36 - 27 = 9$

19. 41, $4 + 3(4) + 25 = 4 + 12 + 25 = 41$

20. 6, $-6 + 3|-4| = -6 + 3(4) = -6 + 12 = 6$

21. 33, $-3(14 + 3(-3) - 16) = -3(14 - 9 - 16) = -3(-11) = 33$

22. 33/13, $3(11 - 9 + 9)/(2^3 + 5) = 3(11)/(8 + 5) = 3(11)/13 = 33/13$

23. For $y = 4$, $x = 100(4) = 400$, for $y = 8$, $x = 100(8) = 800$, for $y = 10$, $x = 100(10) = 1000$

24. For $x = 6$, $y = (1/3)(6)+10 = 12$, for $x = 12$, $y = (1/3)(12)+10 = 14$, for $x = 36$, $y = (1/3)(36)+ 10 = 22$

25. For $b = 12$, $a = (144)/12 = 12$, for $b = 36$, $a = (144/36 = 4$, for $b = 72$, $a = (144)/72 = 2$

26. 2, $(4)(-3) + 14 = 2$

27. -1/5, $(5 - 6)/(11 - 6) = -1/5$

28. -115, $5 + 5(-3) + 5(-3)(7)$

29. 3.92, $0.4(1 - 0.4) + (-1.6)(1 - (-1.6))$

30. 26 in^2, $A = (1/2)bh = (1/2)(10)(5.2)$

31. 151.2 cm^3, $V = lwh = (4.2)(4.5)(8)$

32. 100π in^2, $A = \pi r^2 = \pi(10)^2$

33. 438.012π cm^3, $V = (4/3)\pi r^3 = (4/3)\pi(6.9)^3$ (answer is rounded to 3 decimal places)

34. 72 in^2, $A = (1/2)(b_1 + b_2)h = (1/2)(5 + 7)(12)$

Problem Set 3
Answers and key steps in solution.

1. $-6y + 28$, $4(y + 7) - 10y = 4y + 28 - 10y = -6y + 28$

2. $41m - 72$, $12(3m - 6) + 5m = 36m - 72 + 5m = 41m - 72$

3. $24ab$ $(-6a)(-4b) = (-6)(-4)(a)(b) = 24ab$

4. $6z + 51$, $9(z + 4) - 3(z - 5) = 9(z) + 9(4) + (-3)(z) + (-3)(-5) = 36 - 3z + 15 = 6z + 51$

5. $-x + 4y - 12$,   (with the negative sign outside the parentheses, change signs of all terms inside)

6. $16a - 4b$, $5(a + b) + 4(3a - 4b) = 5(a) + 5(b) + 4(3a) + 4(-4b) = a + 5b + 12a - 16b - a + 7b = 5a +$ $12a - a + 5b - 16b + 7b = 16a - 4b$

7. $50x$ (all terms are like terms, so combine all terms)

8. $(7/6)ab$, $(2/3)ab - (-1/2)ab = (4/6)ab + (3/6)ab = (7/6)ab$

9. $-24ab$, $-3(4a)(2b) = -3(8ab) = -24ab$

10. $-5a - 20$, $-5(a + 4) = -5(a) + (-5)(4) = -5a - 20$

11. $4p + 8$, $(2/3)(6p + 12) = (2/3)(6p) + (2/3)(12) = 4p + 8$

12. $28t + 56$, $(3.5)(8t) + (3.5)(16) = 28t + 56$

13. $-72a - 108b + 36c$, $12(-6a - 9b + 3c) = 12(-6a) + 12(-9b) + 12(3c) = -72a -108b + 36c$

14. $4x - 6y + 8$, $(2/5)(10x - 15y + 20) = (2/5)(10x) + (2/5)(-15y) + (2/5)(20) = 4x - 6y + 8$

15. $99x + 11z$, $(-9x - z)(-11) = (-9x)(-11) + (-z)(-11) = 99x + 11z$

16. $x + 5$,   (with the negative sign outside the parentheses, change signs of all terms inside)

17. Like, $-4x$

18. Unlike

19. Like, $-24xyz$

20. Like, $17x^2y$

21. Like, $-109x$

22. Unlike

Problem Set 4
Answer and key steps in solution.

1. $\dfrac{-5}{3}$, $6x + 10 = 0$, $6x = -10$, $x = \dfrac{-10}{6} = \dfrac{-5}{3}$

2. $\dfrac{-14}{5}$, $-5y + 14 = 0$, $-5y = 14$, $y = \dfrac{-14}{5}$

3. 16, $(3/4)x = 12$, $4(3/4)x = 4(12)$, $3x = 48$, $x = 16$

4. -108, $12 = -x/9$, $-x = 12(9)$, $x = -108$

5. -16, $9 - x = 25$, $-x = 25 - 9$, $-x = 16$, $x = -16$

6. 8, $a + 14 = 3a - 10 + a$, $a + 14 = 4a - 10$, $a = 4a - 24$, $-3a = -24$, $a = 8$

7. $\dfrac{-8}{3}$, $3(x + 2) - 2 = -(4 + x) + x$, $3x + 6 - 2 = -4 - x + x$, $3x + 4 = -4$, $3x = -8$, $x = \dfrac{-8}{3}$

8. 20, $5(x + 10) = 150$, $5x + 50 = 150$, $5x = 100$, $x = 20$

9. -66, $(1/2)x + 3 = (2/3)x + 14$, $(1/2)x = (2/3)x + 11$, $6((1/2)x = (2/3)x + 11))$, $3x = 4x + 66$, $-x = 66$,
    $x = -66$

10. $\dfrac{-23}{3}$, $b + 25 = 4(b + 12)$, $b + 25 = 4b + 48$, $b = 4b + 23$, $-3b = 23$, $b = \dfrac{-23}{3}$

11. no, $3(5+4) \neq 35$

12. no, $2(-2) - 10 \neq -6$

13. yes, $(4/5)(10) - 20 = -12$

14. no, $16 - (2)(-8) \neq 0$

15. yes, $22(1/2) + 19 = 30$

16. $\dfrac{2A}{h}$, $A = (1/2)bh$, $2A = bh$, $b = \dfrac{2A}{h}$

17. $\dfrac{P - 2L}{2}$, $P = 2L + 2W$, $P - 2L = 2W$, $\dfrac{P - 2L}{2}$

18. $\dfrac{E}{c^2}$, $E = mc^2$, divide by c^2 to get m $= \dfrac{E}{c^2}$

19. $\dfrac{I}{Pt}$, $I = Prt$, divide by Pt to get r $= \dfrac{I}{Pt}$

20. $\dfrac{y - b}{x}$, $y = mx + b$, $y - b = mx$, $\dfrac{y - b}{x}$

21. Jack 330 yards, Tom 295 yards,   x is Tom's distance, so $x + x + 35 = 625$, $2x + 35 = 625$, $2x = 590$,
    $x = 295$. Add 35 to get Jack's distance of 325.

22. Height = 10 cm, $A = (1/2)bh$, $30 = (1/2)(6)h$, $30 = 3h$, $10 = h$

23. \$14, \$18, \$19, x = cost of first shirt, $x + 4$ = cost of 2nd shirt, $x + 5$ = cost of 3rd shirt.
    $x + x + 4 + x + 5 = 51$, $3x + 9 = 51$, $3x = 42$, $x = 14$.

24. Length = 140 meters
    Width = 60 meters $w + w + w + 80 + w + 80 = 400$
                $4w + 160 = 400$
                $4w = 240$
                $w = 60$, therefore the length is $60 + 80 = 140$.

25. 6, -14 $|x + 4| = 10$, $x + 4 = 10$, $x = 6$ or $x + 4 = -10$, $x = -14$

26. 6, -18 $|5x - 6| = 24$, $5x - 6 = 24$, $5x = 30$, $x = 6$ or $5x - 6 = -24$, $5x = -18$, $x = -18/5$

27. 3/5 $|-2x + 3| = 3x$, $-2x + 3 = 3x$, $3 = 5x$, $x = 3/5$ or $-2x + 3 = -3x$, $3 = -x$, $-3 = x$.

28. No solution $6|3x - 1| = 18(x - 5)$, $|3x - 1| = (18/6)(x - 5)$, $3x - 1 = 3(x - 5)$, $3x - 1 \neq 3x - 15$, or
$6|3x - 1| = -18(x - 5)$, $|3x - 1| = (-18/6)(x - 5)$, $3x - 1 = -3(x - 5)$, $3x - 1 = -3x + 15$ $6x - 1 = 15$, $6x = 16$, $x = 16/6$
$= 8/3$. But 8/3 does not satisfy the original equation when substituting back in, therefore 8/3 is not a solution.

Chapter 2

Inequalities, Graphs and Equations of Lines

Inequalities and Solving Inequalities

When working with quantities which are not equal, we use **inequalities** to solve the problem instead of equations. We see situations in every day life which can be expressed using **symbols of inequality**. For example, a product is advertised in a store for $2.50 each with a maximum purchase of 3. A traffic sign reads *speed limit 55 miles per hour* or another sign for littering reads *minimum fine of $99*. These are all examples where inequalities can be used to express the statements.

Inequality Symbols:

$x < y$ means *x is less than y*
$x > y$ means *x is greater than y*
$x \leq y$ means *x is less than or equal to y*
$x \geq y$ means *x is greater than or equal to y*
$x \neq y$ means *x does not equal y*

If we think of the inequalities in terms of a number line, $x < y$ means that x is left of y. If $x > y$ then x is right of y on the number line.

Examples:

$x = -1, y = 4 \ (x < y)$

$x = 6, \ y = -7 \ (x > y)$

An easy way to remember what the symbols mean is to think of the direction of the opening. The direction of the opening is the direction of the greater quantity. Adding the line underneath the symbol makes it greater than or equal to or less than or equal to the other quantity. The sign for *does not equal* ≠ is easy to remember if you think of the line through the equals sign as being "not". You often see signs for no walking, no left turn or no smoking and they all have lines through them.

Inequalities can be represented on a graph and they can also be represented in **set notation** or **interval notation**. A set is a group of objects, or in this case numbers. They are put inside parentheses. For example, if you have a set of numbers from 2 to 8, not including 2 or 8, it would be represented as (2,8). If either 2 or 8 are included in the set, you use a bracket to represent this inclusion. For example, if you want to include 2 and 8 then the representation is [2, 8]. If 2 is included but not 8, then it's [2, 8). If 8 is included but not 2, it is (2, 8].

On a number line, inclusion is noted with a solid dot (•), whereas exclusion is noted with an open dot (▫).

Examples:

(2, 8]

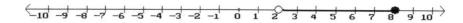

[2, 8)

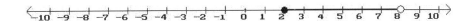

Here's some examples of set notation involving inequalities.

If $y < 5$, set notation is $(-\infty, 5)$
If $y \leq 5$, set notation is $(-\infty, 5]$
If $y \geq 5$, set notation is $[5, \infty)$
If $y > 5$, set notation is $(5, \infty)$

The symbol ∞ stands for **infinity**, which indicates that the interval continues indefinitely in the positive direction. The symbol $-\infty$ stands for **negative infinity**, which indicates that the interval continues indefinitely in the negative direction.

There are some basic properties of inequalities involving mathematical operations.

First take the inequality $a < b$ for any real number a and b. Adding or subtracting the same number from both sides of the $<$ does not change the inequality sign.

Examples: $2 < 4$. Add 3 to both sides of the $<$

$2 + 3 < 4 + 3$
$\quad 5 < 7$

Notice that 5 is less than 7, therefore the inequality sign did not change.

Now subtract 3 from both sides of the $<$

$2 - 3 < 4 - 3$
$\quad -1 < 1$

Once again, the inequality sign did not change.

When multiplying and dividing by the same positive number, the inequality sign does not change. But multiplying and dividing by the same negative number reverses the inequality sign.

Examples: $6 > 3$. Multiply 3 to both sides of the $>$

$6 \cdot 3 > 3 \cdot 3$
$\quad 18 > 9$

Notice that 18 is greater than 9, therefore the inequality sign did not change.

Now divide both sides by 3.

$6/3 > 3/3$
$\quad 2 > 1$

Once again, the inequality sign did not change. Now multiply both sides by -3.
$6 \cdot (-3) > 3 \cdot (-3)$
$\quad -18 > -9$

-18 is not greater than -9 so the sign must be reversed to read $-18 < -9$.

Now divide both sides by -3.

6/(-3) > 3/(-3)
  -2 > -1

-2 is not greater than -1, so the sign must be reversed to read -2 < -1.

• **Note an easy way to remember the sign change is to think of negative as "negating" or "repelling" as in the example with two negative ends of a magnet pushing against each other, moving each magnet in "opposite" directions. So the inequality sign changes to its opposite. (< changes to >, for example)**

When solving linear inequalities, use the properties of real numbers mentioned in the first chapter and the properties of inequalities mentioned above.

Example: Solve $4(2x + 5) > 36$.

$$4(2x +5) > 36$$
$$8x + 20 > 36 \quad \text{(use distributive property of multiplication)}$$
$$8x > 16 \quad \text{(subtract 20 from both sides of the >)}$$
$$x > 2 \quad \text{(divide both sides of the inequality by 8)}$$

In set notation the answer is $(2, \infty)$.

You can check the answer by substituting a value greater than 2 for x in the original problem. For example, substitute 3 in for x.

$$4[2(\mathbf{3}) +5] > 36$$
$$4(6 + 5) > 36$$
$$4 \cdot 11 > 36$$
$$44 > 36. \quad \text{This is a true statement which confirms our answer.}$$

Example: Solve $-3(x + 10) - 4x \geq 19$.

$$-3(x + 10) - 4x \geq 19$$
$$-3x - 30 - 4x \geq 19 \quad \text{(use distributive property of multiplication)}$$
$$-7x - 30 \geq 19 \quad \text{(combine like terms)}$$
$$-7x \geq 49 \quad \text{(add 30 to both sides)}$$
$$x \leq -7 \quad \text{(divide both sides by -7)}$$

Notice that the inequality sign reversed because we had to divide by -7. In set notation the answer is $[-7, \infty)$. To check, choose a number less than or equal to -7 and substitute into the original problem.

Example: Solve $(2/3)(x + 18) < (3/4)x - 2$.

$$(2/3)(x + 18) < (3/4)x - 2$$
$$12(2/3)(x + 18) < 12[(3/4)x - 2] \quad \text{(multiply by common denominator of 12 to remove fractions)}$$
$$8(x + 18) < 9x - 24 \quad \text{(multiply 12 by 2/3 and distribute 12 with (3/4)x - 2)}$$
$$8x + 144 < 9x - 24 \quad \text{(use distributive property of multiplication)}$$
$$8x < 9x - 168 \quad \text{(subtract 144 from both sides)}$$
$$-x < -168 \quad \text{(subtract 9x from both sides)}$$
$$x > 168 \quad \text{(divide by -1, which reverses the sign)}$$

The answer in set notation is $(168 , \infty)$.

Problem Solving With Inequalities

Many times we have to translate words into equations to solve problems with inequalities. Therefore it is important to recognize key words and phrases and how they translate to inequalities. Such statements are as follows:

x is at least *y*	translates to $x \geq y$.
x will exceed *y*	translates to $x > y$.
x is at most *y*	translates to $x \leq y$.
x will not exceed *y*	translates to $x < y$.

Example: Translate the statement into mathematical symbols. The meteorologist forecasts that the high temperature for tomorrow will not exceed 85 degrees.

The temperature, therefore, will be 85 degrees or less. Using *t* to represent temperature, then $t \leq 85$.

Example: A couple wants to rent a social hall for a wedding reception. The cost is $150 for the first two hours and $55 for each additional hour or any part of an hour. How long can the hall be rented if the couple budgeted $350 for this expense?

Solving the problem.

Let *x* = Number of hours after the first two hours.

Cost for first two hours plus cost for additional hours must not exceed $350.

$150	+	55(*x* -2)	$\leq$	$350

$$150 + 55(x - 2) \leq 350$$
$150 + 55x - 110 \leq 350$ (use distributive property of multiplication)
$ 40 + 55x \leq 350$ (combine like terms)
$ 55x \leq 295$ (subtract 40 from both sides)
$ x \leq 5.36$ (divide both sides by 55)

Therefore the social hall can be rented for a maximum of 5 hours.

Compound Inequalities

    A compound inequality is two inequalities joined together with the word *and* or the word *or*. The answer to a compound inequality contains the numbers which satisfy both inequalities. The solution will be the **intersection** between the sets of answers of the two inequalities. The intersection of two sets is all the elements that are in common between the sets. For example the sets (2, ∞) and (-∞, 8) have the numbers 2 to 8 in common, not including 2 and 8. In set notation, the intersection is (2, 8). Intersection between sets is noted with the symbol "∩" between the two sets.

Examples of compound inequalities containing the word *and* are

$y > 6$ and $y < 12$
$x \geq -12$ and $x < 5$
$2x + 4 < 10$ and $3x - 5 > -9$

Solutions to compound inequalities are generally written in interval notation, (ex. (3, 8)) or represented on a graph

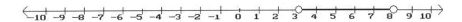

Example: Solve $2x + 6 \leq 8$ and $5(x - 2) > -20$.

Solution:

We start by solving each inequality separately.

$2x + 6 \leq 8$ and $5(x - 2) > -20$

$$2x \leq 2 \qquad\qquad\qquad 5x - 10 > -20$$
$$x \leq 1 \qquad\qquad\qquad\quad 5x > -10$$
$$x > -2$$

In set notation we have (-∞ , 1] ∩ (-2 , ∞), which is the set (-2 , 1].

   If you have trouble obtaining the final answer, you can start by writing out numbers in each set and see what numbers are contained in both sets.   When doing that you'll see that all the numbers between -2 and 1, not including -2, are present in both sets.

The solution can be represented graphically as follows:

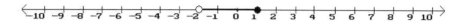

•Note that intervals are said to be *open* if neither endpoints are contained in the solution (a , b). A *half open* interval is open on one end and closed on another (a, b] or [a, b). A *closed* interval contains both endpoints [a, b].

Example: Solve $6x - 8 \geq 16$ and $3x + 6 > 2x + 7$.

Solution:

Solve each inequality separately.

$$6x - 8 \geq 16 \qquad\qquad \text{and} \qquad\qquad 3x + 6 > 2x + 7$$
$$6x \geq 24 \qquad\qquad\qquad\qquad\qquad\quad 3x > 2x + 1$$
$$x \geq 4 \qquad\qquad\qquad\qquad\qquad\qquad x > 1$$

In set notation we have [4, ∞) ∩ (1, ∞)
The graph of the solution is the intersection of the two.

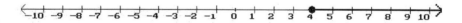

In set notation the solution is [4, ∞).

In some cases, there will be no solution. This happens where there are no numbers which make both parts of the compound inequality true.

Example: Solve $7x < -28$ and $x - 4 > -6$.

Solution:

Solve each inequality separately.

$$7x < -28 \qquad\qquad \text{and} \qquad\qquad x - 4 > -6$$
$$x < -4 \qquad\qquad\qquad\qquad\qquad\qquad x > -2$$

In set notation we have (-∞ , -4) ∩ (-2 , ∞) .

It is clearly evident that there are no numbers which satisfy both inequalities.
   Some compound inequalities contain the word *or*. The solution set for such inequalities are numbers that make either or both of the inequalities true. The solution is said to be the **union** of the two sets and in set notation is noted with the symbol "U".

Some examples of compound inequalities containing the word *or* are

$4x < 10$ or $3(x - 12) > -6$

6x ≤ -18 or 9x + 11 ≥ 10
(2/3)x > 1 or (½)x < -9

Solutions to compound inequalities are generally written in set notation (ex, (-8, -4) U (3, 7)) or represented graphically.

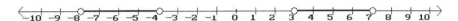

Example: Solve (2/3)x > 1 or (1/2)x < -9.

Solution:

Solve each inequality separately.

   (2/3)x > 1   or   (1/2)x < -2
(3)(2/3)x > (3)(1)   2(1/2)x < 2(-2)
     2x > 3   x < -4
      x > 3/2

In set notation, we have (- ∞, -4) U (3/2, ∞).

Graphically, the solution is represented as follows:

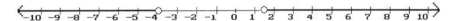

Example: Solve x + 5 ≥ 3 or -x ≥ 7.

Solution:

Solve each inequality separately.

x + 5 ≥ 3   or   -x ≥ -7
    x ≥ -2   x ≤   7

In set notation we have [-2, ∞) U (- ∞, 7]. Notice that this solution is all real numbers and graphically the entire number line would be shaded.

   Inequalities might be written with 2 inequality symbols. Such inequalities are called **double inequalities**. An example of a double inequality is 2 < 4x + 1 < 10. This could also be written as the compound inequality 2 < 4x + 1 and 4x + 1 < 10.

Solving a double inequality is easy. You want to isolate the variable in the middle, so in the above example, you would solve as follows:

    2 < 4x + 1 < 10
2 - 1 < 4x < 10 - 1
    1 < 4x < 9
    ¼ < x < 9/4

The solution would be the set (¼, 9/4).
Example: Solve -10 ≤ -2(x + 2) ≤ 20.

Solution:

   -10 ≤ -2(x + 2) ≤ 20
   -10 ≤ -2x - 4 ≤ 20
-10 + 4 ≤ -2x ≤ 20 + 4

$$-6 \leq -2x \leq 24$$
$$-12 \leq x \leq 3 \quad \text{(dividing by -2 flips the signs)}$$

The solution would be the set [-12, 3].

Solving Inequalities With Absolute Value

The **absolute value inequality** will be in the forms $|x| < h$, $|x| \leq h$, $|x| > h$ or $|x| \geq h$. To solve such equations, we still have a positive and a negative case. To set up the equations for the positive case, we drop the absolute value sign and rewrite the equation . For the negative case, we drop the absolute value sign, take the negative of the other side and reverse the inequality symbol.

Example: Solve $|x| > 5$.

Positive case $x > 5$

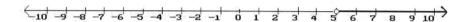

Negative case $x < -5$

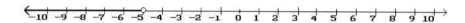

The solution is $(-\infty, -5) \cup (5, \infty)$. The graph of the solution set is

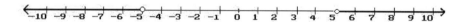

•Note that each case and the solution set is graphed. When we graph inequalities with absolute value, we only need to graph the solution set. Therefore in the upcoming examples, only the solution set will be graphed.

Example: Solve $|2x - 5| < 9$.

Positive case $2x - 5 < 9$
$$2x < 14$$
$$x < 7$$

Negative case $2x - 5 > -9$
$$2x > -4$$
$$x > -2$$

The solution is the set (-2, 7)

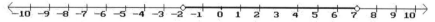

Example: Solve $|3x + 13| \leq 7$

Positive case $3x + 13 \leq 7$
$$3x \leq -6$$
$$x \leq -2$$

Negative case $3x + 13 \geq -7$
$$3x \geq -20$$
$$x \geq -20/3$$

The solution is the set [-20/3, -2]

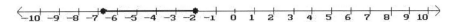

Example: Solve |4x - 3| ≥ 13

Positive case 4x - 3 ≥ 13
                    4x ≥ 16
                      x ≥ 4

Negative case 4x - 3 ≤ -13
                    4x ≤ -10
                      x ≤ -10/4
                      x ≤ -5/2

The solution is (-∞, -5/2] U [4, ∞)

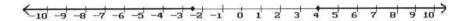

Example: Solve |-3(x + 4)| ≤ -11

Positive case -3(x + 4) ≤ -11
                  -3x - 12 ≤ -11
                      -3x ≤ 1
                        x ≥ -1/3

Negative case -3(x + 4) ≥ 11
                  -3x - 12 ≥ 11
                      -3x ≥ 23
                        x ≤ -23/3

The solution is (-∞, -23/3] U [-1/3, ∞)

Review Problems: Set 1

Solve each inequality and represent the answer in set notation.

1. 4x > 12
2. -6x < 24
3. (2/5) < (8/5)x
4. -3x + 5 ≤ 14
5. -2y + 6 ≥ 32
6. 3(y − 3) < 2y + 4
7. (¼)x + 8 > (1/2)x + 10
8. x < 5 and x > -3
9. y ≤ 14 and y ≥ -9
10. x + 3 < 3x - 1 and 4x - 2 < 2x
11. 2x + 4 < 0 and -4x > -20
12. x ≤ -5 or x > 6
13. y > 11 or y ≤ -2
14. 5x < -15 or (2/3)x > 8

15. $-4 < 2x < 8$
16. $-2 \le 3(x + 2) \le 5$
17. $|x| < 5$
18. $|-3x| > 6$
19. $|2x + 5| \le 12$
20. $|-5x - 4| \ge 18$

The Rectangular Coordinate System

When thinking of the **rectangular coordinate system**, imagine a city that is set up with all streets running north to south and east to west. The streets running north to south are equal distance and parallel to each other as are the streets running east to west. Drawing the streets on the graph would show a grid with equal sized squares. In algebra, the vertical (north to south) line straight through the middle of the is known as the **y-axis** and the horizontal (east to west) line straight through the middle is known as the **x-axis.** The center of the graph is known as the **origin**.

There are four sections of the rectangular coordinate system created by the intersection of the x and y axis. Each section is known as a **quadrant**. It's easy to remember by thinking of "quad", which means four. The quadrants are named I, II, III and IV, starting in the upper right and rotating counter clockwise.

Think of the layout of a city. The north to south streets start at 1 and go to 10 and are avenues. The east to west streets start at 1 and go to 10 and are boulevards. Suppose John lives at the intersection of East 5th boulevard and North 8th avenue and Susie lives at the intersection of West 6th boulevard and South 2nd avenue. You can plot John's location on the graph by staring at the origin, moving right to East 5th boulevard and then up to North 8th street. Likewise, you can plot Susie's location by starting at the origin and moving left to West 6th boulevard and South to 2nd street. Notice how John's location is labeled as (5, 8) in the following graph. This point is called an **ordered pair**. Each number in the ordered pair is known as a **coordinate.**

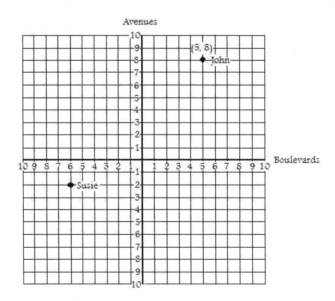

The first number in an ordered pair is the **x- coordinate** and the second number in an ordered pair is the **y-coordinate**.

•**Note that a coordinate is in the form (x, y).**

Coordinates on the x-axis are negative left of the origin and positive right of the origin. Coordinates on the y-axis are negative below the origin and positive above the origin. The coordinate of the origin is (0,0) since it is the middle of the graph. From this information, we can tell what quadrant a point falls. If both coordinates are positive, the point falls in the first quadrant. If both coordinates are negative, the point falls in the third quadrant. If x is negative and y is positive, the point falls in the second quadrant. If x is positive and y is negative, the point falls in the fourth quadrant.

Examples:
(-2, 4) falls in the second quadrant.
(4, 10) falls in the first quadrant.
(-8, -3) falls in the third quadrant.
(9, -6) falls in the fourth quadrant.

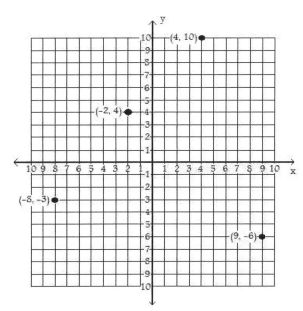

Graphing Linear Equations

A linear equation is an equation with an x and y variable both to the first power. An example of a linear equation is $y = 4x + 7$. Another example is $3x + 4y = 10$. If the linear equation is written in the form $Ax + By = C$ (A, B and C are numbers), then it's called **general form.** The graph of a linear equation will be a straight line.

There are several ways to graph a linear equation. The first way is to pick values for either x or y, substitute them into the equation and solve for the other variable. You need only two ordered pairs to graph a line.

Example: Graph $2x + 4y = 12$.

Many times it's easiest to pick 0 for x and then 0 for y to get the two points.

If $x = 0$, then $2(\mathbf{0}) + 4y = 12$
$$4y = 12$$
$$y = 3$$

The first point to place on the graph is (0, 3).

If $y = 0$, then $2x + 4(\mathbf{0}) = 12$
$$2x = 12$$
$$x = 6$$

The second point to place on the graph is (6, 0).

Draw a straight line through the two points to complete the graph of the line.

•**Note the two coordinates on the graph. One is on the x-axis and one is on the y-axis. Those coordinates are called the x-intercept and y-intercept because the line crosses the x and y axis at those points.** Sometimes it's easier to choose values for x and y other than 0 because it will avoid fractions, which are more difficult to plot on the graph.

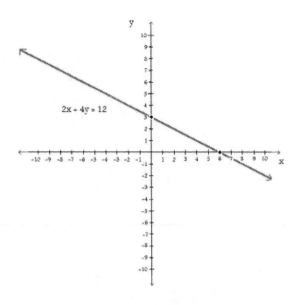

$2x + 4y = 12$

Example: Graph $5x - 2y = 9$.

If $x = 1$, then $5(\mathbf{1}) - 2y = 9$
$5 - 2y = 9$
$-2y = 4$
$y = -2$

The first point to place on the graph is (1, -2).

If $y = 3$, then $5x - 2(\mathbf{3}) = 9$
$5x - 6 = 9$
$5x = 15$
$x = 3$

The second point to place on the graph is (3, 3).
Now connect the dots to draw the line.

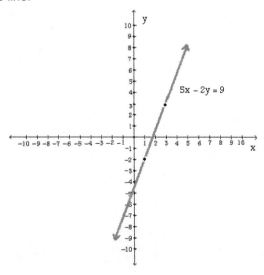

$5x - 2y = 9$

•**Note that you can choose any value to substitute for x and y.**

Some equations have only an x variable or a y variable. The graphs of such equations are either a vertical line or a horizontal line. If the equation contains only x, the graph is a vertical line. If the equation contains only y, the graph is a horizontal line.

Example: Graph $x = 4$

Notice there is no y in this equation, which means that the x coordinate of any point on this line is always 4 no matter what value is chosen for y Therefore, the graph of $x = 4$ is a vertical line with an x-intercept of (4, 0).

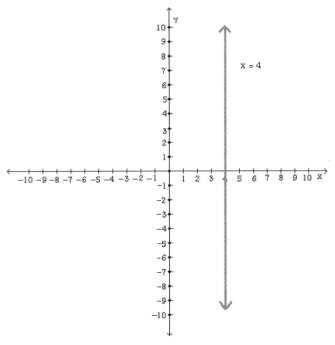

Example: Graph $y = -3$.

Notice there is no x in this equation, which means that the y coordinate of any point on this line is always -3 no matter what value is chosen for x. Therefore, the graph of $y = -3$ is a horizontal line with a y-intercept of (0, -3).

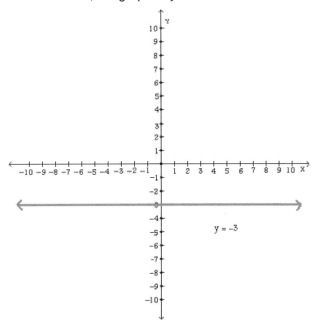

Another way to graph a linear equation is to write it into the form $y = mx + b$, where b is the y-intercept and m is the **slope**. You can think of the slope of the line as the "rise over the run". Rise is the change in the y coordinates, and run is the change in the x coordinates.

Example: Graph $y = 3x + 4$.

    The y–intercept is (0, 4) and the slope is 3. First plot the point (0, 4) on the graph. From that point you use the slope to add a second point. To do that, think of the slope of 3 as 3/1. The rise is 3 and the run is 1. So from the coordinate (0, 4) move up 3 to (0, 7) (rise) and then over to the right 1 to (1,7) (run). Plot another point at (1, 7) and draw the line through those two points.

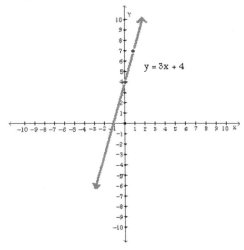

Example: Graph $y = -2x - 5$.

    The y-intercept is (0, -5) and the slope is -2. First plot the point (0, -5) and from there use the slope of -2 to plot the second point. The run is ALWAYS positive, so for a negative slope the rise is downward (or negative). From (0, -5) move down 2 to (0, -7) and over to the right 1 to (1, -7) and plot a point. Then draw a line through the points.

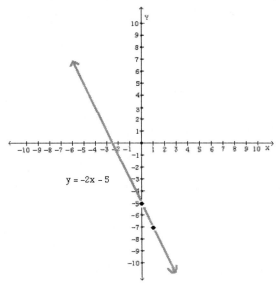

•**Note if you choose to graph using the y-intercept and slope, you must write the equation in the form $y = mx + b$.**

Example: Graph $3x + 4y = -7$

First solve the equation for y.

$3x + 4y = -7$

$$4y = -7 - 3x$$
$$y = \frac{-7 - 3x}{4}$$

$$y = -7/4 - (3/4)x$$

The slope is -3/4 and the y-intercept is (0, -7/4). Plot the points using the same method in the previous examples and draw the line. You could also pick any value for x and solve for y and then any value for y and solve for x. This will also give you two points for the line. The easiest points to choose would be $x = 0$ and $y = 0$, therefore solving for the x and y intercepts.

Substituting 0 for x gives 3(0) + 4y = -7, 4y = -7, y = -7/4. Therefore the y- intercept is (0, -7/4).

Substituting 0 for y gives 3x + 4(0) = -7, 3x = -7, x = -7/3. Therefore the x- intercept is (-7/3, 0).

The graph of the line is below.

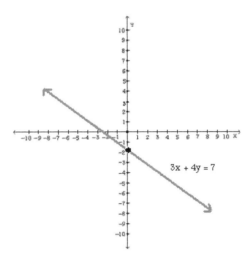

Graphing Linear Inequalities

Graphing a **linear inequality** is much the same as graphing a linear equation. If the equation is in the form $y > mx + b$ or $y < mb + x$ the line is dotted. The line is solid if the equation is in the form $y \le mx + b$ or $y \ge mx + b$. The solution of an inequality is represented as a shaded region on the graph.

Example: Graph $y > 3x$.

This equation is in slope-intercept form, so $m = 3$ and $b = 0$. We can graph this as if the equation was $y = 4x$, except since it's an inequality with a > sign, the line must be dotted. To determine which side of the graph is the solution set and should be shaded on the graph, select a point from one side of the dotted line. In this case, we'll choose the point (1,1).

Substitute 1 for x and 1 for y in the equality and see if it satisfies it.

1 > 3(1)

1 > 3 is a false statement, therefore it does not satisfy the inequality and neither will any other ordered pair on that side of the dotted line. Therefore, the other side of the dotted line must be shaded to represent the solution.

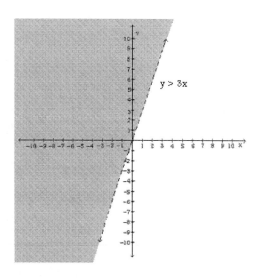

•Note that it doesn't matter what ordered pair to use to check to see which side of the line should be shaded. It's easiest to use (0,0), but in this case (0, 0) lies on the dotted line, so that ordered pair cannot be used in the check.

Example: Graph $4x + 2y \geq 8$.

First we get the equation in slope-intercept form.

$4x + 2y \geq 8$

$\quad 2y \geq 8 - 4x$ (subtract $4x$ from both sides)

$\quad\quad y \geq 4 - 2x$ (combine like terms on the right side)

$\quad\quad y \geq -2x + 4$

The slope of the line is -2 and y-intercept is (0, 4).

Check a point on the graph on either side of the line. The easiest point to check, if possible, is (0, 0).

0 $\geq -2(\mathbf{0}) + 4$. $0 \geq 4$ is a false statement, therefore all points on the same side of the line as (0, 0) are not part of the solution. Shade in the region on the other side of the line to represent the solution.

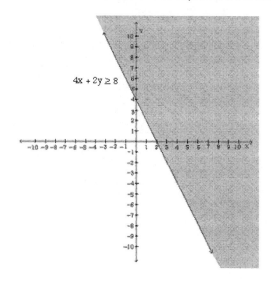

Example: Graph x < 7.

To graph an inequality with only one variable is very simple. Recall that the graph of an equation containing only an x variable is a vertical line. There is no need to check an ordered pair. In this case, since the sign is <, we shade to the left of the dotted line since all values to the left are values for x < 7. If the sign was > or ≥ we would shade to the right of the line. If the inequality involved only a y variable, the shading would be above the line for > or ≥ and below the line of < or ≤.

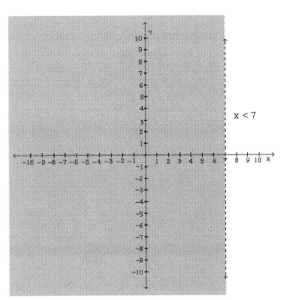

Midpoint Formula

Given two ordered pairs (x, y), how would you find the midpoint ? Think of midpoint as the average or the middle of two points. The distance between each coordinate and the midpoint must be the same. If the x coordinates are 2 and 6, it's easy to determine that the midpoint is 4. You can visualize this on a number line with the midpoint represented at "M".

Notice that the distance between 2 and M is 2 and the distance between 6 and M is also 2.

If you have two ordered pairs in a rectangular coordinate system, the same concept applies. The formula for finding the midpoint is as follows:

For two ordered pairs (x_1, y_1) and (x_2, y_2), the midpoint is $\left(\dfrac{x_1 + x_2}{2}, \dfrac{y_1 + y_2}{2}\right)$.

Example: Find the midpoint of line segment AB.

A (6, 4)
B (18, -6)

Using the midpoint formula we get

(6+18)/2 = 12 for the x coordinate of the midpoint.
(4 - 6)/2 = -1 for the y coordinate of the midpoint.

The midpoint is the ordered pair (12, -1)

Review Problems: Set 2

1. Find the coordinates of each point shown.

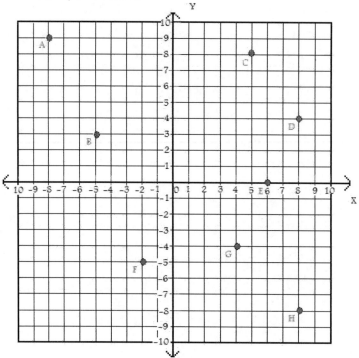

Draw a rectangular coordinate system and plot each ordered pair on the same graph.

2. (-4, -6)
3. (- 9, 5)
4. (5, 7)
5. (2, -8)
6. (0, 7)
7. (8, 0)
8. (-2, -8)

9. Show whether or not the ordered pair (2, 4) is a solution to the equation $3x - 2y = -4$.

On a rectangular coordinate system, graph the following equations using any method you wish.

10. $x = -5$
11. $y = 8$
12. $y = 3x - 4$
13. $y = (2/3)x + 6$
14. $2x + 4y = 10$

Graph the following linear inequalities.

15. $y \geq -3x + 1$
16. $6x + 2y \leq 4$
17. $y \leq 8$

Slope of a Line

The **slope** of a line is the amount which a line slants from lower left to upper right or upper left to lower right. The slope measures the average rate of change between the y variable and the x variable. To calculate the slope given two ordered pairs (x_1, y_1) and (x_2, y_2), use the following formula:

$$\text{slope} = \frac{y_2 - y_1}{x_2 - x_1}$$

The slope of the line containing the points (3, 6) and (-2, 9) is

$\frac{(9 - 6)}{(-2 - 3)}$ which equals -3/5. As a rate of change this means that for every 3 units the y coordinate decreases, the x coordinate increases by 5.

A line with a negative slope slants downward from upper left to lower right and a line with a positive slope slants upward from lower left to upper right. It's easy to remember this if thinking of starting from the left and going uphill as positive and downhill as negative.

A horizontal line has zero slope and a vertical line has an undefined slope. This is shown in the following examples:

Slope of the line containing the points (2, 0) and (4, 0) (horizontal line)

Slope is (0 - 0)/(4 - 2) = 0/2 = 0.

Slope of the line containing the points (1, 5) and (1, 9) (vertical line)

Slope is (9 - 5)/(1 - 1) = 4/0 = undefined (division by zero is undefined)

Example: Find the slope of the line containing the points (6, 11) and (-2, -6).

Solution:

$(x_1, y_1) = (6, 11)$
$(x_2, y_2) = (-2, -6)$

Slope = (11 - (-6))/(6- (-2))

= 17/8

•**Note that either point can be designated as (x_1, y_1) and (x_2, y_2) without affecting the answer.**

•**Note that you can find the slope from the equation, if given, by writing it in y = mx+b form. The slope is m.**

Example:

Suppose a study is conducted to figure out the effect of study time on test scores. Students at several different schools across the country all took the same exam. Each student logged their study time for the exam. The average test scores and average study time is represented on the graph below.

From the graph we can figure out the rate of change between the score on the exam and hours of studying. Notice the endpoint coordinates are (1, 40) and (9, 100). Using these coordinates we can obtain the slope.

(100 – 40)/(9 – 1) = 60/8 = 7.5

This means on average, for every 1 hour of studying, the test score will increase by 7.5.

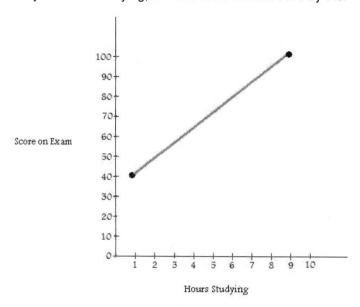

Example: A store sells floor tile for $25 per square yard plus a delivery charge of $10. What is the equation representing the cost of the tile? What is the slope and how much does it cost for 50 square yards of floor tile?

Solution:

Let n = Number of square yards of wall paneling

Cost is equal to 25 dollars times the number of square yards plus 10 dollars.

$$C = 25n + 10$$
For $n = 50$,

$C = 25(\mathbf{50}) + 10$
$C = \$1{,}260$

The slope is 25.

If you forget how to find the slope by looking at the equation, you can think of slope as the change in cost divided by the change in number of square yards. Use (50, 1260) as one point and find another point by picking a value for n and solving for C. Let $n = 10$, therefore $C = 260$ and the next coordinate is (10, 260). Now use the slope formula:

(1260 - 260)/(50 - 10) = 1000/40 = 25.

Slopes of Parallel and Perpendicular Lines

Parallel lines have the same slope. Perpendicular lines are lines that meet to form a right angle. The slopes of perpendicular lines are negative reciprocals of either either. In other words, the slopes of perpendicular lines multiply to -1.

Example: Determine whether the line that passes through the points (1, 8) and (-2, 6) is parallel or perpendicular to the line with slope of 2/3.

•Note that a line that "passes through the points" the line contains the points.

Solving the problem.

We have to find the slope of the line through the points (1, 8) and (-2, 6).

Slope = (6 – 8)/(-2 – 1)
    = - 2/(- 3)
    = 2/3

Therefore, the line through the points is parallel to the line that has a slope of 2/3.

Example: Determine whether the line that passes through the points (5, 10) and (7, -4) is parallel or perpendicular to the line with slope of 1/7.

Solving the problem.

We have to find the slope of the line through the points (5, 10) and (7, -4).

Slope = (-4 – 10)/(7 – 5)
    = -14/2
    = -7

Multiplying the slopes of the two lines gives

(-7)(1/7) = -1, therefore the two lines are perpendicular.

•**Note that if the slopes of two lines are not equal or their products do not equal -1, then the lines are neither parallel nor perpendicular.**

Writing Equations of Lines

There are a few ways in which we can write an equation of a line. If the slope and y-intercept are given, then it's very simple to write the equation. Substitute the value of the slope for m and the y-intercept for b in the equation $y = mx+b$ (**slope-intercept form**).

Example: Write the equation for the line that has a slope of 4 and a y-intercept of 6.

$y = mx + b$

$m = 4, b = 6$

Therefore the equation of the line is $y = 4x + 6$.

The **point-slope form** for the equation of a line may be used when given the slope of the line and a point (x_1, y_1) which the line passes through. The point-slope form is $(y - y_1) = m(x - x_1)$.

Example: Find the equation of the line that passes through (2, 8) and has a slope of -3.

Solution:

$(y - 8) = -3(x - 2)$
$y - 8 = -3x + 6$
    $y = -3x + 14$

The equation of the line is $y = -3x + 14$.

You may also use the point-slope form for the equation of the line when only given two points that the line passes through. The only difference is that you must find the slope of the line using the slope formula.

Example: Find the equation of the line that passes through the points (2, 5) and (0, 10).

Solution:

Slope = (10 - 5)/(0 - 2) = -5/2

Now use the point-slope form with the point (2, 5) to get

$(y - 5) = (-5/2)(x - 2)$
$(y - 5) = (-5/2)x + 5$
$\quad y = (-5/2)x + 10$

•Note that you can use either (2, 5) or (0, 10) in the point-slope form. Use the point which makes the calculations the easiest.

An easy method for finding the equation of a line is to use the form $y = mx + b$ instead of using the point-slope form.

Example: Find the equation of the line that passes through (2, 8) and has a slope of -3.

Substitute 2 for x, 8 for y and -3 for m in the equation $y = mx + b$ and solve for b.

$8 = -3(2) + b$
$8 = -6 + b$
$14 = b$

Now we have $m = -3$, $b = 14$ and the equation of the line is $y = -3x + 14$.

Example: Find the equation of the line that passes through the points (3, 5) and (-2, 8).

Find the slope using the slope formula to get

$(8 - 5)/(-2 - 3) = 3/(-5) = -3/5$

Then choose either ordered pair for x and y and substitute into $y = mx + b$. The easiest to use is (3, 5).

$5 = (-3/5)(3) + b$
$5 = -9/5 + b$
$25/5 + 9/5 = b$
$34/5 = b$

Therefore, the equation of the line is $y = (-3/5)x + 34/5$.

•Note that to write the equation of a line, use whatever method is easiest, unless instructed otherwise.

Equations of Parallel and Perpendicular Lines

Recall that parallel lines have the same slope.

We can find the equation of a line that passes through a given point and is parallel to a second line.

Example: Find the equation of a line that passes through the point (7, 8) and is parallel to the line $y = 4x + 6$.

Solution:

Since the line $y = 4x + 6$ has slope of 4, then the line that is parallel to this line has a slope of 4.

Use $y = mx + b$ with $x = 7$, $y = 8$ and $m = 4$.

8 = **4(7)** + *b*
8 = 28 + *b*
-20 = *b*.

Substitute -20 for *b* and 4 for *m* into *y* = *mx* + *b*.
Therefore the equation of the line is *y* = 4*x* – 20.

Notice the graph of both lines below.

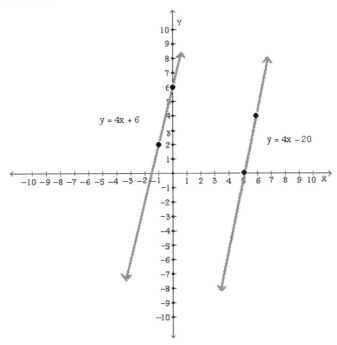

Recall that 2 perpendicular lines have slopes that multiply to -1. We can find the equation of a line that passes through a given point and is perpendicular to a second line.

Example: Find the equation of the line that passes through the point (5, -1) and is perpendicular to the line *y* = 2*x* - 1.

Solution:

The slope of the line *y* = 2*x* - 1 is 2. The slope of the line perpendicular to this line must be -1/2 because the product of the slopes must equal -1.

We know that *m* = -1/2, *x* = 5, *y* = -1.

Substitute these values into *y* = *mx* + *b* to solve for the y- intercept.

-1 = (-1/2)(5) + *b*

-1 = -5/2 + *b*

-1 + 5/2 + *b*

3/2 = *b*

Therefore, the equation of the line perpendicular to *y* = 2*x* - 1 through (5, -1) is *y* = (-1/2)*x* + 3/2.

Example: Find the equation of the line that passes through the point (2, 3) and is perpendicular to the line $y = 3x - 5$.

Solution:

The slope of the line perpendicular to $y = 3x - 5$ must multiply by 3 equal -1. We think of the slope of the first line as m_1 and the slope of the second line as m_2, therefore $3(m_1) = -1$, so $m_1 = -1/3$.

Now we know that $m = -1/3$, $x = 2$ and $y = 3$.

Use the formula $y = mx + b$

3 = (-1/3)(2) + b
$3 = -2/3 + b$
$3\ 2/3 = b$
$11/3 = b$

The equation of the line perpendicular to $y = 3x - 5$ that passes through the point (2, 3) is $y = (-1/3)x + 11/3$.

Notice the graph of both lines below.

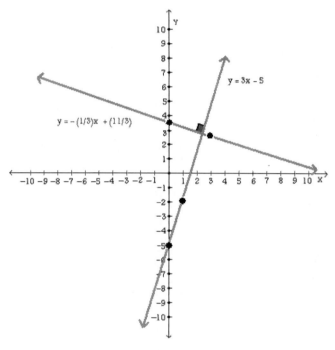

Review Problems: Set 3

Find the slope of the line that passes through the given points.

1. (4, -4), (6, 9)
2. (9, 14), (-3, 14)
3. (-5, -8), (2, 11)
4. (4, -7), (4, 6)
5. (a, b) , (-a, c)

Find the slope of the line.

6. $y = (3/4)x + 6$
7. $3y = 4x + 9$

8. $5x + 3y = 10$
9. $(2/3)x - 4y = -8$
10. $4y = 3(y - 1)$
11. $x = -6$

Determine whether the line that passes through the two points is parallel, perpendicular or neither to a line with the slope of 3.

12. $(2, 5), (9, 4)$
13. $(1, 8), (4, 17)$
14. $(0, 1), (6, 9)$
15. $(5, 10), (2, 11)$

Are the lines with the given slopes perpendicular?

16. $m_1 = 5, m_2 = 5$
17. $m_1 = -1/4, m_2 = 4$
18. $m_1 = 6, m_2 = 2/6$
19. $m_1 = 10, m_2 = -1/10$

Find the equation of the line in $y = mx + b$ form with the given information.

20. $m = 5, b = 6$
21. $m = -7$, passes through $(2, 5)$
22. passes through $(1, 6)$ and $(4, 9)$

Write the equation of the line that passes through the given point and is parallel to the given line. Then write the equation that is perpendicular to the given line that passes through the given point. Each equation must be in $y = mx + b$ form.

23. $(0, 0), \ y = 3x + 10$
24. $(4, 3), \ y = (1/4)x - 6$
25. $(-2, -4), \ y = 4x - 5$

Functions

A **function** is defined as a relationship between input values (x, called the **domain**) and output values (y, called the **range**). In a function, there can only be one y-value assigned to every x-value. If more than one y-value is associated with a single x-value, then the relation is not a function.

Example:

x	y
1	4
2	5
3	6

The above table represents inputs and outputs (domain and range) and represents a function.

x	y
0	3
1	6
2	9
1	4

The above table does not represent a function because there are two different output values for $x = 1$.

x	y
1	-5
2	-8
3	-8
5	-10
6	-12

The above table represents a function. Notice the output values are the same for both x = 2 and x = 3. A function can have the same output values for different input values.   You can determine if the relation is a function by performing the **vertical line test**.   Graph the relation and if you can draw a vertical line anywhere on the graph and it intersects at more than one point, then it is not a function.

Example: Notice the green vertical line passes through the graph at two points. Therefore, the given graph does not represent a function.

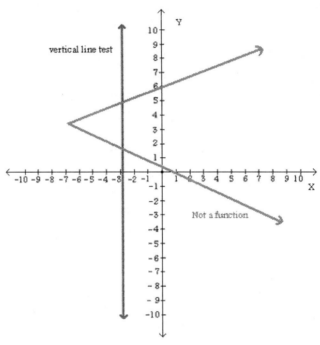

Linear Functions

A linear function is defined as an equation in the form of f(x) = mx + b. It is read *a function of x*. If the variable in the equation is y, then the function is f(y). If the variable in the equation is z, then the function is f(z), etc. Some examples of linear functions are as follows:

f(x) = (1/2)x - 4
g(x) = 2x - 13
f(y) = 0.9y + 2.75

Notice that a function doesn't have to be defined as f(x).
From any function, we can find an output value for any input value.
Example: Given the function f(x) = 4x + 12, find the output for an input of 5.

That means we need to find the value of the function at x = 5, also noted as f(5).
Substitute 5 in for x to get

4(**5**) + 12 = 20 + 12 = 32. Therefore, f(5) = 32.

Example: Given the function $g(x) = -9x + 12$, find $g(3)$ and $g(-6)$.

Substitute 3 in for x to get $-9(3) + 12 = -27 + 12 = -15$. Therefore, $g(3) = -15$.
Likewise, to find $g(-6)$ substitute -6 in for x to get $-9(-6) + 12 = 54 + 12 = 66$. Therefore, $g(-6) = 66$.

Nonlinear Functions

A **nonlinear function** is a function which is not represented graphically by a straight line.
Some examples of nonlinear functions are $f(x) = x^2$, $f(x) = x^3$ and $f(x) = |x|$.

Example: Graph the function $f(x) = x^2$.

The function $f(x) = x^2$ is known as the **squaring function**. To graph the function, we choose values for x and substitute for x in $f(x)$. Notice the values for x and $f(x)$ in the chart below. The values for $f(x) \geq 0$ for any value of x since squaring all real numbers gives a positive result. From the graph below you will notice that the domain is all real numbers and range is all real numbers greater than or equal to zero. The graph of the squaring function is called a **parabola**.

x	$f(x)$	$(x, f(x))$
-2	4	(-2, 4)
-1	1	(-1, 1)
0	0	(0, 0)
1	1	(1, 1)
2	4	(2, 4)

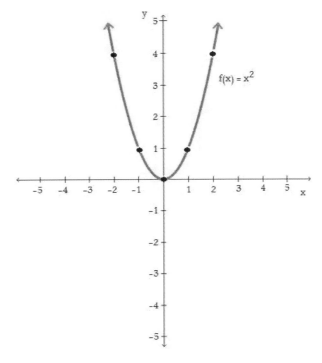

Example: Graph the function $f(x) = |x|$.

The function $f(x) = |x|$ is known as the **absolute value function.** To graph the function we choose values for x and substitute for x in $f(x)$. Notice in the table below that $f(x) \geq 0$. The domain is all real numbers and the range is all real numbers greater than or equal to zero.

x	f(x)	(x, f(x))
-2	2	(-2, 2)
-1	1	(-1, 1)
0	0	(0, 0)
1	1	(1, 1)
2	2	(2, 2)

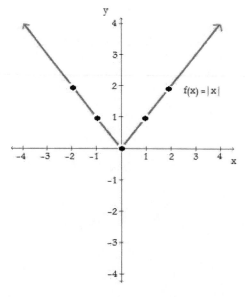

Example: Graph the function $f(x) = x^3$.

    The function $f(x) = x^3$ is known as the **cubing function**. To graph the function we choose values for x and substitute for x in $f(x)$. The domain and range are both all real numbers.

x	f(x)	(x, f(x))
-2	-8	(-2, -8)
-1	-3	(-1, -3)
0	0	(0, 0)
1	1	(1, 1)
2	8	(2, 8)

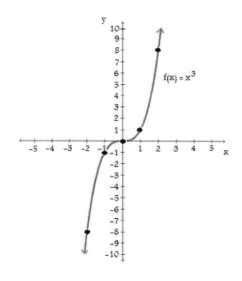

Functions can be shifted up, down, left and right. These shifts are called **translations.**

If $f(x)$ is a function, then $f(x) + k$ has the same graph as $f(x)$ except it is translated up k units. The function $f(x) - k$ has the same graph as $f(x)$ except it is translated down k units.

If $f(x)$ is a function, then $f(x + h)$ has the same graph as $f(x)$ except it is translated h units to the left. The function $f(x - h)$ has the same graph as $f(x)$ except it is translated h units to the right.

Example: Graph $g(x) = x^3 + 2$.

Solution:

The graph of $g(x) = x^3 + 2$ is the same in shape as the graph of $f(x) = x^3$ except that it is translated 2 units up. If $g(x) = x^3 - 2$, then it has the same graph of $f(x) = x^3$ except that it is translated 2 units down. An alternate method to graph $g(x)$ is to pick values for x and substitute into x in $g(x)$ and plot the points.

x	$g(x)$	$(x, g(x))$
-2	-6	(-2, -6)
-1	1	(-1, 1)
0	2	(0, 2)
1	3	(1, 3)
2	10	(2, 10)

•Note that $g(x)$ is 2 higher for each value of x than $f(x)$ in the previous example. This illustrates the vertical translation as well as the graph below.

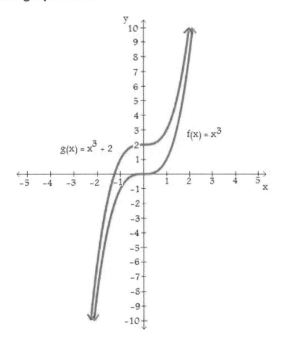

Example: Graph $g(x) = (x - 2)^2$.

Solution:

The graph of $g(x) = (x - 2)^2$ is the same in shape as the graph of $f(x) = x^2$ except that it is translated 2 units to the right.   If $g(x) = (x + 2)^2$, then it has the same graph as $f(x) = x^2$ except that it is translated 2 unites to the right.

An alternate method to graph $g(x)$ is to pick values for x and substitute into x in $g(x)$ and plot the points.

x	$g(x)$	$(x, g(x))$
-1	1	(-1, 1)
0	4	(0, 4)
1	1	(1, 1)
2	0	(2, 0)
3	1	(3, 1)
4	4	(4, 4)
5	9	(5, 9)

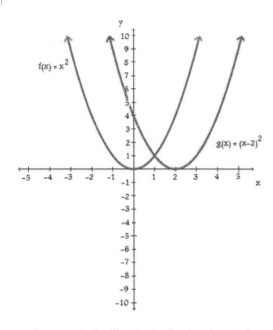

•Note that both f(x) and g(x) are on the graph to illustrate the horizontal translation of 2 units to the right.

Example: Graph $g(x) = |x + 2| - 1$.

Solution:
The graph of $g(x) = |x + 2| - 1$ is the same shape as the graph of $f(x) = |x|$ except that is has multiple translations. The +2 inside the absolute value shows there is a translation of 2 units to the left. The -1 outside of the absolute value shows there is a translation of 1 unit down. An alternate method to graph $g(x)$ is to pick values for x and substitute into x in $g(x)$ and plot the points.

x	$g(x)$	$(x, g(x))$
-3	0	(-3, 0)
-2	-1	(-2, -1)
-1	0	(-1, 0)
0	1	(0, 1)
1	2	(1, 2)
2	3	(2, 3)
3	4	(3, 4)

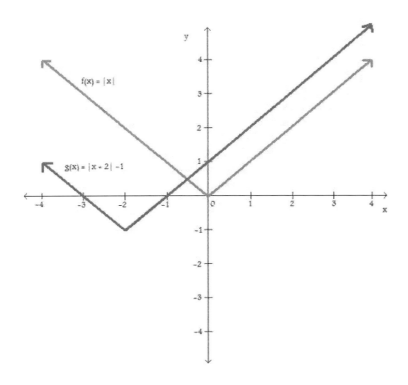

f(x) = |x|

g(x) = |x + 2| −1

Review Problems: Set 4

1. Does the table below represent a function?

x	y
4	8
3	-6
2	-12
1	-17

2. Does the table below represent a function?

x	y
0	2
1	5
1	8
4	11

3. Find the following values of the function indicated.

f(x) = 3x − 12,
f(1), f(3), f(-3), f(-4)

4. Does the following graph represent a function?

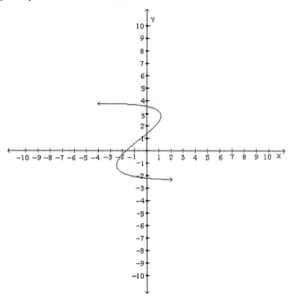

Key Terms and Concepts to Review

- Inequalities
- Symbols of inequalities
- Set notation, interval notation
- Compound inequalities
- Intersection and union
- Double inequalities
- Rectangular coordinate system, quadrants, ordered pairs, coordinates
- General form of a line
- x and y intercepts
- Graphing lines
- Midpoint, slope
- Writing equations of lines, parallel and perpendicular lines
- Functions, linear and nonlinear, vertical line test

Answers to Problem Sets

Problem Set 1
Answers and key steps in solution

1. $x > 3$, $(3, \infty)$, $4x > 12$, divide both sides by 4 to get $x > 3$
2. $x > -4$, $(-4, \infty)$, $-6x < 24$, divide both sides by -6 and reverse sign to get $x > -4$
3. $x > \frac{1}{4}$, $(\frac{1}{4}, \infty)$, $(2/5) < (8/5)x$,   divide by 8/5 so multiply by 5/8 to get $\frac{1}{4} < x$
4. $x \geq -3$, $[-3, \infty)$, $-3x + 5 \leq 14$, $-3x \leq 9$, $x \geq -3$
5. $y \leq -13$, $(-\infty, -13]$, $-2y \geq 26$, $y \leq -13$
6. $y < 13$, $(-\infty, 13)$, $3(y - 3) < 2y + 4$, $3y - 9 < 2y + 4$, $y - 9 < 4$, $y < 13$
7. $x < -8$, $(-\infty, -8)$, $(1/4)x + 8 > (1/2)x + 10$, Multiply by 4 to get $x + 32 > 2x + 40$, $x > 2x + 8$, $-x > 8$, $x < -8$
8. $(-3, 5)$
9. $[-9, 14]$
10. $x < 1$ and $x > 2$, no solution, $x + 3 < 3x - 1$, $3 < 2x - 1$, $4 < 2x$, $x < 2$..... $4x - 2 < 2x$, $-2 < -2x$, $1 > x$
11. $x < -2$ and $x < 5$, $(-\infty, -2)$, $2x + 4 < 0$, $2x < -4$, $x < -2$.......... $-4x > -20$, $x < 5$
12. $(-\infty, -5] \cup (6, \infty)$
13. $(-\infty, -2] \cup (11, \infty)$
14. $x < -3$ or $x > 12$, $(-3, \infty) \cup (12, \infty)$, $5x < -15$ or $(2/3)x > 8$, $5x < -15$, $x < -3$.... $(2/3)x > 8$, multiply by $(3/2)$

to get $x > 12$.

15. $-2 < x < 4$, $(-2, 4)$, $-4 < 2x < 8$, divide everything by 2 to get $-2 < x < 4$

16. $-8/3 \le x \le -1/3$, $[-8/3, -1/3]$, $-2 \le 3(x + 2) \le 5$, $-2 \le 3x + 6 \le 5$, subtract 6 to get $-8 \le 3x \le -1$, divide by 3 to get $-8/3 \le x \le -1/3$

17. $(-5, 5)$ $|x| < 5$, $x < 5$ or $x > -5$

18. $(-\infty, -2) \cup (2, \infty)$ $|-3x > 6|$, $-3x > 6$, $x < -2$ or $-3x < -6$, $x > 2$

19. $[-17/2, 7/2]$ $|2x + 5| \le 12$, $2x + 5 \le 12$, $2x \le 7$, $x \le 7/2$ or $2x + 5 \ge -12$, $2x \ge -17$, $x \ge -17/2$

20. $(-\infty, -22/5] \cup [14/5, \infty)$ $|-5x - 4| \ge 18$, $-5x - 4 \ge 18$, $-5x \ge 22$, $x \le -22/5$ or $-5x - 4 \le -18$, $-5x \le -14$, $x \ge 14/5$

Problem Set 2
Answers and key steps in solution

1. a. $(-8, 9)$, b. $(-5, 3)$, c. $(5, 8)$, d. $(8, 4)$, e. $(6,0)$, f. $(-2, -5)$, g. $(4, -4)$, h. $(8, -8)$

2-8

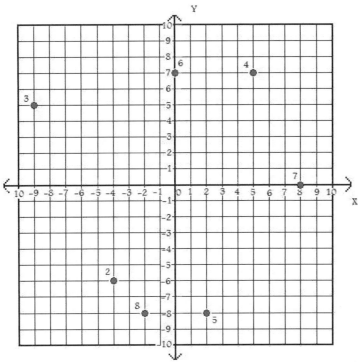

9. $3x - 2y = -4$, for $x = 2$, $y = 4$

    $3(2) - 2(4) = -4$

     $6 - 8 = -4$

     $-2 \ne -4$, therefore 4 is not a solution to the equation.

10.

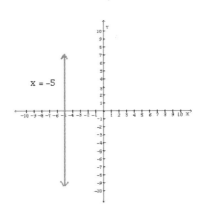

Since *x* = -5, the *x* is -5 regardless what value is for *y*, therefore the graph is vertical line x intercept of (-5, 0).

11.

Since the equation is *y* = 8, the *y* coordinate is 8 regardless of the value for *x*. The y intercept is (0, 8) and the graph is a horizontal line through (0, 8).

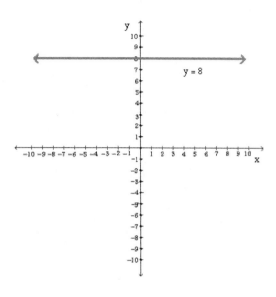

12.

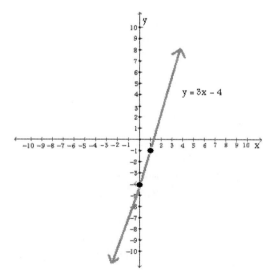

For the graph *y* = 3*x* – 4 notice the point at (0, -4). This is the y- intercept. From this point we can use the slope to go up 3 and to the right 1 and plot a point at (1, -3). Draw a line through those points.

13.

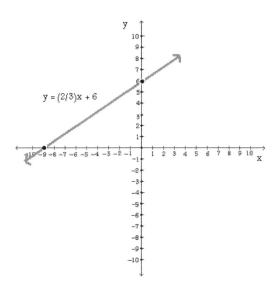

The equation of the line is $y = (2/3)x + 6$. From this equation you can plot a point at $(0, 6)$, which is the y-intercept. We can get the x-intercept by putting 0 in for y and solving for x. That gives us $0 = (2/3)x + 6$, subtract 6 from both sides to get $-6 = (2/3)x$. Divide by $(2/3)$ to get $-9 = x$. Plot another point at $(-9, 0)$ and draw a line through the 2 points.

14.

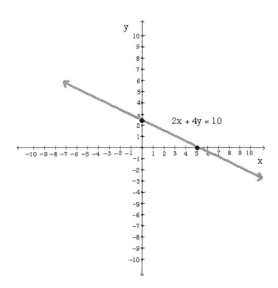

The equation of the line in standard form is $2x + 4y = 10$. You can find the intercepts by putting 0 in for x, then 0 in for y. The intercepts are $(0, 5/2)$ and $(5, 0)$. Plot the intercepts and draw a line through the points.

15. The equation is in the slope-intercept form with $m = -3$ and $b = 1$. Select an ordered pair not on the line to check what region needs to be shaded. Since $(0, 0)$ is not on the line, use this ordered pair to check.

Substitute 0 for x and 0 for y to get $0 \geq -3(0) + 1$.
$0 \geq 1$ is a false statement, therefore $(0, 0)$ and no points on the same side of the line as $(0, 0)$ are in the solution. Therefore, the solution is the region on the other side of the line.

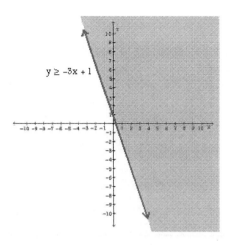

$$y \geq -3x + 1$$

16. $6x - 2y \geq 8$

Write the equation in slope-intercept form.

$-2y \geq 8 - 6x$, $y \leq -4 + 3x$, $y \leq 3x - 4$. Graph the line using the slope and y-intercept.
Choose the ordered pair (0,0) to check for the solution.
$6(\mathbf{0}) - 2(\mathbf{0}) \geq 8$, $0 \geq 8$ is a false statement, therefore (0,0) and all points on the same side of the line as (0,0) are not part of the solution. Therefore, the other side of the line is shaded.

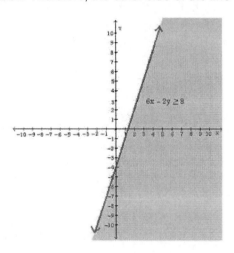

$6x - 2y \geq 8$

17. $y \leq 8$

Graph the line, which is a horizontal line through 8 and the solution is everything below and including the line since all values above the line would be $y > 8$.

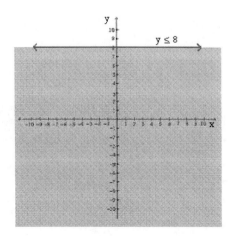

$y \leq 8$

Problem Set 3
Answers and key steps in solution

1. 13/2,   (4, -4), (6, 9) slope = (9 + 4)/(6 – 4) = 13/2
2. 0,   (9, 14), (-3, 14) slope = (14- 14)/(-3 – 9) = 0
3. 19/7,   (-5, -8), (2, 11) slope = (11 + 8)/(2 + 5) = 19/7
4. undefined,   (4, -7), (4, 6) slope = (6 + 7)/(4 -4) = 13/0, undefined because of 0 denominator
5. (b-c)/2a,   (a, b), (-a, c) slope = (c – b)/(-a -a) = (c-b)/(-2a) = (b-c)/2a
6. ¾, $y = (3/4)x + 6$, in slope-intercept form ($y = mx +b$), m is the slope.
7. 4/3, $3y = 4x + 9$, $y = (4/3)x + 9/3$, $y = (4/3)x + 3$
8. -5/3, $5x + 3y = 10$, $3y = 10 – 5x$, $y = (10/3) – (5/3)x$
9. 1/6, $(2/3)x – 4y = -8$, $-4y = -(2/3)x – 8$, $y = (2/12)x + 2$, $y = (1/6)x + 2$
10. 0, $4y = 3(y-1)$, notice there is no x term in this equation, therefore the slope is zero.
11. Undefined, $x = -6$, notice there is no y term in this equation, therefore the slope is undefined.
12. Neither,   (2, 5), (9, 4) slope = (4 – 5)/(9 – 2) = -1/7
13. parallel,   (1, 8), (4, 17) slope = (17 – 8)/(4 – 1) = 9/3 = 3
14. neither,   (0, 1), (6, 9) slope = (9 – 1)/(6 – 0) = 8/6 = 4/3
15. perpendicular, (5, 10), (2, 11) slope = (11 – 10)/(2 – 5) = -1/3, perpendicular because 3(-1/3) = -1
16. no,   The slopes multiply to 25 and not -1.
17. yes,   The slopes multiply to -1.
18. no,   The slopes multiply to 2 and not -1
19. yes,   The slopes multiply to -1
20. $y = 5x+ 6$, $m = 5$ and $b = 6$, put in $y = mx + b$ form
21. $y = -7x + 19$, $m = -7$, passes through (2, 5), 5 = -7(2) + b, 5 = -14 + b, 19 = b, therefore $y = -7x +19$.
22. $y = x + 5$,   slope is (9 – 6)/(4 -1) = 3/3 = 1, choose either point and slope of 1 and put into $y = mx+b$ form to get 6 = (1)(1) + b, 5 = b, therefore $y = x+ 5$.
23. $y = 3x$ (parallel), $y = (-1/3)x$ (perpendicular),   Line passes through (0, 0) and parallel to $y = 3x + 10$, so slope of line parallel is 3, therefore 0 = 0(3) + b and b = 0. So the equation of the line is $y = 3x$. Line passes through (0, 0) and is perpendicular to $y = 3x + 10$, so the slope of line perpendicular is -1/3 since (-1/3)(3) = -1. Therefore 0 = (-1/3)(0) + b, b = 0. So the equation of the line is $y = (-1/3)x$.
24. $y = (1/4)x + 2$ (parallel), $y = -4x + 19$ (perpendicular) Line passes through (4, 3) and parallel to $y = (1/4)x – 6$. Slope is (¼), so 3 = (1/4)(4) + b, 3 = 1 + b, 2 = b. Therefore, the equation of the line is $y = (1/4)x + 2$.
    Line passes through (4, 3) and is perpendicular to $y = (1/4)x – 6$. Slope of line perpendicular is -4 since ((-4) (¼) = -1, so 3 = (-4)(4) + b, 3 = -16 + b, 19 = b. Therefore the equation of the line is $y = -4x + 19$.
25. $y = 4x + 4$ (parallel), $y = (-1/4)x – 9/2$ Line passes through (-2, -4) and is parallel to $y = 4x – 5$. The slope of the line is 4, so -4 = (4)(-2) + b, -4 = -8 + b, 4 = b. Therefore, the equation of the line is $y = 4x + 4$. Line passes through (-2, -4) and is perpendicular to $y = 4x – 5$. The slope of the line is (-1/4) since (-1/4)(4) = -1, so -4 = (-1/4)(-2) + b, -4 = ½ + b, -9/2 = b. Therefore, the equation of the line is $y = (-1/4)x – 9/2$.

Problem Set 4
Answers and key steps in solution

1. Yes, because there is exactly one value in the range for each value in the domain
2. No, because for the domain value of 1, ($x = 1$), there are 2 values for the range ($y = 5$ and $y = 8$)
3. $f(1) = -9$, $f(3) = -3$, $f(-3) = -21$, $f(-4) = -24$ $f(x) = 3x -12$, $f(1) = 3(1) -12$, $f(3) = 3(3) – 12$, $f(-3) = 3(-3) – 12$, $f(-4) = 3(-4) - 12$
4. No, because it does not pass the vertical line test.

Chapter 3

Systems of Linear Equations

Solving Systems of Two and Three Equations

In the last chapter we learned about the rectangular coordinate system, plotting coordinates and graphing a single linear equation. Now, we will consider a **system of linear equations**, (two or more equations), their relationship and solving them graphically and algebraically. The solution to a system of equations can be seen graphically as the point of intersection of the lines. There are some practical uses for solving systems of equations. For example, suppose a company produces watches. One line represents the revenue for selling a certain number of watches and the other line represents the cost for producing the watches. The break even point, (where sales = costs) is the point of intersection. A graph such as this shows when revenues are greater than, less than or equal to costs of production.

Example:

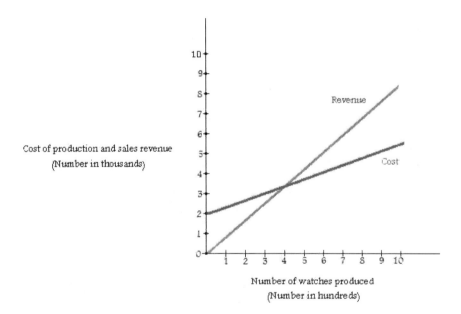

The red line indicates the cost to produce a certain number of watches and the blue line indicates the revenue earned on the sale of a certain number of watches. You can see from the graph that the break even point is the ordered pair (500, 12,500). This is when 500 watches are sold and the cost or production and sales revenue is 12,500. The company will earn money when more than 500 watches are sold and lose money if less than 500 watches are sold.

If a system of equations has no solution (the lines represented on a graph are parallel), then the system is said to be **inconsistent**. A system is said to be **consistent** if it has a solution (the lines represented on a graph intersect). If the lines represented on a graph coincide (they completely cover each other, therefore are the same line), then the consistent equations are said to be **dependent**. If the equations have different graphs, then the equations are said to be **independent**.

Solving Systems Graphically

The previous example shows the solution of a system of linear equations graphically, but how do we graph a system of equations? We learned how to graph a line from a single equation in the previous chapter. Graphing a

system of equations is done by simply graphing each line separately on the same rectangular coordinate system. Their point of intersection is the solution to the system.
Example: Solve the system $6x + 3y = 18$ graphically.
$$x - 2y = 28$$

First graph $6x + 3y = 9$ using any method you choose. Let's get the equation into $y = mx + b$ form and graph using the y-intercept and slope.

$6x + 3y = 18$
$3y = 18 - 6x$ (subtract 6x from both sides)
$y = 6 - 2x$ (divide both sides by 3)
$y = -2x + 6$

Plot the y-intercept of (0, 6) and use the slope of -2 to get the other point. Remember slope is rise over run, so go down 2 units from the ordered pair (0, 6) to (0, 4) and then over 1 to the right to (1, 4) and plot the second point there. Draw a line through the points.

Next graph $x - 2y = 28$.

$x - 2y = 28$
$x - 28 - 2y = 0$ (subtract 28 from both sides)
$x - 28 = 2y$ (add 2y from both sides)
$(1/2)x - 14 = y$ (divide both sides by 2 to solve for y)

Plot the y-intercept of (0, -14) and use the slope of ½ to get another point. Move up 1 and over to the right 2 to get (2, -13). Plot this point and draw a line through the two points.

•**Note that you could graph the equations using point-slope form and also by plotting points by substituting values for the variable into the equation and solve for the other variable.**

Notice on the graph that the lines intersect at the coordinate (8, -10).

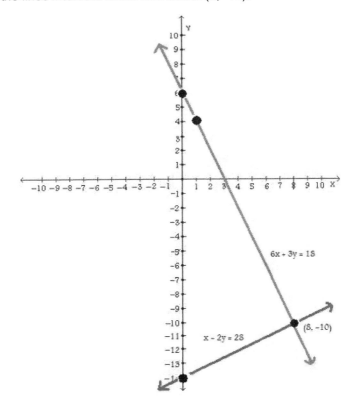

Check the answer obtained on the graph by substituting 8 for x and -10 for y in each equation.

$6 \cdot 8 + 3(-10) = 18$
$\qquad 48 - 30 = 18$
$\qquad\qquad 18 = 18$
and

$8 - 2(-10) = 28$
$\quad 8 + 20 = 28$
$\qquad\quad 28 = 28$

Example: Solve the system graphically.

$\qquad y = (1/2)x - 8$
$- 2x + 4y = -32$

Before graphing, write both equations in $y = mx + b$ form. The first equation is in the proper form.

$-2x + 4y = -32$
$\quad 4y = -32 + 2x \qquad$ (add $2x$ to both sides)
$\qquad y = -8 + (1/2)x \quad$ (divide both sides by 4)
$\qquad y = (1/2)x - 8$

Notice both equations are the same. Therefore, they are dependent equations and have infinitely many solutions. There is no need to graph dependent equations to see where the lines intersect.

•Note that the solution of dependent equations are all real numbers since the lines are the same and intersect at all points.

Example: Solve the system. If the system has a solution, represent it graphically.

$\qquad 6y = -2x - 8$
$3x + 9y = 14$

Write each equation in $y = mx + b$ form

$6y = -2x - 8$
$\quad y = (-2/6)x - 8/6 \qquad$ (divide both sides by 6)
$\quad y = (-1/3)x - 4/3 \qquad$ (simplify -2/6 and -8/6)

$3x + 9y = 14$
$\quad 9y = 14 - 3x \qquad\qquad$ (subtract $3x$ from both sides)
$\qquad y = (14/3) - (3/9)x \qquad$ (divide both sides by 9)
$\qquad y = (-1/3)x + (14/3) \qquad$ (simplify -3/9 and 14/3 and rearrange terms)

Notice both lines have a slope of -1/3 but have different y-intercepts. Therefore the lines are parallel, the system is inconsistent and there is no solution.

Solving Systems Algebraically

Oftentimes it's very difficult to know the exact coordinates of the point of intersection on a graph. In such cases, we can solve systems algebraically. There are two basic methods to do this. One is the **substitution method** and the other is the **elimination** or **addition method**.

Substitution Method

In the substitution method with equations involving 2 variables, solve one equation in terms or either variable. Substitute the expression in for the other variable and solve. Then substitute that value into the other variable and solve. You will then have values for both variables.

Example: Solve the system $x = 3 - 2y$ using the substitution method.
$$5y + 3x = 10$$

Notice the first equation is already solved for x, so simply substitute $3 - 2y$ in for x in the second equation.

$$5y + 3(\mathbf{3 - 2y}) = 10$$

Solve for y.

$$5y + 9 - 6y = 10$$
$$-1y + 9 = 10$$
$$-1y = 1$$
$$y = -1$$

Now that we have a value for y, substitute **-1** in for y in either of the original equations to solve for x.

•Note when substituting, it's best to choose the equation that appears simplest to solve, one that involves the smallest numbers to multiply or divide.

Using the first equation, $x = 3 - 2(\mathbf{-1})$
$$x = 3 + 2$$
$$x = 5$$

Therefore the solution to the system is (5, -1).

To check your answer, substitute **5** for x and **-1** for y in both equations:

$$\mathbf{5} = 3 - 2(\mathbf{-1})$$
$$5 = 3 - (-2)$$
$$5 = 5 \qquad \text{and}$$

$$5(\mathbf{-1}) + 3(\mathbf{5}) = 10$$
$$-5 + 15 = 10$$
$$10 = 10$$

Example: Solve the system $4x + 6y = -4$ using the substitution method.
$$3x - 6y = 39$$

We can solve either equation for either variable, so let's choose the first equation and solve for x.

$$4x + 6y = -4$$
$$4x = -4 - 6y \qquad \text{(subtract } 6y \text{ from both sides)}$$
$$x = (-4/4) - (6/4)y \qquad \text{(divide both sides by 4)}$$
$$x = -1 - (3/2)y \qquad \text{(simplify } -4/4 \text{ and } -6/4)$$

Now substitute **-1 - (3/2)y** in for x in the second equation and solve for y.

$$3[\mathbf{-1 - (3/2)y}] - 6y = 39$$
$$-3 - (9/2)y - 6y = 39$$
$$-3 - (9/2)y - (12/2)y = 39 \qquad \text{(common denominator of y terms is 2, so change 6 to 12/2)}$$
$$-3 - (21/2)y = 39$$
$$-(21/2)y = 42$$
$$y = -4 \qquad \text{(divide by -21/2, which is the same by multiplying 42 by (-2/21))}$$

Now substitute **-4** in for y in for x in either equation and solve for x.

$$4x + 6(\mathbf{-4}) = -4$$
$$4x - 24 = -4$$

$$4x = 20$$
$$x = 5$$

•**Note, remember to check by substituting the values for *x* and *y* back into the original equations.**

Example: Solve the system $14x - 4y = 10$ using the substitution method.
$$y = (7/2)x + 4$$

Since the second equation is already solved for *y*, substitute **(7/2)x + 4** in for *y* in the first equation.

$$14x - 4[(7/2)x + 4] = 10$$
$$14x - (28/2)x - 16 = 10$$
$$14x - 14x - 16 = 10$$
$-16 \neq 10$, therefore the system is inconsistent and has no solution.

Elimination or Addition Method

Sometimes it's not very easy to solve a system of linear equations using the substitution method because of numerous fractions involved in the calculations. In other cases, it isn't clear which variable is easiest to solve for before substituting. In such cases, the **elimination or addition method** is easier to use. In this method, we will add the equations or a multiple of the equations together in order to eliminate one variable. This enables us to solve for the other variable. When using this method you want to get the absolute value of the number in front of the variable you wish to eliminate the same (example 5 and -5, -5 and -5 or 5 and 5).

Example: Take the second example that we used for the substitution method.

Solve the system $4x + 6y = -4$ using the elimination method.
$$3x - 6y = 39$$

Notice the first equation has a **6y** and the second equation has a **-6y.** By adding the equations together, the *y* term will be eliminated because $6y + (-6y) = 0$. That is the idea of the elimination method.

Add the equations together.

$$4x + 6y = -4$$
$$+ 3x - 6y = 39$$
$$7x = 35$$
$$x = 5$$

Now substitute 5 in for *x* in either equation and solve for *y*.

$$4 \cdot 5 + 6y = -4$$
$$20 + 6y = -4$$
$$6y = -24$$
$$y = -4.$$

Notice how using the addition method eliminated fractions and made the calculations easier. Sometimes one or both equations must be multiplied before eliminating one of the variables.

Example: Solve the system $5x - 2y = -8$ by the elimination method.
$$15x - 6y = -24$$
To eliminate the *x* term, multiply both sides of the first equation by 3.

$$3(5x - 2y) = 3(-8)$$
$$15x - 6y = -24$$

Notice the equation is now the same as the second equation in the system. So when subtracting the equations, you get 0 =0. This is a true statement, therefore the system has infinitely many solutions.

Example: Solve the system $(2/3)x + 4y = 10$ by the elimination method.
$$2x - 6y = 19$$

To eliminate y, get the least common multiple between 4 and 6, since they are the coefficients of the y terms. Multiples of 4 are 4, 6, 12, 16 and so on. Multiples of 6 are 6, 12, 18 and so on. Notice the least common multiple is 12. In order to eliminate the y terms, multiply the first equation by 3 and the second equation by 2 to get $12y$ and $-12y$.

$$3[(2/3)x + 4y = 10]$$
$$2(2x - 6y = 19)$$

After multiplying, the system becomes

$$2x + 12y = 30$$
$$4x - 12y = 38$$

Now add the equations to eliminate the y terms.

$$6x = 68$$
$$x = 68/6$$
$$x = 34/3$$

Substitute 34/3 in for x in either equation and solve for y.

$2(\mathbf{34/3}) -6y = 19$
$(68/3) - 6y = 19$
$\quad\quad -6y = 19 - (68/3)$
$\quad\quad -6y = (57/3) - (68/3)$ (change 19 to 57/3 by multiplying 19 by 3/3)
$\quad\quad -6y = -11/3$
$\quad\quad\quad y = 11/18$

This answer can easily be verified by substituting back into the original equations. Note that it may be easier to use a calculator to verify.

We can solve word problems involving 2 variables by writing and solving a system of equations.

Example: Suppose Tom has 30 coins consisting of dimes and quarters. If he has a total of $5.55, how many of each coin does he have?

Solution:

Let x = number of dimes
$\quad y$ = number of quarters

Number of dimes plus number of quarters equals 30 coins.

$\quad\quad x \quad\quad\quad + \quad\quad\quad y \quad\quad\quad\quad = \quad 30$

Value of dimes plus value of quarters equals $5.55.

$\quad\quad 0.10x \quad\quad + \quad\quad 0.25y \quad\quad\quad = 5.55$

The system is $\quad\quad\quad x + y = 30$
$\quad\quad\quad\quad\quad\quad 0.10x + 0.25y = 5.55$

We will solve this system using the elimination method. To eliminate the x terms, multiply the first equation by -0.10. This gives us

$-0.10x - 0.10y = -3$
$0.10x + 0.25y = 5.55$

Next, add the two equations to get $0.15y = 2.55$
$$y = 17$$

Substitute 17 in for y in the first equation to get 13 for x. Therefore, Tom has 13 dimes and 17 quarters.

Example: Suppose you have two containers of saline solution. One is a weak mixture of 1% saline solution and the other is a strong mixture of 5% saline solution. You want to create a mixture that is 16 ounces of 4% saline solution. How much of each mixture must you use to create the 4% solution? (Note that ounces times % saline = amount of solution).

Solution	Ounces	% Saline	Amount of saline
Weak	x	0.01	$0.01x$
Strong	y	0.05	$0.05y$
Mixture	16	0.04	16(0.04)

Using the information from the table, we can set up the system of equations.

Amount of weak mixture plus amount of strong mixture equals 16 ounces.

x $+$ y $=$ 16

Amount of saline in weak plus the amount of saline in strong equals amount of saline in mixture.

$0.01x$ $+$ $0.05y$ $=$ 16(0.04)

Solution:

$x + y = 16$
$0.01x + 0.05y = 0.64$ (16 times 0.04)

We will solve this system using the substitution method. Solve the first equation for x by subtracting y from both sides of the = sign. This gives us $x = 16 - y$. Now substitute $16 - y$ in for x in the second equation and solve for y.

$0.01(\mathbf{16 - y}) + 0.05y = 0.64$
$0.16 - 0.01y + 0.05y = 0.64$
$0.16 + 0.04y = 0.64$
$0.04y = 0.48$
$y = 12$

Substituting 12 for y in the first equation gives a result of $x = 4$.
Therefore you need 4 ounces of the 1% solution and 12 ounces of the 5% solution.

•**Note that it's oftentimes easier to solve problems such as these using a chart like the one above. Then create the system of equations from the chart.**

Review Problems: Set 1

1. Refer to the graph. Name two ordered pairs that satisfy the equation y = (4/3)x + 3. Name two ordered pairs that satisfy the graph y = (-8/7)x + 8.

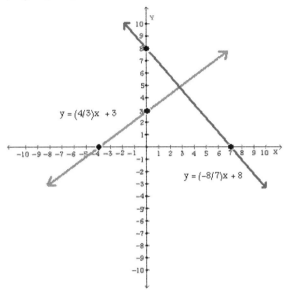

2. Complete the following table for values used to graph 3x + 4y = 12.

x	y	(x,y)
0		
	0	
	2	

Determine whether the ordered pair is a solution to the system of equations.

3. (2, 4) for x + 2y = 10
3x - 5y = -8

4. (½, -1) for 2x + 5y = -4
8x - 9y = 13

Solve each system by graphing.

5.   x + 2y = 10
-2x + 4y = 12

6.   6x - 3y = 12
(1/2)x + 2y = -8

7.   y = 3x
4x + 4y = 0

Answer the following questions using the graph below.

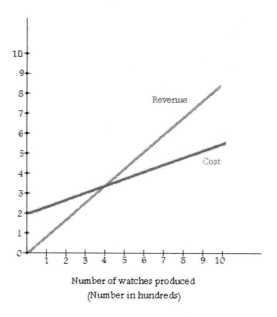

Cost of production and sales revenue
(Number in thousands)

Number of watches produced
(Number in hundreds)

8. Where is the break even point?
9. What does the break even point mean in the context of this problem?
10. What interval is revenue less than cost?

Determine whether the systems are dependent, consistent or inconsistent.

11. $(2/3)y + 6x = 10$
        $2y + 18x = 4$

12. $y = 5x - 8$
       $-10x = -2y - 16$

13. $4x + (2/5)y = 6$
        $-2x - 4y = -9$

14. If you want to use the substitution method to solve the following system, which equation and variable is easiest to solve for and why?

         $2x + y = 9$
         $4x + 3y = 14$

15. If you use elimination method, what must you multiply the first equation by if you want to add to eliminate the *y* variables?

16. If you want to eliminate the *y* variables in the following system, what should you multiply each equation by? If you want to eliminate the *x* variables, what should you multiply each equation by?

         $3x - 10y = 20$
         $-4x + 4y = -2$

17. Solve the system by substitution.

          $y = (2/3)x - 2$
         $6x - 18y = 24$

18. Solve the system by elimination.

$$5x + 2y = 0$$
$$3x - 3y = 21$$

19. Solve the system by any method you wish.

$$3x + y = 12$$
$$2x + 4y = -10$$

20. In the parallelogram below, what are the values of x and y? (Hint, opposite angles of a parallelogram are equal as are alternate interior angles $(x - y)$ and 40 degrees)

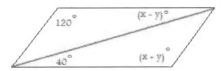

Solving Systems With 3 Variables

We solved systems of two linear equations in two variables. We will now move to three equations with three variables. In an equation with two variables x and y, the graph is a line. In an equation with three variables x, y and z, the graph is a **plane**.   Think of a plane as a wall that extends vertically, horizontally or diagonally indefinitely. The techniques used to solve these systems are basically the same. The first thing you want to do is rewrite all equations in $Ax + By + Cz = D$ form where A, B, C and D are numbers. Choose any two equations and eliminate a variable. Choose two other equations and eliminate the same variable. The idea is to reduce the original system into two equations with two variables. Then you can solve the system as we did in previous section. The solution is the intersection of the planes. A few examples will clarify this process.

Example: Solve the system $x + 2y + 3z = 14$
$$2x + y - 2z = -2$$
$$3x - 4y + z = -2$$

First we choose a variable we wish to eliminate. Let's eliminate the x variable by using the first and second equation.

$$x + 2y + 3z = 14$$
$$2x + y - 2z = -2$$

Multiply the first equation by -2 to get
$$-2x - 4y - 6z = -28$$
$$2x + y - 2z = -2$$

Notice we multiplied by -2 so when we add the equations the x terms are eliminated.
Adding gives us

$-3y - 8z = -30$

Now choose two other equations and eliminate the x terms. Let's use the first equation and the third equation. The reason why we are using the first and third equations is because we only have to multiply the first equation before adding to eliminate the x term. Using the second and third equations would require multiplying both equations or multiplying one or the other equation by a fraction, which is more difficult.

Multiply the first equation by -3 to get

$-3x - 6y - 9z = -42$
$3x - 4y + z = -2$

Add the equations to get

$-10y - 8z = -44$

Now we have a system of equations in two variables.

$-3y - 8z = -30$
$-10y - 8z = -44$

Notice the z terms are the same so it's easy to eliminate them by subtracting the second equation from the first. This gives us

$7y = 14$
$y = 2$

Substitute 2 for y in for either equation to solve for z.

$-3(\mathbf{2}) - 8z = -30$
$-6 - 8z = -30$
$-8z = -24$
$z = 3$

To solve for x, use one of the original 3 equations with $y = 2$ and $z = 3$.

Using the first equation we get

$x + 2(\mathbf{2}) + 3(\mathbf{3}) = 14$
$x + 4 + 9 = 14$
$x + 13 = 14$
$x = 1$

Therefore the solution to the system is $x = 1$, $y = 2$, $z = 3$. Since there is a solution, the system is consistent.

•**Note that you can check your answer by substituting the values for x, y and z in all 3 original equations.**

Example: Solve the system $2x + 3y + 4z = 6$
$2x - 3y - 4z = -4$
$4x + 6y + 8z = 12$

Notice all the terms in the third equation are divisible by 2, so when dividing the equation by 2, we get $2x + 3y + 4z = 6$. That is exactly the same equation as the first. So now we only have to deal with using two equations to solve the system.

Add the first equation to the second equation to get $4x = -2$. Solve for x to get $x = -1/2$.
Substitute -1/2 for x in the first equation to get

$(2)(\mathbf{-1/2}) + 3y + 4z = 6$
$-1 + 3y + 4z = 6$
$3y + 4z = 6 + 1$
$3y + 4z = 7$

$$3y = 7 - 4z$$
$$y = (-4/3)z + 7/3$$

Now we substitute -1/2 for x in the second equation to get

$$(2)(-1/2) - 3y - 4z = -4$$
$$-1 - 3y - 4z = -4$$
$$-3y - 4z = -3$$
$$-3y = -3 + 4z$$
$$y = (-4/3)z + 1$$

Notice that there are different solutions for y in terms of z.

The equations then are dependent with infinite number of solutions. The fact that the first equation in and the third equation in the original system are the same also tells us that the equations are dependent.

Example: Solve the system
$$2x + y - z = 1$$
$$x + 2y + 2z = 2$$
$$4x + 5y + 3z = 3$$

We'll use the first two equations to eliminate the x terms. Multiply the second equation by -2 and combine with the first equation to get

$$-2x - 4y - 4z = -4$$
$$2x + y - z = 1$$

Add the equations to get

-3y - 5z = -3

Use the second and third equations. Multiply the second equation by -4 and combine with the third equation to get

$$-4x - 8y - 8z = -8$$
$$4x + 5y + 3z = 3$$

Add the equations to get

-3y - 5z = -5

Notice the y and z terms are the same in both equations in red. But $-3y - 5z$ cannot equal both -3 and -5, therefore the system is inconsistent and there is no solution.

Systems of equations can help solve real life problems.

Example: A company makes three different types of wrenches. The cost to manufacture each wrench is $5, $4 and $3 and sell for $18 $15 and $10, respectively. The cost of manufacturing 160 wrenches is $670 and the monthly revenue from their sale is $2,410. How many of each type must be sold to achieve the revenue of $2,510?

We start by setting up the three equations.

Let x = number of 1st type of wrench
y = number of 2nd type of wrench
z = number of 3rd type of wrench
The total number of wrenches is 160, so the first equation is

$$x + y + z = 160$$
The cost of the wrenches is $670, with each wrench costing $5, $4 and $3, so the second equation is

$5x + 4y + 3z = 670$

The wrenches sell for $18, $15 and $10, respectively, for a total monthly revenue of $2,410 so the third equation is

$18x + 15y + 10z = 2410$

The system is

$$x + y + z = 160$$
$$5x + 4y + 3z = 670$$
$$18x + 15y + 10z = 2410$$

The easiest way to start solving this system is to use the first two equations. Eliminate the z variable by multiplying the first equation by -3 and adding to the second equation.

$$-3x - 3y - 3z = -480$$
$$5x + 4y + 3z = 670$$

Adding the two equations gives us **$2x + y = 190$**

Now use the first and third equations and eliminate the z variable by multiplying the first equation by -10 and adding to the third equation.

$$-10x - 10y - 10z = -1600$$
$$18x + 15y + 10z = 2410$$

Adding the two equations gives us **$8x + 5y = 810$**

Now we can form a system from the two equations in bold.

$$2x + y = 190$$
$$8x + 5y = 810$$

Let's eliminate the x variables by multiplying the first equation by -4 to get

$-8x - 4y = -760$, then add to the second equation to get

$$-8x - 4y = 760$$
$$8x + 5y = 810$$
$$y = 50$$

Substitute 50 for y into $2x + y = 190$ to get

$$2x + \mathbf{50} = 190$$
$$2x = 140$$
$$x = 70$$

Now substitute for x and y into $x + y + z = 160$ to get

$$70 + 50 + z = 160.$$
$$120 + z = 160$$
$$z = 40$$

Therefore, the number of wrenches produced are 70, 50 and 40.
•Note that you can check the answer by substituting the values for x, y and z back into the original 3 equations.

Systems of Linear Inequalities

Solving systems of linear inequalities graphically is very similar to solving systems of linear equations. We graph the system inequalities on the same rectangular coordinate system. Shade the area which represents the intersection of the graphs. To check, we can pick a point from the shaded region and make sure the coordinates satisfy both inequalities in the system. We will start by graphing both separately and then graphing both on the same rectangular coordinate system.

Example: Solve the system by graphing

$$y \geq 2x + 3$$
$$3x + y < 6$$

The graph of $y \geq 2x + 3$.

Find the shaded region by picking a point on either side of the line to see if it satisfies the inequality. The easiest to choose is $(0, 0)$. Substitute into $y \geq 2x + 3$ to get $\mathbf{0} \geq 2(\mathbf{0}) + 3$. This is a false statement so the solution is on the other side of the line. We can check to make sure the shaded region is correct by choosing a point in that region and see if it satisfies the inequality. We'll choose the point $(-3, 0)$. Therefore $\mathbf{0} \geq 2(\mathbf{-3}) + 3$, $0 \geq -3$ is a true statement, so our solution is correct.
Next we will graph $3x + y < 6$.

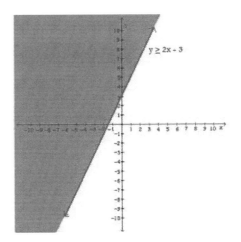

If we choose any point in the unshaded region and substitute into both inequalities, we will notice that the inequalities will not be satisfied. The shaded area in the graph below is the region that only satisfies $3x + y < 6$. We find the shaded region by picking a point on either side of the line to see if it satisfies the inequality. Choose $(0, 0)$ since it's the easiest to work with. Therefore $3(\mathbf{0}) + \mathbf{0} < 6$ is a true statement and is part of the solution set. All points on the same side of the dotted line satisfy the inequality.

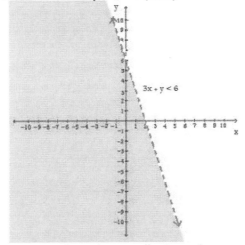

By graphing both inequalities on the same rectangular coordinate system, we will see where the two solutions intersect.

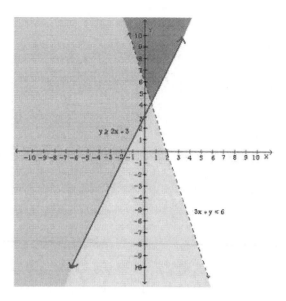

The large shaded area where the inequality $y \geq 2x + 3$ is located satisfies both equations. Therefore it is the solution to the system of inequalities.

•**Note that we show that the green area is the solution by picking a point in the region and testing it in both inequalities. Any point in that region will satisfy both inequalities.**

We'll check by using the point (-3, 0).

$0 \geq 2(-3) + 3$
$0 \geq -3$ is a true statement, so (-3, 0) satisfies $y \geq 2x + 3$

$3(-3) + 0 < 6$
$-9 < 6$ is a true statement, so (-3, 0) satisfies $3x + y < 6$.

Example: Solve the system by graphing

$x \leq 7$
$y > 4$
The graph of $x \leq 7$

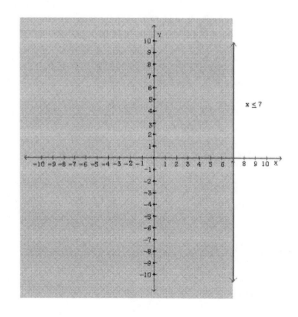

The graph of $y > 4$

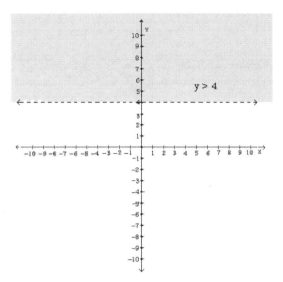

It is not necessary to graph each inequality separately. We graph them separately here to help illustrate how we come up with the solution when combining the graphs on a single rectangular coordinate system. For the final answer, it's sufficient to show only the final solution shaded.

Notice when graphing both on the same rectangular coordinate system, the intersection and solution to the system is shaded region where the inequality $y > 4$ is written. The shaded region in the upper right section of the graph is where only $y > 4$ is satisfied and the largest shaded region is where only $x \leq 7$ is satisfied.

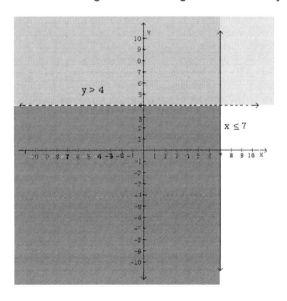

Example: Solve the system by graphing

$x < 5$
$y \leq x$
$y \geq 3$

When dealing with 3 inequalities, sometimes the solution will be an enclosed area bounded by on all sides by the lines. Notice in the above examples with 2 inequalities, the solution was an area bounded on only 2 sides. To solve a system by graphing involving 3 inequalities, graph all 3 inequalities on a single rectangular coordinate system. Check for the area that satisfies all 3 inequalities.

We will begin by graphing each inequality separately and then combine all of them on a single rectangular coordinate system. This will make it easier to visualize the solution.

Graph of $x < 5$

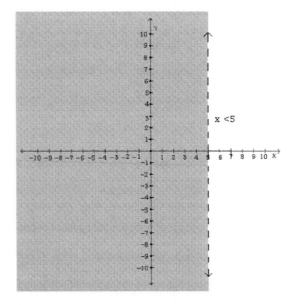

Notice that the region shaded is everything left of the line. That is because all points to the left of the line will have an x coordinate less than 5. It doesn't matter what the y coordinate is, which is why all the y values are included in the solution.

Graph $y \leq x$

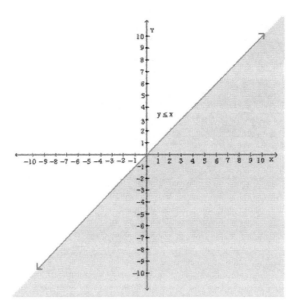

To ensure the correct side of the line is shaded, choose a point in the shaded region and substitute the coordinates into $y \leq x$ to see if it satisfies the inequality. If it does, then the correct side of the line is shaded. If not, the opposite side of the line must be shaded. Let's choose the point (1, -1). Substituting into the inequality gives us $-1 \leq 1$, which satisfies the inequality.

Graph $y \geq 3$

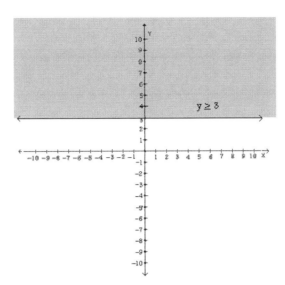

Notice the graph of all 3 inequalities on a single rectangular coordinate system. The solution is the intersection of the solutions of the 3 graphs above and is represented by the small triangular shaded region. You can check the solution by picking a point in that region and substituting into all 3 inequalities. If the point satisfies all 3 inequalities, then it is correct.

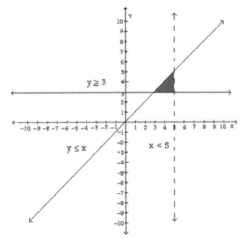

Example: Solve the system of inequalities by graphing

$y \geq 3x + 4$
$y \leq 3x - 2$

$y \geq 3x + 4$ has a slope of 3 and y intercept of 4 and
$y \leq 3x - 2$ has a slope of 3 and y intercept of -2.

Since the slopes are the same, the lines are parallel.

Notice the solution to the graph $y \geq 3x + 4$ and the solution to the graph $y \leq 3x - 2$. Their solutions do not intersect, therefore there is no solution to the system.

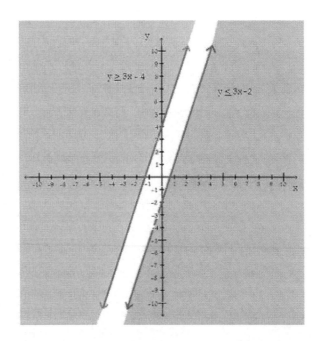

To check, pick a point in the unshaded region and substitute into both inequalities. We choose (0,0) because it's the easiest point to work with. When substituting into $y > 3x + 4$, we get $0 > 3(0) + 4$. Therefore (0, 0) does not satisfy the inequality. When substituting into $y \leq 3x - 2$, we get $0 \leq 3(0) - 2$. Therefore (0, 0) does not satisfy the inequality.

Review Problems: Set 2

Answer the following questions pertaining to the system below.

$$3x + 5y - z = 13$$
$$2x - 3y + 4z = 9$$
$$4x + 4y + z = 18$$

1. If the first and third equations are added together, which variable is eliminated?
2. If you want to eliminate the x variable and use equations 2 and 3, what must you multiply the second equation by before adding to the third equation?
3. The equation $4x + 4y + z = 18$ is a linear equation in how many variables?
4. Is the system consistent or inconsistent?
5. Determine whether or not (3, 2, 4) is a solution to the system

$$x + y + z = 9$$
$$2x + 2y - 3z = -6$$
$$(1/3)x + (3/2)y - 6z = -20$$

6. Determine whether or not (5, 0, -2) is a solution to the system

$$8x + y - 2z = 44$$
$$x + 5z = -2$$
$$y + (3/2)z = -3$$

Is the system inconsistent or consistent?

7. Solve the system

$$2x + 4y - z = 12$$
$$x - 3y + 4z = -17$$
$$-5x + y + 2z = -17$$

8. Solve the system

$$y + z = 13$$
$$2x + y + 2z = 16$$
$$x + y + z = 11$$

9. Solve the system

$$(1/2)x - 2y - 4z = -11$$
$$3x + 2y + z = 3$$
$$x - 4y - 8z = -22$$

10. In a system of 3 equations, after eliminating a variable and forming a system of 2 equations, you get the following :

$$4x - 5y = 10$$
$$4x - 5y = -9$$

What can you conclude from this?

11. Is (-2, 5, -6) a solution to the system

$$(4/3)x + 3y - z = 10$$
$$x + y - z = 9$$
$$4x - 3y + 6z = -35$$

12. Jerry, Joe and Rich have a total of $250 between them. The sum of Rich's and Jerry's money is $10 more than Joe and Jerry has $30 more than Rich. How much do each of them have separately? (Hint : Assign a separate variable for Jerry's money, Joe's money and Rich's money. Write 3   equations with the 3 variables and solve the system)

13. Solve the system of inequalities by graphing

$$x + y \geq 6$$
$$y \geq 2x$$

14. Solve the system of inequalities by graphing

$$x < 3$$
$$y \geq -2$$
$$y > -2x + 7$$

Key Terms and Concepts to Review

•Systems of linear equations (2 variables)
•Inconsistent system
•Consistent system
•Dependent system
•Solving systems by graphing
•Solving systems algebraically
•Elimination method
•Substitution method
•Systems of linear equations (3 variables)
•Systems of linear inequalities

Answers To Problem Sets

Problem Set 1
Answers and key steps in solution

1. (-4, 0) , (0, 3)   x- intercept and y- intercept
   (0, 8) , (7, 0)   x- intercept and y -intercept
2. $3x + 4y = 12$, the table is completed by substituting values in for the given variable and solving for the other variable.

X	Y	(X,Y)
0	3	(0,3)
4	0	(4,0)
(4/3)	2	(4/3,2)

3. No   (2, 4), $x + 2y = 10$ and $3x - 5y = 8$.. $2+2(4) = 10$ but $3(2) -5(4) \neq 8$
4. Yes   (½, -1), $2x + 5y = -4$ and $8x - 9y = 13$.. $2(1/2) + 5(-1) = -4$ and $8(1/2) -9(-1) = 13$
5. Graph both equations by any method and locate the point of intersection. It's easy to graph by finding the x and y- intercepts by substituting 0 for x and solving for y, then substituting 0 for y and solving for x. Plot the intercepts and draw a line through the points. Notice the solution is (2, 4).

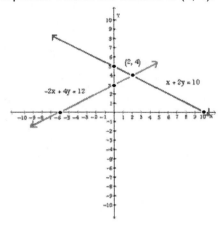

6. For $6x - 3y = 12$, it's easy to find the intercepts by substituting 0 for x and solving for y, then substituting 0 for y and solving for x. For $(1/2)x + 2y = -8$, it's easier to write the equation in $y = mx + b$ form, $2y = -8 - (1/2)x$, divide by 2 to get $y = -4 - (1/4)x$. Then plot the y- intercept of (0, -4) and use the slope of -1/4 to plot a second point. From there, you can draw the line. Notice the point of intersection is (0, -4).

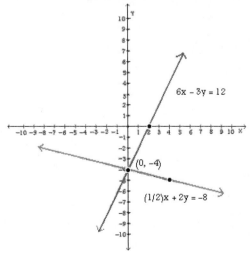

7. The equations $y = 3x$ and $4x + 4y = 0$ are easiest to graph writing it into $y = mx + b$ form and using the y- intercept and slope. After graphing, you notice the lines intersect at (0, 0).

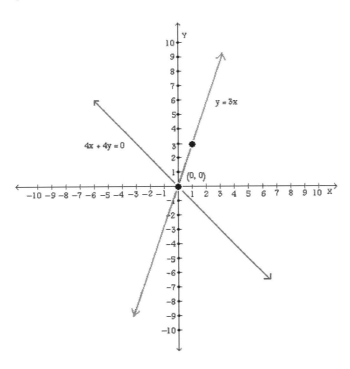

8. (4, 3 ½), the break even point is the point of intersection.
9. Where cost equals revenue.
10. (0, 3 ½), this occurs when the revenue line is lower than the cost line.
11. Inconsistent because when multiplying first equation by 3, the slope is the same as the slope of the second equation but the y- intercepts are different.
12. Dependent because when multiplying the first equation by 2, the equation is the same as the second equation.
13. Consistent because there is one solution, slopes are not the same and equations are not identical.
14. Solve the first equation for y because all you need to do is subtract $2x$ from both sides. There is no division needed.
15. Multiply by -3 and add to the second equation or multiply by 3 and subtract from the second equation.
16. Multiply the first equation by 2 and the second by 5 and add. Multiply the first equation by 4 and the second by 3 and add.
17. (2, -2/3), $6x - 18[(2/3)x - 2] = 24$, $6x - 12x + 36 = 24$, $-6x = -12$, $x = 2$.... $y = (2/3)(2) - 2 = (4/3) - 2 = -2/3$
18. (-2, 5), First step to eliminate x variables is to multiply first equation by -3 and second by 5 and add equations. Solve for y and substitute back in to an original equation and solve for x.
19. (5 4/5, -5 2/5), easiest method, solve for y in first equation and substitute in second equation or eliminate y variables by multiplying first equation by -4 and add to second equation. Then solve for x and substitute back into an original equation to solve for y.
20. $x = 80$, $y = 40$, $x - y = 40$ and $x + y = 120$. Add equations to get $2x = 160$, $x = 80$. Therefore $80 + y = 120$, $y = 40$.

Problem Set 2
Answers and key steps in solution
1. z because $-z + z = 0$.
2. -2 because $-2(2x) = -4x$ and $-4x + 4x = 0$.
3. 3, (x, y, and z)
4. Consistent, because there is only 1 solution.
5. No, because in the second equation $2(\mathbf{3}) + 2(\mathbf{2}) - 3(\mathbf{4}) \neq -6$
6. Yes, consistent because x, y and z satisfy each equation. There is a solution, so it's consistent.
7. $x = 2$, $y = 1$, $z = -4$ (2, 1, -4)
8. $x = -2$, $y = 6$, $z = 7$ (-2, 6, 7)

9. $x = 2$, $y = -4$, $z = 5$ (2, -4, 5)
   (For 7, 8 and 9 review examples for methods on how to solve and substitute values back into the equations to check. If they don't satisfy all the equations, the answer is incorrect.)

10. No solution, inconsistent because both lines have the same slope.

11. No, because $(4/3)(-2) + 3(5) - 6 \neq 10$

12. Joe $120, Jerry $80, Rich $50.. Let x = Jerry's money, y = Joe's money and z = Rich's money
   $x + y + z = 250$
   $x + z - y = 10$
   $x - z = 30$
   Solve the system.

13.

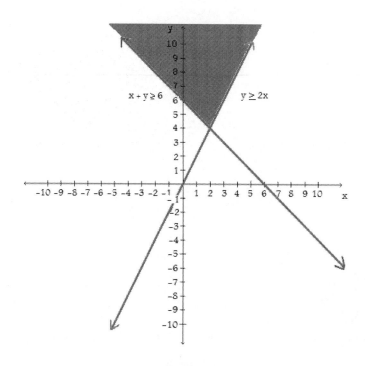

14.

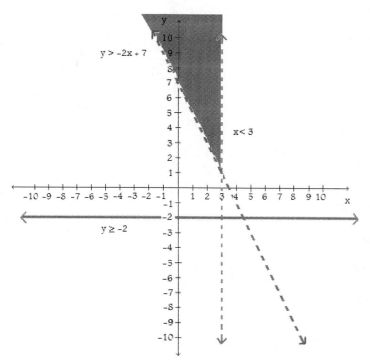

Chapter 4

Exponents and Polynomials

Positive Exponents

Suppose you wish to multiply a number, variable or expression a repeated number of times. Exponents allow you to write these products in a simpler form. For example,

$5 \cdot 5 \cdot 5 \cdot 5 = 5^4$

$y \cdot y \cdot y \cdot y \cdot y = y^5$

$(x - 3) \cdot (x - 3) \cdot (x - 3) \cdot (x - 3) \cdot (x - 3) \cdot (x - 3) = (x - 3)^6$

Each of the simplified expressions are called **exponential expressions**. The number being raised to the exponent is known as the **base** and the exponent is known as the **power**. When the exponent is one, it is not shown ($x^1 = x$).

Examples: State the base and the exponent in each of the following:

x^4 : The base is x and the exponent is 4.

$(5x)^5$: The base is $5x$ and the exponent is 5.

$-y^3$: The base is y and the exponent is 3.

$(-y)^3$: The base is $-y$ and the exponent is 3.

•**Note whatever is inside the parentheses being raised to the power is the base.**

There are several rules for exponents. When multiplying two exponential expressions, add the exponents. This is called the **power rule.** When dividing two exponential expressions, subtract the exponents. This is known as the **quotient rule for exponents**. When raising an exponential expression to a power, multiply the exponents. The examples below will clarify the reasoning behind this and help make the rules easier to remember.

Example: Simplify the expression $x^3 \cdot x^4$.

Recall that $x^3 = x \cdot x \cdot x$ and $x^4 = x \cdot x \cdot x \cdot x$
Therefore $x^3 \cdot x^4 = x \cdot x \cdot x \cdot x \cdot x \cdot x \cdot x$
Count the number of x's and you'll see there are 7. So the answer is x^7.

•**Note that this rule only applies to exponential expressions with the same base. For example, you cannot add exponents when you have $x^5 \cdot y^2$.**

Example: Simplify the expression.

$$y^4 \cdot x^3 \cdot y^6 \cdot x^2$$

Gather the x's together and the y's together and simplify.

$x^3 \cdot x^2 = x^5$
$y^4 \cdot y^6 = y^{10}$

Therefore the simplified form is $x^5 y^{10}$.

Example: Simplify the expression.

$$(-y)^5 (-x)^2$$

$(-y)^5 = (-y) \cdot (-y) \cdot (-y) \cdot (-y) \cdot (-y) = -y^5$

$(-x)^2 = (-x) \cdot (-x) = x^2$

Therefore the simplified form is $-y^5 x^2$.

Example: Simplify the expression.

$$(x^6)^3$$

In this case, we multiply the exponents to get x^{18}. If the rule is hard to remember, you can rewrite this problem as $x^6 \cdot x^6 \cdot x^6$ and using the rule for adding the exponents. Taking this a step further, you don't even need to remember the rule for adding. You can simply break down each x^6 as $x \cdot x \cdot x \cdot x \cdot x \cdot x$ and count the x's.

•**Note on a problem with large exponents, it will be very time consuming to write down all the x's and count them.**

A common mistake is found in a problem where the coefficient in front of the base is not 1. For example, $(4x^2)^3$. Oftentimes people will think of the multiplication rule for a power raised to another power, which is correct with the exponents. But the error is taking 4 times 3 instead of 4^3. The correct solution to this problem is

$(4x^2)^3 = 4x^2 \cdot 4x^2 \cdot 4x^2 = 64x^6$

Notice this is the same as $4^3 \cdot (x^2)^3$.

Example: Simplify the expression.

$$(-4x^2)^3(x^4)^5$$

$(-4x^2)^3 = (-4)^3 \cdot (x^2)^3$
$\quad\quad = -64x^6$

$(x^4)^5 = x^{20}$

So $(-4x^2)^3(x^4)^5 = -64x^6 \cdot x^{20}$
$\quad\quad\quad\quad\quad\quad = -64x^{26}$

Example: Simplify the expression.

$$(x^4/y^5)^3$$

We simplify this in two parts. Simplify the numerator, then simplify the denominator.

$(x^4)^3 = x^{12}$
$(y^5)^3 = y^{15}$

Therefore the simplified form is (x^{12}/y^{15}), $y \neq 0$.

•**Note that $y \neq 0$ because division by 0 is undefined.**

Example: Simplify the expression

$$\frac{x^3 y^6}{xy^4}$$

In the problem we use the quotient rule for exponents and subtract exponents to simplify. Therefore,

$$\frac{x^3}{x} = x^{(3-1)} = x^2 \text{ and } \frac{y^6}{y^4} = y^{(6-4)} = y^2$$

The answer is $x^2 y^2$.

If the rule is confusing, you can rewrite the problem as $\dfrac{x \cdot x \cdot x \cdot y \cdot y \cdot y \cdot y \cdot y \cdot y}{x \cdot y \cdot y \cdot y \cdot y}$

Now, cancel the x and the y's to get $x \cdot x \cdot y \cdot y = x^2 y^2$.

Example: Simplify the expression

$$\frac{(5x^3)^2 \cdot (2y^4)^3}{14x^3 y^6}$$

$(5x^3)^2 = (5x^3)(5x^3) = 25x^6$
$(2y^4)^3 = (2y^4)(2y^4)(2y^4) = 8y^{12}$

$$\frac{(5x^3)^2 \cdot (2y^4)^3}{14x^3 y^6} = \frac{25x^6 \cdot 8y^{12}}{14x^3 y^6}$$

$$= \frac{200x^6 y^{12}}{14x^3 y^6} \quad (25 \cdot 8 = 200)$$

$$= \frac{100x^3 y^6}{7} \quad \text{(divide numerator and denominator by 2, } x \text{ and } y \text{ in denominator cancel out)}$$

Example: Simplify the expression

$$\frac{-3(xy^3)^7}{81(2x^3 y^2)^3}$$

$-3(xy^3)^7 = -3(x^7 y^{21}) = -3x^7 y^{21}$
$81(2x^3 y^2)^3 = 81(8x^9 y^6) = 648x^9 y^6$

$$\frac{-3(xy^3)^7}{81(2x^3 y^2)^3} = \frac{-3x^7 y^{21}}{648x^9 y^6}$$

$$= \frac{-y^{15}}{216x^2} \quad \text{(divide numerator and denominator by 3, the } x\text{'s in numerator and } y\text{'s in denominator cancel)}$$

Zero Exponents

If $x \neq 0$, then $x^0 = 1$. To explain why this is the case, we'll choose a value for x, say $x = 2$. Now we'll choose a power for x that is greater than 1.

If the exponent is 5, then

$2^5 = 32$.

Now, we'll decrease the exponent by increments of 1 down to 1.

$2^4 = 16$
$2^3 = 8$
$2^2 = 4$
$2^1 = 2$

As you would expect, as the exponent n decreases 2^n decreases.
Now cut n in half each time starting with $n = 1$.

$2^{1/2} = 1.414$
$2^{1/4} = 1.189$
$2^{1/8} = 1.091$
$2^{1/16} = 1.044$
$2^{1/32} = 1.022$

Notice as the exponent gets smaller and smaller (approaching 0), 2^n approaches zero.

•**Note that 0^0 is undefined.**

Negative Exponents

The general rules for positive exponents hold true for negative exponents. If x is an integer and $n \neq 0$, then x^{-n} = $1/x^n$. To see why this holds true, multiply the equation by x^n to get $x^{-n} \cdot x^n = 1$. Remember when multiplying exponential expressions, you add the exponents, so $-n + n = 0$ and $x^0 = 1$.

The important thing to remember is $x^{-n} = 1/x^n$.

You can think of this as the reciprocal of x^{-n} and changing the exponent from negative to positive. Generally speaking, you want to make sure you have all positive exponents in the expression in simplest form.

Examples: Write each expression with only positive exponents.

3^{-4} , $(2a)^{-2}$, $5x^{-3}$

$3^{-4} = 1/(3^4) = 1/81$

$(2a)^{-2} = 1/(2a)^2 = 1/4a^2$

$5x^{-3} = 5/(x^3)$

•**Note when raising a fraction to a negative exponent, take the reciprocal of the fraction and change the exponent to positive.**

Example: Simplify the expression using only positive exponents.

$(x/y)^{-3}$

Take the reciprocal first then change the negative -3 to 3.

(y/x)
$(y/x)^3$

Then apply the rule for raising an exponent to an exponent (remember y is y^1 and x is x^1)

y^3/x^3

Example: Simplify the expression using only positive exponents.

$4x^{-3}/(x^{10})$

There are two ways to solve this.

You can apply the rule for dividing exponential expressions and subtract the exponents.

$$4x^{-3}/(x^{10}) = 4x^{(-3-10)} = 4x^{-13}$$

Then change the negative exponent to positive by changing x^{-13} to $1/x^{13}$.

The simplified form is $\dfrac{4}{x^{13}}$.

You can change the negative exponent to positive first to get $4/(x^3x^{10})$, then apply the rule for multiplying exponential expressions to get $\dfrac{4}{x^{13}}$.

Example: Simplify the expression using only positive exponents.

$$(x^5x^6)/(x^{-4})$$

Keep the common base x in the numerator and add the exponents to get

$$x^{11}/x^{-4}$$

Subtract the exponents to get

$$x^{(11+4)} = x^{15}$$

You could also use the rules for negative exponents to get

$$x^5x^6x^4 = x^{15}$$

Scientific Notation

When numbers get very large or very small, they become difficult to work with and read. Examples of such numbers are 0.0000000000043425 and 546,245,000,000,000,000,000. Oftentimes these types of numbers appear in science, such as the distance planets are from Earth or the mass of atoms. **Scientific notation** is a method to make using such numbers easier by writing them in a simpler form. A positive number in the form N X 10^x, where $1 \le N < 10$ and x is an integer, is said to be in scientific notation.

•Note that X represents multiplication and not a variable.

When a number is in scientific notation, the decimal point is always after the first non zero number. Some examples of numbers in scientific notation are

3.5 X 10^3, 5.89 X 10^{-4} and 2.9123 X 10^6

To change a number into scientific notation, we move the decimal point between the first two non zero numbers. Then we count the number and direction that the decimal point must move to get the original number. The number of decimal places moved will be the exponent. If we move the decimal point to the right, the exponent is positive. If we move the decimal point to the left, the exponent is negative.

Examples: Write the following numbers in scientific notation.

1.   567,325,000,000,000,000
     First place the decimal point between the 5 and 6. Count how many decimal places we have to move to the right to get to the end of the number. Notice we have to move 17 decimal places. Therefore, 567,325,000,000,000,000 written in scientific notation is 5.67325 X 10^{17}.

•Note that the zeros after the 5 are not written when changing to scientific notation. When all the rest of the numbers are zero they are not written.

2.   0.0000000007982

First place the decimal point between the 7 and 9. Count how many decimal places we have to move to the left to get back to the beginning of the number. Notice we have to move 10 decimal places. Therefore 0.0000000007982 written in scientific notation is 7.982×10^{-10} .

Be sure to be careful with numbers such as 65.8×10^3 and 254.69×10^{-4}. At first glance, these appear to be in scientific notation, but the decimal point is not after the first non zero number.

To write in scientific notation, multiply the problem out and then convert to scientific notation.

$65.8 \times 10^3 = 65.8 \times 1000 = 65,800$

Another way to simplify the above is to move the decimal point 3 places to the right since the exponent is 3.

Now we can change 65,800 into scientific notation, which is 6.58×10^4.

In the example 254.69×10^{-4} , multiply to get $254.69 \times 0.0001 = 0.025469$.

Another way to simplify the above is to move the decimal point 4 places to the left since the exponent is -4.

Now we can change 0.025469 into scientific notation, which is 2.5469×10^{-2} .

In some cases, using scientific notation makes multiplying and dividing very large or very small numbers easier.

Example: Evaluate $\dfrac{(500,000,000,000)(0.000000004)}{(20,000,000,000,000)(0.00000000025)}$

First step is to write each number in scientific notation.

$\dfrac{(5 \times 10^{11})(4 \times 10^{-9})}{(2 \times 10^{13})(2.5 \times 10^{-10})}$

Regroup to make the multiplication easier.

$\dfrac{(5)(4)(10^{11})(10^{-9})}{(2)(2.5)(10^{13})(10^{-10})} = \dfrac{(20)(10^{11})(10^{-9})}{(5)(10^{13})(10^{-10})}$

Use the rule for exponents when multiplying to get

$\dfrac{(20)(10^{11-9})}{(5)(10^{13-10})} = \dfrac{(20)(10^2)}{(5)(10^3)}$

Use the rule for dividing exponents to get

$\dfrac{20}{5(10)} = \dfrac{20}{50} = \dfrac{2}{5}$

Review Problems: Set 1

State the base and the exponent for each of the following expressions.

1. $2x^4$
2. $(3x)^5$
3. $-r^8$
4. $(-ab)^2$

Simplify each expression using only positive exponents.

5. 4^4
6. -4^3
7. $(-2)^4(3)^3$
8. 11^0
9. $10^0 5^2$
10. $x^4 x^2 x^6$
11. $(x^3 y)(x^2 y^3)$
12. $(3xyz^2)^2$
13. $(5x)^3$
14. x^{-2}
15. $(x^3)/x$
16. $(x^4 y^2)/(x^2 y)$
17. $(a^2/b)^4$
18. $(2/3)^{-2}$
19. $(b^4)^{-3}$
20. $3/(b^{-2})$
21. $(c^3)^2 c^{-1}$
22. $(a^{20} a^{11})/a^3$

Write the following in scientific notation.

23. 432,900,000,000
24. 0.0000006934
25. 938.35 X 10^3
26. 92.6 X 10^{-2}

Change from scientific to standard notation.

27. 4.5 X 10^3
28. 9.77 X 10^{-8}
29. 5.387 X 10^7

Evaluate the following.

30. $\dfrac{(60,000,000,000,000)(0.00000000003)}{(20,000,000,000)(0.0000000004)}$

Polynomials

In algebra, a **term** is a variable, number or a product of a number and a variable raised to a power. When a term is just a number, it is called a **constant**. The **coefficient** of the term can be thought of as the number in front of the variable. The **leading coefficient** is the coefficient in front of the term with the highest variable exponent In the expression $4x^2 + 3x + 2$, the leading coefficient is 4 since $4x^2$ is the term with the highest variable exponent. A **polynomial** is a term or a sum of terms whose exponents are whole numbers and no variables in the denominator. If a polynomial has one term it is known as a **monomial.** If it has two terms, it is known as a **binomial** and if it has three terms, it is known as a **trinomial.** The **degree** of monomial is the exponent of the variable. The degree of a polynomial is the degree of the term with the highest degree.

•**Note an easy way to remember the classification of polynomials is that** *mon* **means one,** *bi* **means two and** *tri* **means three.**

Examples:

Terms: x, $3xy$, $-5x$, 17, $(10/11)x^4 y^2$, $0.3y$ (coefficients of these terms are 1, 3, -5, 17, 10/11, 0.3)

Polynomials: $-5x$, $3x + 2xy$, $(1/2)x^2 + 2x + 3$, $13xy - \sqrt{14} + 3y$

The following are not polynomials: $(x - 2)/x^2$, $14x^{-1/4} + 2x$, $6x^{1/3} + 4$

 The first expression is not a polynomial because there is a variable in the denominator. The last two expressions are not polynomials because they have exponents that are not whole numbers.

Examples:

What are the degrees of the following polynomials?

 1. x^4 , the degree is 4 because the exponent is 4.
 2. $5x^4y^3$, the degree is 7 because the sum of the exponents of the variables is 7.
 3. 5, the degree is 0 because there are no variables, 5 is a constant.
 4. $4x^6y^4 + 10xy^3 + 20y$, the degree is 10 because the term with the highest degree is $4x^6y^4$, which is 10. The degree of the second term is 4 and the degree of the third term is 1.

•**Note that terms in polynomials are generally written with the exponents in decreasing order.**

Adding and Subtracting Polynomials

 When adding or subtracting polynomials, look for like terms and add or subtract them. Recall that like terms are terms that have the same variables with the same exponents.

Example: Add the polynomials by combining like terms.

$4x^2 + 3x - 5$ and $-6x^2 - 7x + 10$

Solution:

$(4x^2 + 3x - 5) + (-6x^2 - 7x + 10)$

$4x^2 + 3x - 5$

$- 6x^2 - 7x + 10$

Add the like terms. Notice the like terms have the same color for easy identification.

$4x^2 - 6x^2 = -2x^2$

 $3x - 7x = -4x$

 $-5 + 10 = 5$

None of the terms remaining are like terms, so the answer is $-2x^2 - 4x + 5$.

Example: Add the polynomials.

$5x^4y^3 + 3y^2 + 6x^4y^3 - 2y^2 + x + y$
Add the like terms

$5x^4y^3 + 6x^4y^3 = 11x^4y^3$

 $3y^2 - 2y^2 = y^2$
Notice there is an x and a y left, cannot add them since they are not like terms.

Therefore the answer is $11x^4y^3 + y^2 + x + y$.

Example: Subtract the polynomials.

$(-3x^2y + 2xy + x) - (2x^2y - 4xy + 3x)$

$-3x^2y + 2xy + x - 2x^2y + 4xy - 3x$

Combine like terms

$-3x^2y - 2x^2y = -5x^2y$

$2xy + 4xy = 6xy$

$x - 3x = -2x$

The terms remaining are not like, so the answer is $-5x^2y + 6xy - 2x$.

Example: Subtract the polynomials.

$(-13x^5y^4z^3 - 7x^5y^4z) - (10x^5y^4z^3 + 14x^5y^4z)$

Combine like terms

$-13x^5y^4z^3 - 10x^5y^4z^3 = -23x^5y^4z^3$

$-7x^5y^4z - 14x^5y^4z = -21x^5y^4z$

Therefore the answer is $-23x^5y^4z^3 - 21x^5y^4z$

Example: Perform the given operations to the polynomials below.

$(x^2y + 2y + 3x + 5) - (2x^2y + 3y + 4x + 1) + (3x^2y - 2y + 5x + 7)$

Combine like terms

$x^2y - 2x^2y + 3x^2y = 2x^2y$

$2y - 3y - 2y = -3y$

$3x - 4x + 5x = 4x$

$5 - 1 + 7 = 11$

Therefore, the answer is $2x^2y - 3y + 4x + 11$.

Multiplying Polynomials

When multiplying a monomial by a polynomial, use the distributive property of multiplication. If you don't recall the distributive property, think of this as multiplying the monomial by each term in the polynomial and combining like terms.

Example: Multiply the following.

$5x^2(3xy + 2x)$

Multiply $5x^2$ by each term of the polynomial.
$5x^2(3xy) = 15x^3y$

$5x^2(2x) = 10x^3$

Since $15x^3y$ and $10x^3$ are not like terms, they cannot be added. Therefore, the answer is $15x^3y + 10x^3$.

Example: Multiply the following.

$-3y^3(7xy + 4x - 5y^3)$

Multiply $-3y^3$ by each term in the polynomial.

$-3y^3(7xy) = -21xy^4$

$-3y^3(4x) = -12xy^3$

$-3y^3(-5y^3) = 15y^6$

There are no like terms, so we cannot add them. Therefore the answer is $15y^6 - 21xy^4 - 12xy^3$.

The FOIL Method

When multiplying two binomials, we can use a method known as **FOIL**. F means "first", O means "outer", I means "inner" and L means "last". This refers to the terms in the binomials. Basically, we are just multiplying each term in the first binomial with each term in the second binomial and combining like terms.

Example: Multiply the following.

$(2x + 3y)(4 - 3x)$

F (first terms) $(2x)(4) = 8x$

O (outer terms) $(2x)(-3x) = -6x^2$

I (inner terms) $(3y)(4) = 12y$

L (last terms) $(3y)(-3x) = -9xy$

There are no like terms, therefore the answer is $-6x^2 - 9xy + 8x + 12y$.

Notice that we just multiplied $2x$ by each term in the second binomial, then multiplied the $3x$ by each term in the second binomial and combined like terms.

Example: Multiply the following.

$(3x^2 - 5y)(2y - 6x)$

$(3x^2)(2y) = 6x^2y$

$(3x^2)(-6x) = -18x^3$

$(-5y)(2y) = -10y^2$

$(-5y)(-6x) = -30xy$

There are no like terms, therefore the answer is $-18x^3 + 6x^2y - 10y^2 - 30xy$.

Example: Multiply the following.

$(x + 5)(2x - 4)$

$x(2x) + x(-4) + 5(2x) + 5(-4)$

$2x^2 - 4x + 10x - 20$

Combine like terms to get

$2x^2 + 6x - 20$

Multiplying a Binomial With a Trinomial

When multiplying a binomial with a trinomial, we use the distributive property. Basically, we multiply the first term in the binomial with each term in the trinomial, then the second term in the binomial with each term in the trinomial and combine like terms.

Example: Multiply the following.

$(3x + 6y)(x^2 - 4xy + y^2)$

Multiply $3x$ by each term in the trinomial

$(3x)(x^2) + (3x)(-4xy) + (3x)(y^2) = 3x^3 - \mathbf{12x^2y} + \mathbf{3xy^2}$

Now multiply $6y$ by each term in the trinomial

$(6y)(x^2) + (6y)(-4xy) + (6y)(y^2) = \mathbf{6x^2y} - \mathbf{24xy^2} + 6y^3$

Combine like terms marked in bold

$3x^3 + 6y^3 - \mathbf{12x^2y} + \mathbf{6x^2y} + \mathbf{3xy^2} - \mathbf{24xy^2}$

$3x^3 + 6y^3 - 6x^2y - 21xy^2$

Example: Multiply the following.

$(2x - 2y + 4)(x + y)$

Multiply each term in the trinomial with each of the two terms in the binomial.

$(2x)(x) + (2x)(y) + (-2y)(x) + (-2y)(y) + 4(x) + 4(y)$

$2x^2 + 2xy - 2xy - 2y^2 + 4x + 4y$

Combine like terms to get $2x^2 - 2y^2 + 4x + 4y$.

Multiplying Two Trinomials

To multiply two trinomials, use the same method as when multiplying a binomial with a trinomial. Multiply each term in the first trinomial with each term in the second trinomial and combine like terms.

Example: Multiply the following trinomials.

$(3x + y - z)(4x + 2y + 3z)$

1st term in first trinomial with each term in second trinomial $(3x)(4x) + (3x)(2y) + (3x)(3z) = 12x^2 + 6xy + 9xz$
2nd term in first trinomial with each term in second trinomial $(y)(4x) + (y)(2y) + (y)(3z) = 4xy + 2y^2 + 3yz$

3rd term in first trinomial with each term in second trinomial $(-z)(4x) + (-z)(2y) + (-z)(3z) = -4xz - 2yz - 3z^2$

Now combine like terms.

$12x^2 + 2y^2 - 3z^2 + 6xy + 4xy + 9xz - 4xz + 3yz - 2yz$

$12x^2 + 2y^2 - 3z^2 + 10xy + 5xz + yz$

Multiplying Three Polynomials

When multiplying three polynomials, multiply any two polynomials first. Get the result, then multiply the third polynomial to the result and combine like terms.

Example: Multiply the following polynomials.

$5xy(3x + 2y - 3)(7x + 4)$

Multiply $(3x + 2y - 3)(7x + 4)$ first.

$(3x)(7x) + (3x)(4) + (2y)(7x) + (2y)(4) + (-3)(7x) + (-3)(4)$

$21x^2 + 12x + 14xy + 8y - 21x - 12$

Combine like terms to get

$21x^2 + 14xy - 9x + 8y - 12$

Now multiply $5xy(21x^2 + 14xy - 9x + 8y - 12)$

$(5xy)(21x^2) + (5xy)(14xy) + (5xy)(-9x) + (5xy)(8y) + (5xy)(-12)$

$105x^3y + 70x^2y^2 - 45x^2y + 40xy^2 - 60xy$

Special Kinds of Products

$(x + y)(x - y) = x^2 - y^2$

$(x + y)^2 = (x + y)(x + y) = x^2 + 2xy + y^2$

$(x - y)^2 = (x - y)(x - y) = x^2 - 2xy + y^2$

•**Note that the result of all of these special products can be obtained by using the FOIL method.**

Review Problems : Set 2

Tell whether each of the following is a monomial, binomial or trinomial and determine its degree.

1. $3x$
2. $4x^2 + 2y$
3. $5x^4y^3 - 2xy + y^2$
4. $-17x^7y^4$
5. 23
6. $6y^4 - 3x^2$

Write the polynomial that represents the perimeter of the rectangle.

7.

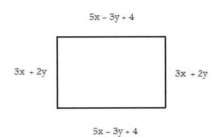

Add or subtract the polynomials as indicated.

8. $(2x + 5y) + (3x - 8y)$
9. $(8x - 2y) - (5x + 7y)$
10. $(3xy + 4y) + (9xy - 8y)$
11. $(6xy - x) - (-4xy + 2x)$
12. $(x^2y + 3xy + y^2) + (2x^2y^2 - 9xy - 4y^2)$
13. $(3x^2y^2 + 2xy - xy^2) - (8x^2y^2 - 4xy + 2xy^2)$
14. $(-ab - a - b) + (2ab + 2a + 3b)$
15. $(-2ab + 3a + 5b) - (-2ab - 3a + 6b)$

Write the polynomial that represents the area of the square.

16.

$x + 2y$

Write the polynomial that represents the area of the rectangle.

17.

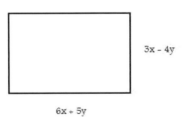

Multiply each of the following polynomials.

18. $(3x - 7y)(2x + 5y)$
19. $(xy + y)(3xy - 9y)$
20. $(2m - n)(2n + 3m)$
21. $(6z + 7)(5z - 2)$
22. $(2x^2 + 3x + 4)(x - 5)$
23. $(x^2y - 2y - 5)(xy + 2x)$
24. $(4x^2 + 5x + 1)(x - y)$
25. $(x + y)(2x + 3y + 2)$
26. $(ab + b - 3)(a - b - 5)$
27. $3x(x - 2)(x + 6)$

28. $4y(x + 5)(x - 4)$
29. $(x + 2)(x - 2)$
30. $(x + 4)(x + 4)$
31. $(x - 5)(x - 5)$

Finding the Greatest Common Factor

A **factor** is a number that divides evenly into another number. For example, 2 divides evenly into 12, so 2 is a factor of 12. Finding the factors is known as **factoring.**

1, 2, 3, 4, 6 and 12 are all factors of 12.
When each factor of a number is a prime number, the number is said to be in **prime factored form.**

Examples: Find the prime factored form (or prime factorization) of each of the following

1. 24
   Divide 24 by 2 to get 12.
   Then 12 can also be divided by 2 to get 6.
   Next, 6 can be divided by 2 to get 3.
   That leaves us with $2 \cdot 2 \cdot 2 \cdot 3$.
   Therefore the prime factorization is $2^3 \cdot 3$.

2. 72
   Divide 72 by 2 to get 36.
   Then 36 can be divided by 2 to get 18.
   Next, 18 can be divided by 2 to get 9.
   Finally, 9 can be divided by 3 to get 3.
   That leaves us with $2 \cdot 2 \cdot 2 \cdot 3 \cdot 3$.
   Therefore the prime factorization is $2^3 \cdot 3^2$

•**Note how multiples of the same factor are written in exponential form.**
•**Note that if you are unsure what number divides evenly into another number, if the number is even it is divisible by 2. If the sum of the digits in the number is divisible by 3, then the entire number is divisible by 3. (18... 1 + 8 = 9, 9 is divisible by 3, so 18 is divisible by 3).**

3. 250
   Divide 250 by 10 to get 25
   Next divide the 10 by 2 to get 5. That leaves us with 2, 5 and 25 as factors.
   Finally divide 25 by 5 to get $2 \cdot 5 \cdot 5 \cdot 5$ as the factors of 250.
   Therefore the prime factorization is $5^3 \cdot 2$.

•**Note that any number ending in 0 is divisible by 10. Any number ending in 0 or 5 is divisible by 5. If a number ends in 00, it is divisible by 100. If it ends in 000 it is divisible by 1,000, etc.**

Suppose we want to find the largest number that is a factor or two or more numbers. That number is called the **greatest common factor (GCF)** of the numbers. To find the greatest common factor, do the prime factorization of each number and find the lowest power of common factors and multiply them together.

Example: Find the greatest common factor of 40 and 72.

40/5 = 8, so we have $5 \cdot 8$ as factors of 40.
Notice that 8 can be factored into $2 \cdot 2 \cdot 2$
Therefore the prime factorization of 40 is $5 \cdot 2 \cdot 2 \cdot 2$

The prime factorization of 72 is $2 \cdot 2 \cdot 2 \cdot 3 \cdot 3$ from example 2 above.
Notice the common factors are marked in red.

Therefore, the GCF of 40 and 72 is $2 \cdot 2 \cdot 2 = 8$.

Example: Find the greatest common factor of 45 and 135.

$45/5 = 9$, so we have $5 \cdot 9$ as factors of 45.
Notice that 9 is $3 \cdot 3$.
Therefore, the prime factorization of 45 is $3 \cdot 3 \cdot 5$.

$135/5 = 27$, so we have $27 \cdot 5$ as factors of 135.
Notice that 27 is $3 \cdot 3 \cdot 3$.
Therefore, the prime factorization of 135 is $3 \cdot 3 \cdot 3 \cdot 5$.

Notice the common factors are 3 and 5. The lowest power of each factor gives us $3 \cdot 3 \cdot 5$.

Therefore, the GCF of 45 and 135 is 45.

Example: Find the GCF of $6a^2b$, $24a^2b^2$ and $48a^3b^3$.

$6a^2b = 3 \cdot 2 \cdot a \cdot a \cdot b$

$24a^2b^2 = 3 \cdot 2 \cdot 2 \cdot 2 \cdot a \cdot a \cdot b \cdot b$

$48a^3b^3 = 3 \cdot 2 \cdot 2 \cdot 2 \cdot 2 \cdot a \cdot a \cdot a \cdot b \cdot b \cdot b$

Notice the common factors are 3, 2, a and b.

The lowest power of each factor is $3 \cdot 2 \cdot a \cdot a \cdot b$.

Therefore, the GCF is $6a^2b$.

Example: Find the GCF of $15x^2y^3$, $20y^2$ and $45xy$.

$15x^2y^3 = 3 \cdot 5 \cdot x \cdot x \cdot y \cdot y \cdot y$

$20y^2 = 2 \cdot 2 \cdot 5 \cdot y \cdot y$

$45xy = 3 \cdot 3 \cdot 5 \cdot x \cdot y$

Notice the common factors are 5 and y.

$20y^2$ has 2 as a factor but the other 2 don't and $45xy$ and $15x^2y^3$ have 3 and x as a factor but $20y^2$ doesn't. The lowest power of each common factor is 5 and y.

Therefore, the GCF is $5y$.

Factoring Out the GCF

In a previous section of this chapter, we showed how to multiply a monomial by a polynomial. For example,

$$3xy(x^2 + 6y^3) = (3xy)(x^2) + (3xy)(6y^3)$$
$$= 3x^3y + 18xy^4$$

In this section, we will learn how to reverse this process by taking the binomial $3x^3y + 18xy^4$ and factor out the GCF to get $3xy(x^2 + 6y^3)$.
    To factor out the GCF, first factor each term of the binomial separately. Then find the GCF. Once you have the GCF, you factor it out. Factoring out the GCF is basically dividing each term in the polynomial by the GCF. As a result, the polynomial inside the parentheses will be in lowest terms.

Example: Factor $20xy + 35xy^3$.

$20xy = 2 \cdot 2 \cdot 5 \cdot x \cdot y$

$35xy^3 = 5 \cdot 7 \cdot x \cdot y \cdot y \cdot y$

Notice the common factors are 5, x and y. The lowest power of each factor gives us a GCF of $5 \cdot x \cdot y = 5xy$.

Now divide each term of the polynomial by the GCF.

$20xy/5xy = 4$

$35xy^3/5xy = 7y^2$

Therefore, $4 + 7y^2$ becomes the new polynomial and $5xy$ is factored out. The factored form of $20xy + 35y^3$ is $5xy(4 + 7y^2)$.

Example: Factor $2xyz^3 + 14y^2z^2 - 16xz^4$.

$2xyz^3 = 2 \cdot x \cdot y \cdot z \cdot z \cdot z$

$14y^2z^2 = 7 \cdot 2 \cdot y \cdot y \cdot z \cdot z$

$-16xz^4 = -2 \cdot 2 \cdot 2 \cdot 2 \cdot x \cdot z \cdot z \cdot z \cdot z$

Notice the common factors are 2 and z. The lowest power of each factor gives us a GCF of $2 \cdot z \cdot z = 2z^2$.

Now divide each term of the polynomial by $2z^2$.

$2xyz^3/2z^2 = xyz$

$14y^2z^2/2z^2 = 7y^2$

$-16xz^4/2z^2 = -8xz^2$

The factored form of $2xyz^3 + 14y^2z^2 - 16xz^4$ is $2z^2(xyz + 7y^2 - 8xz^2)$.

Example: Factor $5x + 7y + 9$, if possible.

$5x = 5 \cdot x$

$7y = 7 \cdot y$

$9 = 3 \cdot 3$

Notice there are no factors in common other than 1, therefore $5x + 7y + 9$ cannot be factored.

A polynomial which cannot be factored is called a prime polynomial.

•**Note in some cases the opposite or negative of the GCF may be factored out. An example is $-2x + 6xy$. The GCF is $2x$ but because of the – in front of the $2x$, you factor out $-2x$ to get $-2x(1 - 3y)$.**

Factoring By Grouping

Suppose you wish to factor an expression such as $wx + wz + yx + yz$. Notice there are no common factors among the four terms. But there is a way to factor such an expression. Group terms that have common factors. Basically treat this as two separate binomials to factor and then combine the factored binomials and factor again. First factor $wx + wz$. Notice the common factor is w. Factor out the w to get $w(x + z)$.

Next factor $yx + yz$. Notice the common factor is y. Factor out the y to get $y(x + z)$.

Now combine to get $w(x + z) + y(x + z)$.

Notice that the common factor in bold is $(x + z)$.
Factor out $(x + z)$ to get $(x + z)(w + y)$.

   You can check the answer by applying the FOIL method to $(x + z)(w + y)$. When doing so, you'll notice you get $wx + wz + yx + yz$. Since the result of the FOIL method matches the original polynomial, the factoring is correct.

Example: Factor $5x^3y + 5x^3z + 7xy + 7xz + y + z$.

   There are no factors in common amongst all the terms, so we start grouping terms together that have common factors. Notice $5x$ is in the first 2 terms, so group $5y^3x$ and $5z^3x$. Notice $7x$ is common in $7xy$ and $7xz$, so group them together. The terms y and z have no factors in common.

Factor $5x^3$ out of $5x^3y + 5x^3z$ to get $5x^3(y + z)$.

Factor $7x$ out of $7xy + 7xz$ to get $7x(y + z)$.

Think of the $y + z$ at the end as one term, $(y + z)$

Combine everything to get $5xz^3(y + z) + 7x(y + z) + (y + z)$.

Notice the common factor in bold is $(y + z)$.

Factor out $(y + z)$ to get $(y + z)(5xz^3 + 7x + 1)$.

•**Note when factoring to factor completely so that all remaining terms are completely simplified.**
•**Note that $(y + z)$ is one term, whereas $y + z$ is two terms.**

Review Problems: Set 3

   1. Below shows the prime factorization of 3 monomials. What is their GCF?

   $3 \cdot 3 \cdot 5 \cdot x \cdot x \cdot y$
   $2 \cdot 3 \cdot 3 \cdot x \cdot y \cdot y \cdot y$
   $5 \cdot 7 \cdot y \cdot y$

Find the prime factored form of each of the following numbers.

   2. 45
   3. 68
   4. 122
   5. 72
   6. 48
   7. 225

Find the missing part of each factorization below.

   8. $2x + 6 = 2(\square + 3)$
   9. $5xy - 10x^2 + 15 = 5(xy - \square + 3)$
   10. $-12a^2b + 24ab^2 + 48a^3 = -12a(ab - 2b^2 \square\square)$
   11. $ax + bx + ay + by = (a + b)(\square + \square)$
Find the GCF of each of the following.

   12. 14, 56

13. 16, 48, 72
14. 5, 20, 125
15. $2x^3yz$, $4xyz^3$, $8x^2yz^2$
16. $6ab$, $12ab^2$, $45a^4$

Factor each polynomial, if possible.

17. $3x^2 + 18$
18. $6ab - 19xy$
19. $12x^2y - 36xy + 48$
20. $2z^2 + 4z$
21. $15xy - 16wz$
22. $25x^4 - 10x^2 - 5x$

Factor each polynomial.

23. $5(a + b) - c(a + b)$
24. $(x - y)5z + (x - y)w$
25. $ax - bx + ay - by$
26. $x^2 + 2y + xy + 2x$

Factoring Trinomials

Oftentimes trinomials can be written as a product of two binomials. Because of this fact, there are several techniques we can use to factor trinomials. Sometimes a trinomial can be factored into a binomial multiplied by itself. In such cases, the trinomial is called a **perfect square trinomial.**

A perfect square trinomial is in one of two forms

$(x + y)(x + y) = x^2 + 2xy + y^2$
$(x - y)(x - y) = x^2 - 2xy + y^2$

The easy way to identify a perfect square trinomial is to look at the last term and the coefficient of the middle term, when the coefficient of the first term is one. If you take the square root of the last term and get a whole number and double that number to get the middle term coefficient, then it's a perfect square trinomial. The factored form will look like two binomials that you can FOIL. In fact, factoring a trinomial in such a way is often called the reverse FOIL method.

Example: Factor the following trinomial.

$x^2 + 8x + 16$

Notice the square root of 16 is 4, which is a whole number. The coefficient of the middle term is 8, which is 2 times 4. Therefore $x^2 + 8x + 16$ is a perfect square trinomial.

The factored form is $(x + 4)(x + 4)$ or $(x + 4)^2$.

Example: Factor the following trinomial.

$x^2 - 6x + 9$

Notice the principal square root of 9 is 3, but the square root of 9 is also -3. The coefficient of the middle term is -6. Double the -3 to get -6. Using the above formula for a perfect square trinomial with a negative coefficient in the second term gives us $(x - 3)(x - 3)$.
If you use the FOIL method, you will notice that you have $(-3x) + (-3x)$ to get the middle term, which is $-6x$. Sometimes you can factor out a GCF from a trinomial and still have a perfect square trinomial as the factor remaining.

Example: Factor the trinomial.

$2x^2 + 16x + 32$

Notice 2 is the GCF, factor it out to get $2(x^2 + 8x + 16)$. In the first example, we showed that $x^2 + 8x + 16$ is a perfect square trinomial factored as $(x + 4)(x + 4)$. Therefore $2x^2 + 16x + 32$ is factored to $2(x + 4)(x + 4)$.

Trinomials With Leading Coefficient of 1

When the coefficient of the squared term (x^2, y^2 etc) is 1, you take the following steps to factor the trinomial. Make sure the terms are written from term with highest power of the variable to lowest power of the variable. Get the factorization of the last term of the trinomial. Add the factors to get the coefficient of the second term. The factored form will look like two binomials multiplied together.

Example: Factor $x^2 + 8x + 12$.

The terms are from highest power to lowest power.

The factorization of 12 is $1 \cdot 12$, $3 \cdot 4$, $6 \cdot 2$ (and their negatives, if you multiply two negative numbers you get a positive number, so -2 times -6 is 12. But two negatives added together will not give a positive result, so the negative factors cannot be used in this problem)

The factors must now add to 8. The factors that multiply to 12 and add to 8 are 6 and 2.

The factored form of $x^2 + 8x + 12$ is $(x + 6)(x + 2)$.

•**Note that you can check your answer by using the FOIL method to see if you get the original trinomial. If so, then the answer is correct.**

Example: Factor $y^2 - 6y + 5$.

The factorization of 5 is $1 \cdot 5$, $-1 \cdot (-5)$. Notice that $-1 + (-5) = -6$.

Therefore, the factored form of $y^2 - 6y + 5 = (x - 1)(x - 5)$.

Example: Factor $x^2 - x - 20$.

The factorization of -20 is $1 \cdot (-20)$, $-1 \cdot 20$, $2 \cdot (-10)$, $-2 \cdot 10$, $-4 \cdot 5$, $4 \cdot (-5)$.

Notice that $4 + (-5) = -1$ which is the coefficient of the middle term (1 is assumed when only the variable is present, $x = 1x$, $-x = -1x$, etc). Therefore, the factored form of $x^2 - x - 20 = (x + 4)(x - 5)$.

•**Note that it's easier to sometimes not list all the factorizations. In the above problem, the coefficient of the middle term is -1. The factors must be only 1 number apart becauses it's the only way for them to add to -1. So it isn't important to consider the factorizations with 1 and 20 or 2 and 10).**

Example: Factor $y^2 + 6y - 16$.

The factorization of -16 is $1 \cdot (-16)$, $-1 \cdot 16$, $2 \cdot (-8)$, $-2 \cdot 8$, $4 \cdot (-4)$

Notice that $8 + (-2) = 6$

Therefore, the factored form of $y^2 + 6y - 16 = (y - 2)(y + 8)$.
Here are the possibilities for a factored trinomial.

The sign of the last term is + and the sign of the middle coefficient is positive

(+)(+)

Example: $(x + 4)(x + 5)$ is the factored form of $x^2 + 9x + 20$.

The sign of the last term is negative and the sign of the middle term is either positive of negative.

(+)(-)
(-)(+)

Examples: $(y + 6)(y - 3)$ is the factored form of $y^2 + 3y - 18$.

$(y - 6)(y + 3)$ is the factored form of $y^2 - 3y - 18$.

The sign of the last term is positive and the sign of the middle term is negative.

(-)(-)

Example: $(x - 5)(x - 7)$ is the factored form of $x^2 - 12x + 35$.

Trinomials With Leading Coefficient Not 1

Oftentimes a trinomial will not have a leading coefficient of 1. For example, suppose we want to factor the trinomial $3x^2 + 2x - 5$.

First check to see if there is a GCF other than 1. If so, factor it out. There isn't in this problem and there are a few more possibilities to consider. In this case with a leading coefficient of 3 and last term of -5, we have the following possibilities.

$(3x + 1)(x - 5)$
$(3x - 1)(x + 5)$
$(3x + 5)(x - 1)$
$(3x - 5)(x + 1)$

You could use FOIL method on all 4 possibilities to see which one gives the original trinomial of $3x^2 + 2x - 5$. But you don't need to do that. All you need to do is multiply the outer terms and inner terms and see which terms add to $2x$.

$(3x)(-5) + 1(x) = -15x + 1x = -14x$
$(3x)(5) + (-1)(x) = 15x - 1x = 14x$
$(3x)(-1) + (5)(x) = -3x + 5x = 2x$

Notice that the third possibility gives $2x$ as the middle term. Therefore, the factored form of $3x^2 + 2x - 5$ is $(3x + 5)(x - 1)$.

There is a way to test to see if a trinomial can be factored. You could go through all the possibilities as in the previous problem to see if any of them work, but that can be very time consuming. The easiest way is to think of the trinomial in the form $ax^2 + bx + c$. Identify a, b and c and substitute into $b^2 - 4ac$. If the result is a perfect square (has a square root that is a whole number), then it can be factored using integer coefficients. If not, then we say the trinomial is prime.

Example: Factor $5x^2 - 10x + 2$, if possible.

The equation is already in the correct form, so $a = 5$, $b = -10$, $c = 2$

$b^2 - 4ac = (-10)^2 - 4(5)(2) = 100 - 40 = 60$.

Since 60 is not a perfect square, we cannot factor using the above methods.

Example: Factor $24x^2 + 28x - 12$.

First check to see if the trinomial is factorable.

$a = 24$, $b = 28$, $c = -12$.
$b^2 - 4ac = (28)^2 - 4(24)(-12)$
$= 1936$ and $\sqrt{1936} = 44$, therefore it is factorable.

Next we look for a GCF. Get the prime factorization of 24, 28 and 12.

$24 = 2 \cdot 2 \cdot 2 \cdot 3$
$28 = 2 \cdot 2 \cdot 7$
$12 = 2 \cdot 2 \cdot 3$

Therefore the GCF is 4. Factor out the 4 to get

$4(6x^2 + 7x - 3)$

The possibilities to factor $(6x^2 + 7x - 3)$. (Remember the first terms must multiply to $6x^2$ and the last terms must multiply to -3)

$(3x + 3)(2x - 1)$
$(3x + 1)(2x - 3)$
$(3x - 3)(2x + 1)$
$(3x - 1)(2x + 3)$
$(6x + 3)(x - 1)$
$(6x + 1)(x - 3)$
$(6x - 1)(x + 3)$
$(6x - 3)(x + 1)$

Check all the possibilities by multiplying the outer terms and inner terms and combining like terms. Notice that multiplying the outer and inner terms of $(2x + 3)(3x - 1)$ gives $(2x)(-1) + 3(3x) = 7x$. Therefore, the factored form of $24x^2 + 28x - 12$ is $4(2x + 3)(3x - 1)$.

Difference of Squares and Sum and Difference of Cubes

Difference of Squares

Some binomials can be written as the **difference of two squares**. In order to factor a difference of two squares, it's important to recognize some **perfect squares**. The first 25 perfect squares are as follows:

1, 4, 9, 16, 25, 36, 49, 64, 81, 100, 121, 144, 169, 196, 225, 256, 289, 324, 361, 400, 441, 484, 529, 576 and 625.

The formula for factoring the difference of two squares is

$(x^2 - y^2) = (x - y)(x + y)$
It's easy to think of this as just taking $\sqrt{x^2}$ and $\sqrt{y^2}$, which is x and y. Both binomials in the factored form will have x and y, one with a "-" between them and one with a "+" between them.
Example: Factor $x^2 - 16$.

Notice that x^2 and 16 are both perfect squares.

$\sqrt{x^2} = x$ and $\sqrt{16} = 4$, therefore the factored form of $x^2 - 16$ is $(x - 4)(x + 4)$.

Example: Factor $4x^2 - 25$.

$\sqrt{4x^2} = 2x$ and $\sqrt{25} = 5$, therefore the factored form of $4x^2 - 25$ is $(2x - 5)(2x + 5)$.

Example: Factor $25y^2 - 49x^2$.

$\sqrt{25y^2} = 5y$ and $\sqrt{49x^2} = 7x$, therefore the factored form of $25y^2 - 49x^2$ is $(5y - 7x)(5y + 7x)$.

Example: Factor $x^4 - 16$.

$\sqrt{x^4} = x^2$ and $\sqrt{16} = 4$, so that gives us $(x^2 - 4)(x^2 + 4)$. But this is not simplified yet. Notice $(x^2 - 4)$ in blue.

That factor is also a difference of squares, so we must factor that as well.

$\sqrt{x^2} = x$ and $\sqrt{4} = x$, so $(x^2 - 4) = (x + 2)(x - 2)$

Therefore the factored form of $x^4 - 16$ is $(x + 2)(x - 2)(x^2 + 4)$.

Sum and Difference of Cubes

Just as some binomials can be written as a difference of two squares, some binomials can be written as a **sum and difference of cubes.** A number such as 64 is a perfect cube since $4^3 = 64$. A expression such as y^3 is a perfect cube because $(y)^3 = y^3$. It's important to recognize some of the first few perfect cubes to make factoring easier. The first 10 prefect cubes are 1, 8, 27, 64, 125, 216, 343, 512, 729 and 1000.

The formulas for factoring the sum and difference of cubes are as follows:

$$(x^3 + y^3) = (x + y)(x^2 - xy + y^2)$$
$$(x^3 - y^3) = (x - y)(x^2 + xy + y^2)$$

Example: Factor $x^3 + 27$.

If you look at the formula for sum of cubes, notice that you need to take the cube root of x^3 to get x and the cube root of y^3 to get y. It's important to do this because you need to use x and the value for y in the formula. In this problem use the formula

$(x^3 + y^3) = (x + y)(x^2 - xy + y^2)$
$(x^3 + 27)$
$\sqrt[3]{x^3} = x$ and $\sqrt[3]{27} = 3$.

Substitute x and 3 into the formula to get

$(x^3 + 27) = (x + 3)(x^2 - (x)(3) + (3)^2)$

$\qquad = (x + 3)(x^2 - 3x + 9)$

•**Note that you can check your answer by multiplication.** $(x + 3)(x^2 - 3x + 9) = x(x^2) + x(-3x) + x(9) + 3(x^2) + 3(-3x) + 3(9) = x^2 - 3x^2 + 9x + 3x^2 - 9x + 27 = x^3 + 27.$

Example: Factor $8x^3 - 125y^3$.

For this problem, we need to use the formula for difference of cubes.
$(x^3 - y^3) = (x - y)(x^2 + xy + y^2)$
$(8x^3 - 125y^3)$
$\sqrt[3]{8x^3} = 2x$ (because $2x \cdot 2x \cdot 2x = 8x^3$) and $\sqrt[3]{125y^3} = 5y$ (because $5y \cdot 5y \cdot 5y = 125y^3$)

Now substitute $2x$ for x and $4y$ for y in the formula to get

$8x^3 - 125y^3 = (2x - 5y)[(2x)^2 + (2x)(5y) + (5y)^2]$

$\qquad = (2x - 5y)(4x^2 + 10xy + 25y^2)$

Example: Factor $4a^6 + 32a^3$.

First get the factorization of each term.

$4a^6 = \mathbf{2} \cdot \mathbf{2} \cdot \mathbf{a} \cdot \mathbf{a} \cdot \mathbf{a} \cdot a \cdot a \cdot a \cdot a$
$32a^3 = 2 \cdot 2 \cdot 2 \cdot \mathbf{2} \cdot \mathbf{2} \cdot \mathbf{a} \cdot \mathbf{a} \cdot \mathbf{a}$

Notice the common factors in bold. Factor out the GCF of $4a^3$.

$4a^3(a^3 + 8)$

Now factor $(a^3 + 8)$

$\sqrt[3]{a^3} = a$ and $\sqrt[3]{8} = 2$.   Therefore $(a^3 + 8) = (a + 2)(a^2 - 2a + 4)$.

The factored form of $4a^6 + 32a^3$ is $4a^3(a + 2)(a^2 - 2a + 4)$.

   Sometimes we encounter problems that are the difference of squares and the difference of cubes. In such cases, it's easier to factor as difference of squares first.

Example: Factor $x^6 - 64$.

Factor this as difference of squares first to get $(x^3 - 8)(x^3 + 8)$.

Notice that $(x^3 - 8)$ is the difference of cubes and $(x^3 + 8)$ is the sum of cubes ($\sqrt[3]{x^3} = x$ and $\sqrt[3]{8} = 2$).

$(x^3 - 8) = (x - 2)(x^2 + 2x + 4)$
$(x^3 + 8) = (x + 2)(x^2 - 2x + 4)$
The factored form of $x^6 - 64$ is $(x - 2)(x + 2)(x^2 + 2x + 4)(x^2 - 2x + 4)$.

Solving Equations By Factoring

   Equations in the form $ax^2 + bx + c = 0$, where a, b and c are real numbers and $a \neq 0$, are called **quadratic equations**. The techniques we used to solve linear equations cannot be used to solve quadratic equations. Instead, we can often use the factoring methods learned in this chapter to solve quadratic equations. In general, if a and b are real numbers and $ab = 0$, then $a = 0$ or $b = 0$. We will apply this same concept when solving quadratic equations by factoring.

Example: Solve $x^2 + 8x + 7 = 0$.

First we want to factor the equation.

$(x + 7)(x + 1) = 0$
Now applying the rule above that if $ab=0$, then $a = 0$ or $b = 0$, we get

$(x + 7) = 0$ or $(x + 1) = 0$

Solving each equation gives us

$x = -7$ or $x = -1$

To check, substitute both answers back into the equation.

$(-7)^2 + 8(-7) + 7 = 0$ $(-1)^2 + 8(-1) + 7 = 0$
$49 - 56 + 7 = 0$ $1 - 8 + 7 = 0$
$0 = 0$ $0 = 0$

Since -7 and -1 both satisfy the equation, they are solutions.

Example: Solve $4x^2 + 12x = 0$.

In this case, you can factor out the GCF of $4x$ first

$4x(x + 3) = 0$

Therefore, $4x = 0$ or $(x + 3) = 0$

$$x = 0 \text{ or } x = -3$$

Substituting 0 and -3 for x verifies that they are both solutions.

$4(0)^2 + 12(0) = 0$ $\qquad\qquad$ $4(-3)^2 + 12(-3) = 0$
$\qquad\quad 0 = 0$ $\qquad\qquad\qquad\qquad$ $4(9) - 36 = 0$
$\qquad\qquad\qquad\qquad\qquad\qquad\qquad\qquad 0 = 0$

Example: Solve $9x^2 - 25 = 0$.

Notice that this is a difference of squares, so factoring gives us

$(3x - 5)(3x + 5) = 0$

$3x - 5 = 0$ $\qquad\qquad$ or $\qquad$ $3x + 5 = 0$
$\quad 3x = 5$ $\qquad\qquad\qquad\qquad\quad 3x = -5$
$\qquad x = 5/3$ $\qquad\qquad\qquad\qquad\quad x = -5/3$

Substituting 5/3 and -5/3 back into the equation will verify the answers.

$9(5/3)^2 - 25 = 0$ $\qquad\qquad$ $9(-5/3)^2 - 25 = 0$
$9(25/9) - 25 = 0$ $\qquad\qquad$ $9(25/9) - 25 = 0$
$\qquad\quad 0 = 0$ $\qquad\qquad\qquad\qquad\quad 0 = 0$

Sometimes there are fractional coefficients. In such cases, you can multiply by the common denominator to remove the fractions before factoring.

Example: Solve $x = (6/7)x^2 - 3/7$.

Multiply the equation by 7 to remove fractions.

$7[x = (6/7)x^2 - 3/7]$
$7x = 6x^2 - 3$

Rewrite the equation in the form $ax^2 + b + c = 0$ to factor.
$6x^2 - 7x - 3 = 0$

The possibilities for factoring the equation are

$(3x - 3)(2x + 1)$
$(3x + 3)(2x - 1)$
$(3x + 1)(2x - 3)$
$(3x - 1)(2x + 3)$
$(6x - 3)(x + 1)$
$(6x + 3)(x - 1)$
$(6x - 1)(x + 3)$
$(6x + 1)(x - 3)$

The choice above that works is $(3x + 1)(2x - 3)$. You can check this by multiplying the outer terms and the inner terms and simplifying $(3x)(-3) + 1(2x) = -9x + 2x = -7x$.

Therefore, $(3x + 1)(2x - 3) = 0$

$3x + 1 = 0$ $\qquad$ or $\qquad$ $2x - 3 = 0$
$\quad 3x = -1$ $\qquad\qquad\qquad\qquad 2x = 3$

$x = -1/3$ $x = 3/2$

Substituting both answers for x in the original equation verifies the solution.

Example: Suppose a golf ball is thrown straight up into the air at 120 feet per second. After how many seconds will he ball hit the ground? The height of the object is given by the equation $h = -16t^2 + vt$, where v is the velocity, t is the time after the ball is released and h is the height of the ball.

Substitute 120 for v and 0 for h (the height is 0 when the ball hits the ground).

$0 = -16t^2 + 120t$
$16t^2 - 120t = 0$
$t(16t - 120) = 0$

$t = 0$ or $16t - 120 = 0$
                $16t = 120$
                  $t = 7.5$

At $t = 0$ the ball has just been released, so the answer is 7.5 seconds.

Solving Higher Degree Equations

Suppose you have equations of the third or fourth degree to solve. You can solve most third and fourth degree equations by factoring out a common factor and then factoring as in the examples above. Sometimes fourth degree equations will be a difference of squares.

Example: Solve $x^3 + 4x^2 + 3x = 0$.

Notice each term has an x in it, so factor out an x. Then factor the remaining trinomial.
$x(x^2 + 4x + 3) = 0$

$x(x + 3)(x + 1) = 0$

$x = 0$ or $x + 3 = 0$ or $x + 1 = 0$
                     $x = -3$ $x = -1$

Substituting the values for x back into the original equation verifies the solutions.

•Note that there are 3 answers for x. That is because this is a third degree equation. A linear equation has 1 solution, a quadratic equation has 2 solutions and so on.

Example: Solve $x^4 - 1 = 0$.

Notice that this is a difference of squares because $(x^2)^2 = x^4$ and $1^2 = 1$.

$(x^2 - 1)(x^2 + 1) = 0$

Notice that $x^2 - 1$ is also a difference of squares.

$(x - 1)(x + 1)(x^2 + 1) = 0$

$(x - 1) = 0$ or $(x + 1) = 0$ or $(x^2 + 1) = 0$
      $x = 1$ $x = -1$ $x^2 = -1$

$x^2 = -1$ will not give a real number solution.

The answers are 1 and -1. (real number solutions)

Example: Solve $x^4 - 13x^2 - 36 = 0$.

$(x^2 - 4)(x^2 - 9) = 0$ $(x^2 \cdot x^2 = x^4, -4(--9) = 36$ and $-4 + (-9) = -13)$

Notice we have differences of squares with both factors.

$(x - 2)(x + 2)(x - 3)(x + 3) = 0$

$x - 2 = 0$ or $x + 2 = 0$ or $x - 3 = 0$ or $x + 3 = 0$
    $x = 2$ $x = -2$ $x = 3$ $x = -3$

All the answers can be checked by substituting into the original equation.

Review Problems: Set 4

Complete the factorization of each of the following.

1. $x^2 + 8x + 7 = (x + 7)\square$
2. $x^2 - 6x + 8 = (x - 2)\square$
3. $6x^2 - 7x - 3 = (3x + 1)\square$
4. $4a^2 - 13a - 12 = (4a + 3)\square$

Factor each of the following, if possible.

5. $y^2 + 6y + 9$
6. $x^2 - 7x + 10$
7. $x^2 + 5x + 8$
8. $x^2 + 8x - 48$
9. $b^2 + 12b - 36$
10. $a^2 - 9a + 20$

Factor each of the following (Factor out all common factors first).

11. $6x^2 + 7x + 2$
12. $4y^2 + 20y + 24$
13. $2x^2 + 12x + 18$
14. $3x^2 + 21x + 36$
15. $4y^2 - 32y + 60$
16. $5a^2 + 15ab - 20b^2$
17. $x^4 + 8x^2 + 15$

Factor each of the following (Difference of squares and sum and difference of cubes).

18. $x^2 - 9$
19. $4x^2 - 36$
20. $9x^2 - 25y^2$
21. $81x^2y^2 - 64z^2$
22. $a^4 - b^4$
23. $8x^2 - 72y^2$
24. $x^3 - 8$
25. $y^3 + 64$
26. $5a^3 + 125$
27. $4y^3 - 256$
28. $x^3 + 27y^3$

Solve each of the following by factoring.

29. $x^2 - 5x + 4 = 0$

30. $y^2 + 9x + 14 = 0$
31. $4x^2 + 40x + 84 = 0$
32. $6y^2 - 21y + 9 = 0$
33. $x^2 - 144 = 0$
34. $9y^2 - 81 = 0$
35. $2x^2 - 3x - 5 = 0$
36. $4x^3 + 8x^2 + 4x = 0$

Key Terms and Concepts to Review

•Exponential expressions, base, power
•Scientific notation
•Negative exponents
•Constants
•Monomial, binomial, trinomial, polynomial
•Degree of polynomial
•FOIL method
•Factoring, prime factored form
•Greatest common factor (GCF)
•Factoring by grouping
•Perfect square trinomial
•Difference of squares, perfect squares
•Sum and difference of cubes, perfect cubes
•Quadratic equations, solving quadratic equations by factoring.

Answers to Problem Sets

Problem Set 1
Answers and key steps in solution

1. base = x, exponent = 4. The base is the term that is being raised to the power and the power is 4.
2. base = $3x$, exponent = 5
3. base = r, exponent = 8. If the problem was $(-r)^8$, then the base would be $-r$.
4. base = $(-ab)$, exponent = 2
5. 256, $4(4)(4)(4) = 256$
6. -64, $4(4)(4) = 64$, then apply the – sign to get -64.
7. 432, $(-2)^4 = 16$ and $3^3 = 27$ and $16(27) = 432$
8. 1,   any nonzero number raised to the 0 power is 1.
9. 25 $5^2 = 25$ and $10^0 = 1$ so $(1)25 = 25$.
10. x^{12} same base, add exponents
11. x^5y^4 add exponents for common bases $(x^3x^2)(y^1y^3)$
12. $9x^2y^2z^4$ take 3 to the 2nd power and multiply the exponents for the variables.
13. $125x^3$ take 5 to the 3rd power and multiply the exponent of x by 3.
14. $1/(x^2)$ remember the rules for negative exponents. Take the reciprocal and change the negative exponent to positive.
15. x^2 when dividing subtract the exponents.
16. x^2y subtract exponents from common bases (4 -2 for the x's and 2 -1 for the y's)
17. a^8b^4 multiply 2 by 4 for the a variable and 1 times 4 for the b variable.
18. 9/4   take reciprocal and change sign of exponent to get $1/(2/3)^2 = 1/(4/9) = 9/4$.
19. $1/b^{12}$ multiply exponents to get b^{12}, then take reciprocal and change exponent from negative to positive.
20. $3b^2$ take reciprocal of $1/b^{-2}$ and change negative exponent to positive.
21. c^5 $(c^3)^2 = c^6$ and $c^6c^{-1} = c^5$
22. a^{28} add exponents in numerator to get a^{31} then subtract the exponent in the denominator.
23. 4.329×10^{11}

24. 6.934×10^{-7}

25. 9.3835×10^5 $938.35 \times 10^3 = 938.35 \times 1000 = 938,500$. Rewrite in scientific notation.

26. 9.26×10^{-1} $92.6 \times 10^{-2} = 92.6 \times 0.01 = 0.926$. Rewrite in scientific notation.

27. $4,500$ $4.5 \times 10^3 = 4.5 \times 1000 = 4,500$ (move decimal 3 places to the right)

28. 0.0000000977 9.77×10^{-8}, move decimal 8 places to the left.

29. $53,870,000$ 5.387×10^7, move decimal 7 places to the right.

30. 225 Change each to number to scientific notation, multiply and apply rules for exponents.

Problem Set 2
Answers and key steps in solution

1. Monomial, degree 1   (one term with exponent of 1)
2. Binomial, degree 2   (two terms, degree of first term is 2)
3. Trinomial, degree 7   (three terms, degree of first term is 7)
4. Monomial, degree 11   (one term with exponents adding to 11)
5. Monomial, degree 0   (one term with no variable)
6. Binomial, degree 4   (two terms, degree of first term is 4)
7. $16x - 2y + 8$,   Perimeter is $2L + 2W = 2(3x + 2y) + 2(5x - 3y + 4) = 6x + 4y + 10x - 6y + 8 = 16x - 2y + 8$
8. $5x - 3y$ $(2x + 5y) + (3x - 8y) = 2x + 3x + 5y - 8y = 5x - 3y$
9. $3x - 9y$ $(8x - 2y) - (5x + 7y) = 8x - 5x - 2y - 7y = 3x - 9y$
10. $12xy - 4y$ $(3xy + 4y) + (9xy - 8y) = 3xy + 9xy + 4y - 8y = 12xy - 4y$
11. $10xy - 3x$ $(6xy - x) - (-4xy + 2x) = 6xy + 4xy - x - 2x = 10xy - 3x$
12. $2x^2y^2 + x^2y - 6xy - 3y^2$ $(x^2y + 3xy + y^2) + (2x^2y^2 - 9xy - 4y^2) = 2x^2y^2 + x^2y + 3xy - 9xy + y^2 - 4y^2 = 2x^2y^2 + x^2y - 6xy - 3y^2$
13. $-5x^2y^2 + 6xy - 3xy^2$ $(3x^2y^2 + 2xy - xy^2) - (8x^2y^2 - 4xy + 2xy^2) = 3x^2y^2 - 8x^2y^2 + 2xy + 4xy - xy^2 - 2xy^2 = -5x^2y^2 + 6xy - 3xy^2$
14. $ab + a + 2b$ $(-ab - a - b) + (2ab + 2a + 3b) = -ab + 2ab - a + 2a - b + 3b = ab + a + 2b$
15. $6a - b$ $(-2ab + 3a + 5b) - (-2ab -3a + 6b) = -2ab + 2ab + 3a + 3b + 5b - 6b = 6a - b$
16. $x^2 + 4xy + 4y^2$ $(x + 2y)(x + 2y) = (x)(x) + (x)(2y) + (2y)(x) + (2y)(2y) = x^2 + 4xy + 4y^2$
17. $18x^2 - 9xy - 20y^2$ $(3x - 4y)(6x + 5y) = (3x)(6x) + (3x)(5y) + (-4y)(6x) + (-4y)(5y) = 18x^2 - 9xy - 20y^2$
18. $6x^2 + xy - 35y^2$ $(3x - 7y)(2x + 5y) = (3x)(2x) + (3x)(5y) + (-7y)(2x) + (-7y)(5y) = 6x^2 + xy - 35y^2$
19. $3x^2y^2 - 6xy^2 - 9y^2$ $(xy + y)(3xy - 9y) = (xy)(3xy) + (xy)(-9y) + (y)(3xy) + (y)(-9y) = 3x^2y^2 - 6xy^2 - 9y^2$
20. $6m^2 + mn - 2n^2$ $(2m - n)(2n + 3m) = (2m)(2n) + (2m)(3m) + (-n)(2n) + (-n)(3m) = 6m^2 + mn - 2n^2$
21. $30z^2 + 23z - 14$ $(6z + 7)(5z - 2) = (6z)(5z) + (6z)(-2) + (7)(5z) + (7)(-2) = 30z^2 + 23z - 14$
22. $2x^3 - 7x^2 - 11x - 20$ $(2x^2 + 3x + 4)(x - 5) = (2x^2)(x) + (2x^2)(-5) + (3x)(x) + (3x)(-5) + (4)(x) + (4)(-5) = 2x^3 - 10x^2 + 3x^2 - 15x + 4x - 20 = 2x^3 - 7x^2 - 11x - 20$
23. $x^3y^2 + 2x^3y - 2xy^2 - 9xy - 10x$ $(x^2y - 2y - 5)(xy + 2x) = (x^2y)(xy) + (x^2y)(2x) + (-2y)(xy) + (-2y)(2x) + (-5)(xy) + (-5)(2x)$
24. $4x^3 - 4x^2y + 5x^2 - 5xy + x - y$ $(4x^2 + 5x + 1)(x - y) = (4x^2)(x) + (4x^2)(-y) + (5x)(x) + (5x)(-y) + 1(x) + 1(-y)$
25. $2x^2 + 3y^2 + 5xy + 2x + 2y$ $(x + y)(2x + 3y + 2) = (x)(2x) + (x)(3y) + (x)(2) + (y)(2x) + (y)(3y) + (y)(2)$
26. $a^2b - ab^2 - b^2 - 4ab - 3a - 2b + 15$ $(ab + b - 3)(a - b - 5) = (ab)(a) + (ab)(-b) + (ab)(-5) + (b)(a) + (b)(-b) + (b)(-5) + (-3)(a) + (-3)(-b) + (-3)(-5)$
27. $3x^3 + 12x^2 - 36x$ $3x(x - 2)(x + 6) = 3x[(x)(x) + (x)(6) + (-2)(x) + (-2)(6)] = 3x(x^2 + 4x - 12)$
28. $4x^2y + 4xy - 80y$ $4y(x + 5)(x - 4) = 4y[(x)(x) + (x)(-4) + (5)(x) + (5)(-4)] = 4y(x^2 + x - 20)$
29. $x^2 - 4$ $(x + 2)(x - 2) = (x)(x) + (x)(-2) + (2)(x) + (2)(-2)$
30. $x^2 + 8x + 16$ $(x + 4)(x + 4) = (x)(x) + (x)(4) + (4)(x) + (4)(4)$
31. $x^2 - 10x + 25$ $(x - 5)(x - 5) = (x)(x) + (x)(-5) + (-5)(x) + (-5)(-5)$

Problem Set 3
Answers and key steps in solution

1. y $2, 3, 5, 7, x$ and y are all the factors but only y appears in all 3 monomials.
2. $3 \cdot 3 \cdot 5$ 45 divided by 5 is 9 and 9 divided by 3 is 3, so 5, 3 and 3 are the prime factors.
3. $2 \cdot 2 \cdot 17$ 68 divided by 4 is 17 and 4 is $2 \cdot 2$, so 2, 2 and 17 are the prime factors.
4. $2 \cdot 61$ 122 divided by 2 is 61 and 61 is prime, so 2 and 61 are the prime factors.
5. $2 \cdot 2 \cdot 2 \cdot 3 \cdot 3$ 72 divided by 8 is 9, 8 is $2 \cdot 2 \cdot 2$ and 9 is $3 \cdot 3$.

6. $2 \cdot 2 \cdot 2 \cdot 2 \cdot 3$ 48 divided by 16 is 3 and 16 is $2 \cdot 2 \cdot 2 \cdot 2$.
7. $5 \cdot 5 \cdot 3 \cdot 3$ 225 divided by 5 is 45 and 45 is $5 \cdot 3 \cdot 3$, so 5, 5, 3 and 3 are the prime factors.
8. x $2x + 6 = 2(x + 3)$ (check by multiplying $2(x) + 2(3) = 2x + 6$).
9. $2x^2$ $10x^2/5 = 2x^2$
10. $-4a^2$ $48a^3/(-12a) = -4a^2$
11. x, y $(a + b)(x + y) = (a)x + (a)y + (b)x + (b)y = ax + ay + bx + by$
12. 14 $14 = \mathbf{2 \cdot 7}$, $56 = 2 \cdot 2 \cdot \mathbf{2 \cdot 7}$
13. 8 $16 = \mathbf{2 \cdot 2 \cdot 2} \cdot 2$, $48 = \mathbf{2 \cdot 2 \cdot 2} \cdot 2 \cdot 3$, $72 = \mathbf{2 \cdot 2 \cdot 2} \cdot 3 \cdot 3$
14. 5 $5 = \mathbf{5}$, $20 = \mathbf{5} \cdot 2 \cdot 2$, $125 = \mathbf{5} \cdot 5 \cdot 5$
15. $2xyz$ $2xyz = \mathbf{2 \cdot x \cdot y \cdot z}$, $4xyz^3 = \mathbf{2} \cdot 2 \cdot \mathbf{x \cdot y \cdot z} \cdot z \cdot z$, $8x^2yz^2 = \mathbf{2} \cdot 2 \cdot 2 \cdot \mathbf{x} \cdot x \cdot \mathbf{y \cdot z} \cdot z \cdot z$
16. $3a$ $6ab = \mathbf{3} \cdot 2 \cdot \mathbf{a} \cdot b$, $12ab^2 = 2 \cdot 2 \cdot \mathbf{3} \cdot \mathbf{a} \cdot b \cdot b$, $45a^4 = \mathbf{3} \cdot 3 \cdot 5 \cdot \mathbf{a} \cdot a \cdot a \cdot a$
17. $3(x^2 + 6)$ $3x^2 + 18$,   3 is the GCF, $3x^2/3 = x^2$, $18/3 = 6$
18. Cannot be factored, there are no factors in common between the two terms besides 1.
19. $12(x^2y - 3xy + 4)$ $12x^2y - 36xy + 48$, 12 is the GCF and divide each term by 12.
20. $2z(z + 2)$ $2z^2 + 4z$,   2z is the GCF, $2z^2/2z = z$, $4z/2z = 2$
21. Cannot be factored, there are no factors in common between the two terms besides 1.
22. $5x(5x^3 - 2x - 1)$ $25x^4 - 10x^2 - 5x$, the GCF is 5x, $25x^4/5x = 5x^3$, $10x^2/5x = 2x$, $5x/5x = 1$
23. $(a + b)(5 - c)$ $5(a + b) - c(a + b)$, $(a + b)$ is the common factor, take that out and $(5 - c)$ is left.
24. $(x - y)(5z + w)$ $(x - y)5z + (x - y)w$, $(x - y)$ is the common factor, take that out and $(5z + w)$ is left.
25. $(a - b)(x + y)$ take x out from first two terms, take y out from next two terms, then take out
     $(a - b)$ to get $ax - bx + ay - by = x(a - b) + y(a - b) = (a - b)(x + y)$
26. $(x + y)(x + 2)$ $x^2 + 2y + xy + 2x$, regroup as $x^2 + xy + 2x + 2y$, factor x from the first 2 terms to get
     $x(x + y)$, then factor 2 from next 2 terms to get $2(x + y)$. Notice now $(x + y)$ is the
     common factor, so factor that out to get $(x + y)(x + 2)$.

Problem Set 4
Answers and key steps in solution

1. $(x + 1)$ $x^2 + 8x + 7 = (x + 7)(x + 1)$, $7(1) = 7$ (last term) and add to 8 (middle coefficient)
2. $(x - 4)$ $x^2 - 6x + 8 = (x - 2)(x - 4)$, $(-2)(-4) = 8$ (last term) and add to -6 (middle coefficient)
3. $(2x - 3)$ $6x^2 - 7x - 3 = (3x + 1)(2x - 3)$, $(1)(-3) = -3$ (last term) $(3x)(-3) + (1)(2x) = -7x$, middle term
4. $(a - 4)$ $4a^2 - 13a - 12 = (4a + 3)(a - 4)$, $(3)(-4) = -12$ (last) and $(4a)(-4) + (3)(a) = -13a$ (middle)
5. $(y + 3)(y + 3)$ $y^2 + 6y + 9$, $(3)(3) = 9$ (last term) and add to 6 (middle term coefficient)
6. $(x - 5)(x - 2)$ $x^2 - 7x + 10$, $(-5)(-2) = 10$ (last term) and add to -7 (middle term coefficient)
7. Not factorable using integer coefficients, $x^2 + 5x + 8$, no integers multiply to 8 and add to 5.
8. $(x - 4)(x + 12)$ $x^2 + 8x - 48$, $(-4)(12) = -48$ (last term) and add to 8 (middle term coefficient)
9. Not factorable using integer coefficients, $b^2 + 12b - 36$, no integers multiply to -36 and add to 12.
10. $(a - 4)(a - 5)$ $a^2 - 9a + 20$, $(-4)(-5) = 20$ (last term) and add to -9 (middle term coefficient)
11. $(3x + 1)(2x + 2)$ $6x^2 + 7x + 2$, $(3x)(2x) = 6x^2$, $3x(2) + 1(2x) = 7x$ and $1(2) = 2$..
12. $4(y + 3)(y + 2)$ $4y^2 + 20y + 24$, factor out 4 to get $4(y^2 + 5y + 6)$, then factor $y^2 + 5y + 6 =$
     $(y + 3)(y + 2)$ because $y(y) = y^2$, $3(2) = 6$ (last term) and add to 5 (middle term
     coefficient.
13. $2(x + 3)(x + 3)$ $2x^2 + 12x + 18$, factor out 2 to get $2(x^2 + 6x + 9)$, then factor $x^2 + 6x + 9$ to get
     $2(x + 3)(x + 3)$
14. $3(x + 4)(x + 3)$ $3x^2 + 21x + 36$, factor out 3 to get $3(x^2 + 7x + 12)$, then factor $x^2 + 7x + 12$ to get
     $3(x + 4)(x + 3)$
15. $4(y - 3)(y - 5)$ $4y^2 - 32y + 60$, factor out 4 to get $4(y^2 - 8y + 15)$, then factor $y^2 - 8y + 15$ to get
     $4(y - 3)(y - 5)$
16. $5(a - b)(a + 4b)$ $5a^2 + 15ab - 20b^2$, factor out 5 to get $5(a^2 + 3ab - 4b^2)$, then factor $a^2 + 3ab - 4b^2$ to
     get $5(a - b)(a + 4b)$. (notice $a(a) = a^2$, $a(4b) + (-b)(a) = 3ab$ and $(-b)(4b) = -4b^2$)
17. $(x^2 + 5)(x^2 + 3)$ $x^4 + 8x^2 + 15$, $x^2(x^2) = x^4$, $(5)(x^2) + (x^2)(3) = 8x^2$ and $(5)(3) = 15$
18. $(x - 3)(x + 3)$ $x^2 - 9$, use difference of squares formula $(x^2 - y^2) = (x - y)(x + y)$
19. $4(x - 3)(x + 3)$ $4x^2 - 36 = 0$, factor out 4 to get $4(x^2 - 9) = 0$, then use difference of squares formula
20. $(3x - 5y)(3x + 5y)$ $9x^2 - 25y^2 = 0$, use difference of squares formula
21. $(9xy - 8z)(9xy + 8z)$ $81x^2y^2 - 64z^2 = 0$, use difference of squares formula
22. $(a - b)(a + b)(a^2 + b^2)$ $a^4 - b^4$, use difference of squares formula to get $(a^2 - b^2)(a^2 + b^2)$, then use it
     again on $a^2 - b^2 = (a - b)(a + b)$. Final answer is $(a - b)(a + b)(a^2 + b^2)$

23. $8(x - 3y)(x + 3y)$ $8x^2 - 72y^2$, factor out an 8 to get $8(x^2 - 9y^2)$, the use difference of squares formula

24. $(x - 2)(x^2 + 2x + 4)$ $x^3 - 8$, use difference of cubes formula $(x^3 - y^3) = (x - y)(x^2 + 2xy + y^2)$

25. $(y + 4)(y^2 - 4y + 16)$ $y^3 + 64$, use sum of cubes formula $(x^3 + y^3) = (x + y)(x^2 - 2xy + y^2)$

26. $5(a + 5)(a^2 - 5a + 25)$ $5a^3 + 625$, use sum of cubes formula

27. $4(y - 4)(y^2 + 4y + 16)$ $4y^3 - 256$, use difference of cubes formula

28. $(x + 3y)(x^2 - 3xy + 9y^2)$ $x^3 + 27y^3$, use sum of cubes formula

29. $x = 1$ or $x = 4$ $x^2 - 5x + 4 = 0$, factor to get $(x - 1)(x - 4) = 0$, $x - 1 = 0$ or $x - 4 = 0$, solve for x.

30. $y = -2$ or $y = -7$ $y^2 + 9y + 14 = 0$, factor to get $(y + 2)(y + 7) = 0$, $y + 2 = 0$ or $y + 7 = 0$, solve for y.

31. $x = -3$ or $x = -7$ $4x^2 + 40x + 84 = 0$, factor out 4 to get $4(x^2 + 10x + 21) = 0$, then factor $x^2 + 10x + 21$
to get $4(x + 3)(x + 7) = 0$, $x + 3 = 0$ or $x + 7 = 0$, solve for x.

32. $y = \frac{1}{2}$ or $y = 3$ $6y^2 - 21y + 9 = 0$, factor out 3 to get $3(2y^2 - 7y + 3) = 0$, factor $2y^2 - 7y + 3$ to get
$3(2y - 1)(y - 3) = 0$, $2y - 1 = 0$ or $y - 3 = 0$, solve for y.

33. $x = 12$ or $x = -12$ $x^2 - 144 = 0$, use difference of squares formula.

34. $y = 3$ or $y = -3$ $9y^2 - 81 = 0$, factor out 9 to get $9(y^2 - 9) = 0$, then use difference of squares formula.

35. $x = -1/2$ or $x = 3$ $2x^2 - 3x - 5 = 0$, factor to get $(2x + 1)(x - 3) = 0$, $2x + 1 = 0$ or $x - 3 = 0$, solve for x.

36. $x = 0$ or $x = -1$ $4x^3 + 8x^2 + 4x = 0$, factor out $4x$ to get $4x(x^2 + 2x + 1) = 0$, factor $x^2 + 2x + 1$ to get
$4x(x + 1)(x + 1) = 0$, $4x = 0$ or $x + 1 = 0$, solve for x.

Chapter 5

Radicals and Radical Expressions

Square Roots

    The process of squaring a number is multiplying the number by itself. We will learn how to reverse this procedure to find the **square roots** of numbers. Suppose we want to find a number when squared equals a number x. Such a number is called the *square root of x*.

•**Note that the negative of the number is also the square root because a negative number times a negative number equals a positive number.**

    For example, 5 and -5 are both the square root of 25 since 5^2 and $(-5)^2$ both equal 25.
2x and -2x are both the square root of $4x^2$ since $(2x)^2$ and $(-2x)^2$ both equal $4x^2$.

    The **principal square root** of a number is just the positive square root. In the above examples, the principal square roots are 5 and 2x, respectively.

    The mathematical symbol used to represent the square root is $\sqrt{\ }$. The symbol is known as the **radical symbol**. Therefore, any expression containing a radical symbol is known as a **radical expression**.

•**Note that the square root of a positive number is a real number and the square root of a negative number is not a real number. We will not deal with the square roots of negative numbers in this book. It is a topic for a second course in algebra.**

Examples: Simplify each of the following radicals.

$\sqrt{144}$ = 12 and -12 since $(12)^2$ and $(-12)^2$ equals 144. The principal square root is 12.

$\sqrt{49}$ = 7 and -7 since $(7)^2$ and $(-7)^2$ equals 49. The principal square root is 7.

$-\sqrt{121}$ = 11 and -11.   ($\sqrt{121}$ is 11 and -11, then apply the - in front to get -11 and 11. So it's really the same answer)

$\sqrt{0.04}$ = 0.2 and -0.2 since $(0.2)^2$ and $(-0.2)^2$ equals 0.04. The principal square root is 0.2. Another way to simplify this is to change $\sqrt{0.04}$ to $\sqrt{(1/25)}$ and simplify to 1/5 and -(1/5).

$\sqrt{(4/9)}$ = 2/3 and -2/3 since $(2/3)^2$ and $(-2/3)^2$ equals 4/9. The principal square root is 2/3.

•**Note that you can also simplify the square root of a fraction by taking the square root of the numerator and then the square root of the denominator instead of the square root of the fraction as a whole. In the previous example, you can take the square root of 4 first, then the square root of 9.**

•**Note that the square root of many positive integers are not whole numbers or rational numbers. For example, $\sqrt{13}$ can be found on a calculator or by leaving the answer as $\sqrt{13}$.**

    We just learned how to simplify the square root of positive numbers, now we will learn how to find the square root of expressions containing variables. For a variable x, where $x \neq 0$, $\sqrt{x^2}$ = x and -x. If we are dealing with just the principal square root, then the answer is $|x|$. Recall that $|x|$ is the *absolute value of x*.

Examples: Find the square root of the following. Express all answers as the principal square root.

  a. $\sqrt{9x^2}$

A good way to solve this is to simply the numerical part and the variable part separately.
$\sqrt{9} = 3$ since $3^2 = 9$ and $\sqrt{x^2} = x$ since $(x)^2 = x^2$.

Therefore, $\sqrt{9x^2} = 3x$.

  b. $\sqrt{16y^4x^2}$

$\sqrt{16} = \mathbf{4}$ since $4^2 = 16$, $\sqrt{y^4} = \mathbf{y^2}$ since $(y^2)^2 = y^4$ and $\sqrt{x^2} = \mathbf{x}$ since $(x)^2 = x^2$.

Therefore, multiply the terms in bold to get $\sqrt{16y^4x^2} = 4xy^2$.

  c. $\sqrt{(x + 2)^2} = (x + 2)$ because $(x + 2)(x + 2) = (x + 2)^2$

•**Note the the square root of any number or expression squared is just that number. For example, notice in the previous examples that $\sqrt{(x + 2)^2} = (x + 2)$ and $\sqrt{16} = \sqrt{(4)^2} = 4$.**

  d. $\sqrt{(x^2 + 6x + 9)} = \sqrt{(x + 3)(x + 3)}$

      Notice that we factored $(x^2 + 6x + 9)$ to get $(x + 3)(x + 3)$. That is a perfect square which enables us to simplify the radical expression.

      $\sqrt{(x^2 + 6x + 9)} = \sqrt{(x + 3)(x + 3)} = \sqrt{(x + 3)^2} = (x + 3)$

•**Note that you can check by squaring your answer. After squaring, you should get the expression under the $\sqrt{\ }$.**

      In the previous examples, we simplified radicals that were perfect squares. Many times we can simplify radicals that are not perfect squares. The idea is to break down the number or variable into factors, one of which is a perfect square. By the **multiplication property of radicals** $\sqrt[n]{(ab)} = \sqrt[n]{a} \cdot \sqrt[n]{b}$, where $\sqrt[n]{a}$ and $\sqrt[n]{b}$ are real numbers.

•**Note that in a square root n is 2 but is not written. When solving any root higher than 2, it is noted in the upper left of the radical. For example, the cube root ($n = 3$) of a is noted as $\sqrt[3]{a}$.**

•**Note that all the answers for square roots will be the principal square root unless otherwise noted.**

Example: Simplify the following radical.

$\sqrt{12}$

Get the factors of 12. One of the factors should be a perfect square, if possible.

$12 = 4 \cdot 3$

Therefore $\sqrt{12} = \sqrt{(4 \cdot 3)} = \sqrt{4} \cdot \sqrt{3} = \mathbf{2}\sqrt{3}$
                    ($\sqrt{4} = \mathbf{2}$)

Example: Simplify the following radical.

$\sqrt{84}$

$84 = 4 \cdot 21$

Therefore $\sqrt{84} = \sqrt{(4 \cdot 21)} = \sqrt{4} \cdot \sqrt{21} = \mathbf{2}\sqrt{21}$
                    ($\sqrt{4} = \mathbf{2}$)

Example: Simplify the following radical.

$\sqrt{(50x^3)}$
$50 = 2 \cdot 25, \quad x^3 = x^2 \cdot x$

$\sqrt{50} = \sqrt{(2 \cdot 25)} = \sqrt{2} \cdot \sqrt{25} = \mathbf{5\sqrt{2}}$
$\qquad\qquad\qquad (\sqrt{25} = \mathbf{5})$
$\sqrt{x^3} = \sqrt{(x^2 \cdot x)} = \sqrt{x^2} \cdot \sqrt{x} = \mathbf{x\sqrt{x}}$
$\qquad\qquad\quad (\sqrt{x^2} = \mathbf{x})$

Therefore $\sqrt{(50x^3)} = 5\sqrt{2} \cdot x\sqrt{x} = 5x\sqrt{(2x)}$

Notice that we multiplied the terms $5 \cdot x = 5x$ and $\sqrt{2} \cdot \sqrt{x} = \sqrt{(2x)}$.

Example: Simplify the following.

$\sqrt{(288x^4y^5)}$

$288 = 2 \cdot 144$ and we know 144 is a perfect square, therefore $\sqrt{288} = \sqrt{2} \cdot \sqrt{144} = \mathbf{12\sqrt{2}}$

x^4 is a perfect square since $x^2 \cdot x^2 = x^4$, so $\sqrt{x^4} = \mathbf{x^2}$

$y^5 = y^4 \cdot y$, therefore $\sqrt{y^5} = \sqrt{y^4} \cdot \sqrt{y} = \mathbf{y^2\sqrt{y}}$

Multiply $\mathbf{12\sqrt{2} \cdot x^2 \cdot y^2\sqrt{y}}$ to get

$12 \cdot x^2 \cdot y^2 \cdot \sqrt{2} \cdot \sqrt{y}$

$12x^2y^2\sqrt{(2y)}$

You can check your answer by squaring it to make sure you get $288x^4y^5$.

In some cases, radicals will be the form of a ratio of two numbers or expressions. In these cases, you might be able to simplify the ratio first. The **division property of radicals** states that $\sqrt{(x/y)} = \sqrt{x}/\sqrt{y}$, where $y \neq 0$ because we can't have a 0 in the denominator of a fraction.

Example: Simplify the following.

$\sqrt{(7x^2/36)}$

Use the division property of radicals to get

$\sqrt{(7x^2)}/\sqrt{36}$

The numerator can be simplified to $x\sqrt{7}$ and the denominator can be simplified to 6.

Therefore, $\sqrt{(7x^2/36)} = (x\sqrt{7})/6$.

Check by squaring the answer $(x\sqrt{7})/6 \cdot (x\sqrt{7})/6 = x^2\sqrt{49}/36 = 7x^2/36$.

Example: Simplify the following.

$\sqrt{(64x^4/16y^2)}$

By the division property of radicals we get

$\sqrt{(64x^4)}/\sqrt{(16y^2)}$

Notice that $64x^4$ is a perfect square since $8 \cdot 8 = 64$ and $x^2 \cdot x^2 = x^4$.

Therefore $\sqrt{(64x^4)} = \mathbf{8x^2}$.
Likewise, $16y^2$ is a perfect square, so $\sqrt{(16y^2)} = \mathbf{4y}$.

The radical $\sqrt{(64x^4/16y^2)}$ becomes $(\mathbf{8x^2})/\mathbf{4y}$, which is simplified to $2x^2/y$. The restriction is that $y \neq 0$ because there cannot be a 0 in the denominator.

Example: Simplify the following.

$\sqrt{(125x^3)}/\sqrt{(5x)}$

By the division property of radicals we get $\sqrt{(125x^3/5x)}$

$(125x^3/5x)$ simplifies to $\mathbf{25x^2}$ since $125/5 = 25$ and $x^3/x = x^2$

Therefore $\sqrt{(125x^3/5x)} = \sqrt{(\mathbf{25x^2})}$

$25x^2$ is a perfect square so $\sqrt{(25x^2)}$ simplifies to $5x$.

Review Problems: Set 1

Find each square root, if possible. Give only the principal square root.

    1. $\sqrt{121}$
    2. $\sqrt{49}$
    3. $\sqrt{225}$
    4. $\sqrt{(4/9)}$
    5. $\sqrt{(-9)}$
    6. $\sqrt{(-5)^2}$
    7. $\sqrt{(16/64)}$
    8. $\sqrt{(0.09)}$
    9. $-\sqrt{81}$
    10. $\sqrt{(-100)}$

Find each square root. Assume that there are no restrictions on the value of any variable.

    11. $\sqrt{(25x^4)}$
    12. $\sqrt{(121y^2)}$
    13. $\sqrt{(x + 4)^2}$
    14. $\sqrt{(2y - 7)^2}$
    15. $\sqrt{(x^2 - 10x + 25)}$
    16. $\sqrt{(y^2 + 12y + 36)}$

Simplify the following square roots.

    17. $\sqrt{24}$
    18. $\sqrt{48}$
    19. $\sqrt{72}$
    20. $\sqrt{(8x^2)}$
    21. $\sqrt{(28x^3)}$
    22. $\sqrt{(36x^2y^4)}$
    23. $\sqrt{(125x^3y^5)}$

Simplify the following. Assume none of the variables equal zero.

    24. $\sqrt{(49x^2/25)}$

25. $\sqrt{121/36y^4}$
26. $\sqrt{225x^2y^2/5xy}$
27. $\sqrt{68x^2y^3}/\sqrt{17y}$
28. $\sqrt{50x^2y^3}/\sqrt{2y^3}$

Cube Roots

In the previous section, we learned how to solve square roots. In this section, we will learn how to solve cube roots. The **cube root** of a number n is the number when multiplied by itself 3 times equals n. For example, the cube root of -125 is -5 because $(-5) \cdot (-5) \cdot (-5) = 125$, or $(-5)^3 = -125$.

By definition, the cube root of a is defined as

$\sqrt[3]{a} = b$, if $b^3 = a$.

Examples:

$\sqrt[3]{64} = 4$ since $4^3 = 64$

$\sqrt[3]{(-64)} = -4$ since $(-4)^3 = -64$

$\sqrt[3]{216} = 6$ since $6^3 = 216$

$\sqrt[3]{(-216)} = -6$ since $(-6)^3 = -216$

•Note that 64 and 216 have 1 real number cube root and 2 real number square roots. Any negative number will have a cube root that is negative and any positive number will have a cube root that is positive.

Examples: Simplify the following.

a. $\sqrt[3]{8}$

To solve this, think of what number multiplied by itself 3 times gives you 8. Notice that $2 \cdot 2 \cdot 2 = 8$. Therefore, $\sqrt[3]{8} = 2$.

b. $\sqrt[3]{729} = 9$ since $9 \cdot 9 \cdot 9 = 729$.

How do we know that $9 \cdot 9 \cdot 9 = 729$?

•Note that if the sum of the digits of a number is divisible by 9, the number is divisible by 9.

The sum of the digits of 729 is 18, which is divisible by 9. Therefore, 729 is divisible by 9.

729/9 = 81 and we know the square root of 81 is 9.

c. $\sqrt[3]{512} = 8$ since $8 \cdot 8 \cdot 8 = 512$.

d. $\sqrt[3]{(-125)} = -5$ since $(-5)^3 = -125$.

We just learned how to take the cube root of positive and negative numbers. Now we will learn how to take the cube root involving variables. By definition, if x is a variable representing a real number, $\sqrt[3]{x^3} = x$.

Examples: Simplify the following.

$\sqrt[3]{(64x^3)} = \sqrt[3]{(64)} \cdot \sqrt[3]{(x^3)} = 4 \cdot x = 4x$

Check by taking the cube of $4x$.
$(4x)^3 = 4x \cdot 4x \cdot 4x = 64x^3$.

$\sqrt[3]{(2x + 3y)^3} = (2x + 3y)$ because of the rule that $\sqrt[3]{x^3} = x$.

$\sqrt[3]{(-27x^6y^9)}$

$\sqrt[3]{(-27)} = \textbf{-3}$, $\sqrt[3]{(x^6)} = \boldsymbol{x^2}$ since $(x^2)^3 = x^6$ and $\sqrt[3]{(y^9)} = \boldsymbol{y^3}$ since $(y^3)^3 = y^9$

Multiply the terms in bold to get

$\sqrt[3]{(-27x^6y^9)} = -3x^2y^3$.

$\sqrt[3]{(8x^3y^6z^{12})}$

$\sqrt[3]{(8x^3)} = \textbf{2x}$, $\sqrt[3]{(y^6)} = \boldsymbol{y^2}$ and $\sqrt[3]{(z^{12})} = \boldsymbol{z^4}$

Multiply the terms in blue to get

$\sqrt[3]{(8x^3y^6z^{12})} = 2xy^2z^4$.

   All of the above examples were perfect cubes, but many times we can find the cube root of expressions that are not perfect cubes. The idea is to break down the number or variable into factors, one of which is a perfect cube. For example, if you solve $\sqrt[3]{16}$, break it down into $\sqrt[3]{8} \cdot \sqrt[3]{2}$ because $\sqrt[3]{8} = 2$. If you solve $\sqrt[3]{(x^4)}$, break it down into $\sqrt[3]{(x^3)} \cdot \sqrt[3]{x}$ because $\sqrt[3]{(x^3)} = x$. Remember from the multiplication property of radicals that $\sqrt[3]{ab} = \sqrt[3]{a} \cdot \sqrt[3]{b}$.

Example: Simplify the following.

$\sqrt[3]{(81x^4)}$

$\sqrt[3]{81} = \sqrt[3]{27} \cdot \sqrt[3]{3} = \textbf{3} \cdot \sqrt[3]{\textbf{3}}$ $(\sqrt[3]{27} = 3$ because $3^3 = 27)$

$\sqrt[3]{(x^4)} = \sqrt[3]{(x^3)} \cdot \sqrt[3]{x} = \boldsymbol{x} \cdot \sqrt[3]{\boldsymbol{x}}$ $(\sqrt[3]{(x^3)} = x$ by the definition of cube root $(x)^3 = x^3)$

Multiply like terms to get $\sqrt[3]{(81x^4)} = 3x \cdot \sqrt[3]{(3x)}$

•**Note that you can check by cubing the answer, $[3x \cdot \sqrt[3]{(3x)}]^3 = 27x^3 \cdot 3x = 81x^4$.**

Example: Simply the following.

$\sqrt[3]{(-48x^5y^4)}$
$\sqrt[3]{(-48)} = \sqrt[3]{(-8)} \cdot \sqrt[3]{(6)} = \textbf{-2} \cdot \sqrt[3]{\textbf{(6)}}$ (note that $-8 \cdot 6 = -48$ and $-2^3 = -8$)

$\sqrt[3]{(x^5)} = \sqrt[3]{(x^3)} \cdot \sqrt[3]{(x^2)} = \boldsymbol{x} \cdot \sqrt[3]{\boldsymbol{(x^2)}}$ (note that $x^3 \cdot x^2 = x^5$ and $(x)^3 = x^3)$

$\sqrt[3]{(y^4)} = \sqrt[3]{(y^3)} \cdot \sqrt[3]{y} = \boldsymbol{y} \cdot \sqrt[3]{\boldsymbol{y}}$ (note that $y^3 \cdot y = y^4$ and $(y)^3 = y^3)$

Now multiply the terms in bold to get $-2xy \cdot \sqrt[3]{(6x^2y)}$.
Example: Simplify the following.

$\sqrt[3]{(16x^3y^3z)}$

$\sqrt[3]{16} = \sqrt[3]{8} \cdot \sqrt[3]{2} = \textbf{3} \cdot \sqrt[3]{\textbf{2}}$

$\sqrt[3]{(x^3)} = \boldsymbol{x}$, $\sqrt[3]{(y^3)} = \boldsymbol{y}$ and $\sqrt[3]{z}$ is in simplest form.

Multiply the terms in blue and then the terms in red to get

$3xy \cdot \sqrt[3]{(2z)}$

As with square roots, in some cases cube roots will be the form of a ratio of two numbers, a number and a expression or two expressions. In these cases, you might be able to simplify the ratio first. Recall that by the division property of radicals $\sqrt[3]{(x/y)} = \sqrt[3]{x} / \sqrt[3]{y}$.

Example: Simplify the following.

$\sqrt[3]{(64x^3/8y^6)}$

By the division property of radicals $\sqrt[3]{(64x^3/8y^6)} = \sqrt[3]{(64x^3)} / \sqrt[3]{(8y^6)}$

$\sqrt[3]{(64x^3)} = 4x$ because $(4x)^3 = 64x^3$

$\sqrt[3]{(8y^6)} = 2y^2$ because $(2y^2)^3 = 8y^6$

Therefore $\sqrt[3]{(64x^3/8y^6)} = (4x)/(2y^2) = (2x)/y^2$.

Example: Simplify the following.

$\sqrt[3]{(108x^6y^8/4y^5)}$

By the division property of radicals $\sqrt[3]{(108x^6y^8/4y^5)} = \sqrt[3]{(27x^6y^3)}$ because $108/4 = 27$ and $(y^8)/(y^5) = y^3$.

$\sqrt[3]{(27)} = 3$, $\sqrt[3]{(x^6)} = x^2$ and $\sqrt[3]{(y^3)} = y$.

Therefore $\sqrt[3]{(108x^6y^8/4y^5)} = 3x^2y$.

Example: Simplify the following.

$\sqrt[3]{(128y^9)} / \sqrt[3]{(2y^3)}$

By the division property of radicals $\sqrt[3]{(128y^9)} /^3 \sqrt{(2y^3)} = \sqrt[3]{(128y^9/2y^3)} = \sqrt[3]{(64y^6)}$

$\sqrt[3]{(64)} = 4$ since $4^3 = 64$

$\sqrt[3]{(y^6)} = y^2$ since $(y^2)^3 = y^6$

Therefore, $\sqrt[3]{(128y^9)} / \sqrt[3]{(2y^3)} = 4y^2$.

We learned how to solve square roots and cube roots. There are also fourth roots, fifth roots, sixth roots, seventh roots and so on. The procedure for solving these roots is the same as for square roots and cube roots. For example, a fourth root of a natural number x is a number multiplied by itself four times to equal x, and so on for higher roots. If n is an odd natural number greater than 1 ($n > 1$), then $\sqrt[n]{(x)}$ is an **odd root**. When n is an even natural number greater than 1 ($n > 1$) and $x > 0$, then $\sqrt[n]{(x)}$ is an **even root**.

Review Problems: Set 2

Find each cube root.

1. $\sqrt[3]{64}$
2. $\sqrt[3]{(-27)}$

   3. $\sqrt[3]{125}$
   4. $\sqrt[3]{(-216)}$
   5. $\sqrt[3]{729}$
   6. $\sqrt[3]{(-343)}$
   7. $\sqrt[3]{(27/8)}$
   8. $\sqrt[3]{(-64/27)}$
   9. $-\sqrt[3]{(-8)}$

Find each cube root.

   10. $\sqrt[3]{(125x^3y^3)}$
   11. $\sqrt[3]{(x-6)^3}$
   12. $\sqrt[3]{(2x+9)^3}$
   13. $-\sqrt[3]{(4x-3)^3}$
   14. $\sqrt[3]{(1000y^6)}$
   15. $\sqrt[3]{(216x^6y^9)}$

Simplify the following cube roots.

   16. $\sqrt[3]{(24x^5)}$
   17. $\sqrt[3]{(108y^4)}$
   18. $\sqrt[3]{(40)}$
   19. $\sqrt[3]{(54)}$
   20. $\sqrt[3]{(-48)}$
   21. $\sqrt[3]{(80x^4y^7)}$
   22. $\sqrt[3]{(-81x^6)}$

Simplify the following cube roots.

   23. $\sqrt[3]{(128x^4/2x)}$
   24. $\sqrt[3]{(24x^5y^3/3x^2)}$
   25. $\sqrt[3]{(48y^6/6)}$
   26. $\sqrt[3]{(81x^3y^5)} / \sqrt[3]{(3y^2)}$
   27. $\sqrt[3]{(-250y^8)} / \sqrt[3]{(2y^2)}$
   28. $\sqrt[3]{(256x^7y^3)} / \sqrt[3]{(4x^4)}$

Adding and Subtracting Radical Expressions

   Suppose we wish to add or subtract radical expressions. In order to do so, we first need to recognize the **like radicals**, which are radicals that have the same index and same radicand. To make it simpler to understand, like radicals are those with the same term under the radical sign and same number in the upper left corner of the sign.

For example, $4\cdot\sqrt[3]{x}$ and $\sqrt[3]{x}$, $\sqrt[3]{5}$ and $2\cdot\sqrt[3]{5}$, $4\sqrt{2}$ and $\sqrt{2}$ are like radicals, whereas $\sqrt[3]{y}$ and $\sqrt[3]{x}$, $\sqrt[3]{5}$ and $\sqrt[4]{5}$, $\sqrt{6}$ and $\sqrt{7}$ are not like radicals.
To add radical expressions, you first simplify the expression and then combine all like radicals.

Example: Simplify the following expression.

$3\sqrt{2} + 5\sqrt{2} - 6\sqrt{2}$

Notice that all of the terms are like radicals. When adding, keep the $\sqrt{2}$ and add and subtract the coefficients marked in bold.

Therefore, the answer is $2\sqrt{2}$.

Example: Simplify the following expression.

$\sqrt[3]{x} + 2\sqrt{3} + 3\cdot\sqrt[3]{x} - 5\sqrt{3}$.

Notice the like terms are $2\sqrt{3}$ and $-5\sqrt{3}$, $\sqrt[3]{x}$ and $3\cdot\sqrt[3]{x}$

Combine like terms to get $4\cdot\sqrt[3]{x} - 3\sqrt{3}$.

Example: Simplify the following expression.

$\sqrt{(xy)} + 3\sqrt{(xy)} - \sqrt{(x^2y)} + \sqrt[3]{(xy)} + \sqrt[3]{(x^2y)}$.

   Notice the terms are very similar. In such cases we have to be very careful. The only like terms in this expression are $\sqrt{(xy)}$ and $3\sqrt{(xy)}$. Combine these terms to get

$4\sqrt{(xy)} - \sqrt{(x^2y)} + \sqrt[3]{(xy)} + \sqrt[3]{(x^2y)}$.

   Sometimes on first inspection of a radical expression, it appears that it cannot be simplified. Before we conclude that it cannot be simplified, look to simplify each radical first and then combine like terms.

Example: Simplify the following expression.

$\sqrt{12} + \sqrt{27} - 4\sqrt{3}$.

$\sqrt{12} = \sqrt{4} \cdot \sqrt{3}, \qquad \sqrt{27} = \sqrt{9} \cdot \sqrt{3}$
$\quad\ = 2\sqrt{3} \qquad\qquad\quad = 3\sqrt{3}$

Notice that the terms are now like terms, so we can combine them to get

$2\sqrt{3} + 3\sqrt{3} - 4\sqrt{3} = \sqrt{3}$.

Example: Simplify the following expression.

$\sqrt{125} + 4\sqrt{5} - 2\sqrt{50}$

$\sqrt{125} = \sqrt{25} \cdot \sqrt{5},\qquad 4\sqrt{5}$ cannot be simplified, $\qquad -2\sqrt{50} = -2 \cdot \sqrt{25} \cdot \sqrt{2}$
$\qquad = 5\sqrt{5} \qquad\qquad\qquad\qquad\qquad\qquad\qquad\qquad\qquad\qquad\ = -2(5)\sqrt{2}$
$\qquad\qquad\qquad\qquad\qquad\qquad\qquad\qquad\qquad\qquad\qquad\qquad\qquad\qquad = -10\sqrt{2}$

Combine like terms to get $9\sqrt{5} - 10\sqrt{2}$.

•Note that we are only interested in the principal square root when simplifying before combining like terms. Recall the principal square root is the positive value. Remember that a square root has both a positive and negative value.

Example: Simplify the following expression.

$\sqrt[3]{8} - 2 \cdot \sqrt[3]{16} + \sqrt[3]{48}$
$\sqrt[3]{8} = 2, \qquad -2 \cdot \sqrt[3]{16} = -2 \cdot \sqrt[3]{8} \cdot \sqrt[3]{2}, \qquad \sqrt[3]{48} = \sqrt[3]{8} \cdot \sqrt[3]{6}$
$\qquad\qquad\qquad\qquad\quad = -2(2) \cdot \sqrt[3]{2} \qquad\qquad\quad = 2\cdot\sqrt[3]{6}$
$\qquad\qquad\qquad\qquad\quad = -4\cdot\sqrt[3]{2}$

Notice there are no like terms. We did simplify each term separately but cannot combine any of the terms, so the simplified expression is

$2 - 4\cdot\sqrt[3]{2} + 2\cdot\sqrt[3]{6}$.

Example: Simplify the following expression.

$-^3\sqrt{24} - ^3\sqrt{81} + ^3\sqrt{375}$

$-^3\sqrt{24} = -^3\sqrt{8}\cdot {}^3\sqrt{3},$ $\quad\quad -^3\sqrt{81} = -^3\sqrt{27}\cdot {}^3\sqrt{3},$ $\quad\quad ^3\sqrt{375} = {}^3\sqrt{125}\cdot {}^3\sqrt{3}$
$\quad\quad = -2\cdot{}^3\sqrt{3},$ $\quad\quad\quad\quad\quad = -3\cdot{}^3\sqrt{3}$ $\quad\quad\quad\quad\quad\quad = 5\cdot{}^3\sqrt{3}$

Combine the like terms

$(-2\cdot{}^3\sqrt{3}) - (3\cdot{}^3\sqrt{3}) + (5\cdot{}^3\sqrt{3})$

$\quad\quad -(5\cdot{}^3\sqrt{3}) + (5\cdot{}^3\sqrt{3}) = 0.$

Example: Simplify the following expression.

$\sqrt{(32x^4)} - \sqrt{(72x^4)} + \sqrt{(18x^4)}$

$\sqrt{(32x^4)} = \sqrt{16}\cdot\sqrt{2}\cdot\sqrt{(x^4)} = 4x^2\cdot\sqrt{2}$

$-\sqrt{(72x^4)} = -\sqrt{36}\cdot\sqrt{2}\cdot\sqrt{(x^4)} = -6x^2\cdot\sqrt{2}$

$\sqrt{(18x^4)} = \sqrt{9}\cdot\sqrt{2}\cdot\sqrt{(x^4)} = 3x^2\cdot\sqrt{2}$

Combine like terms to get

$4x^2\cdot\sqrt{2} - 6x^2\cdot\sqrt{2} + 3x^2\cdot\sqrt{2} = x^2\cdot\sqrt{2}$

Multiplying and Dividing Radical Expressions

Multiplying

When multiplying and dividing radical expressions, we use many of the same properties we learned previously. The main property we will use are the distributive property as well as the FOIL method. After applying these, simplify the radicals and combine like terms. The first important rule when multiplying radical expressions is that the index of the terms being multiplied must be the same. For example, we can multiply $\sqrt{2}$ and $\sqrt{10}$ but we cannot multiply $\sqrt{2}$ and $^3\sqrt{10}$.

Example: Multiply and simplify.

$4\sqrt{10}\cdot 5\sqrt{5}$
$4\cdot 5 = 20,\quad \sqrt{10}\cdot\sqrt{5} = \sqrt{50}$
$\quad\quad\quad\quad\quad\quad = \sqrt{25}\cdot\sqrt{2}$
$\quad\quad\quad\quad\quad\quad = 5\sqrt{2}$

Therefore $4\sqrt{10}\cdot 5\sqrt{5} = 20\cdot 5\sqrt{2} = 100\sqrt{2}$
Example: Multiply and simplify.

$\sqrt{(20x^3)}\cdot\sqrt{(5xy^2)}$

$\sqrt{20}\cdot\sqrt{5} = \sqrt{100},\quad\quad \sqrt{(x^3)}\cdot\sqrt{x}\cdot\sqrt{(y^2)} = \sqrt{(x^4)}\cdot\sqrt{(y^2)}$
$\quad\quad\quad = 10$ $\quad\quad\quad\quad\quad\quad\quad\quad = x^2y$

Therefore, $\sqrt{(20x^3)}\cdot\sqrt{(5xy^2)} = 10x^2y.$

Example: Multiply and simplify.

$^3\sqrt{(5xy^4)}\cdot {}^3\sqrt{(25x^2y^5)}$

$\sqrt[3]{5} \cdot \sqrt[3]{25} = \sqrt[3]{125}$,　　　$\sqrt[3]{(x)} \cdot \sqrt[3]{(x^2)} = \sqrt[3]{(x^3)}$,　　　$\sqrt[3]{(y^4)} \cdot \sqrt[3]{(y^5)} = \sqrt[3]{(y^9)}$
　　　$= 5$ 　　　　　　　　　　　　　　$= x$ 　　　　　　　　　　　　　$= y^3$
Therefore, $\sqrt[3]{(5xy^4)} \cdot \sqrt[3]{(25x^2y^5)} = 5xy^3$.

　　We'll now show a couple examples where you use the distributive property to multiply a radical expression with one term by a radical expression with two or more terms.

Example: Simplify $4\sqrt{5}(3\sqrt{7} + 2\sqrt{2})$

Distribute the $4\sqrt{5}$ to get

$4\sqrt{5}(3\sqrt{7}) + 4\sqrt{5}(2\sqrt{2})$

$12\sqrt{35} + 8\sqrt{10}$ 　　(multiply the coefficients and multiply the radicals)

Example: Simplify $3\sqrt{2}(9\sqrt{8} - 5\sqrt{10})$

Distribute the $3\sqrt{2}$ to get

$27\sqrt{16} - 15\sqrt{20}$

$27 \cdot 4 - 15(\sqrt{5} \cdot \sqrt{4})$　(simplify $\sqrt{16}$ and break down $\sqrt{20}$)

$108 - 15(\sqrt{5} \cdot 2)$　　　(multiply 27 by 4 and simplify $\sqrt{4}$)

$108 - 30\sqrt{5}$.　　　　(multiply 15 by 2)

　　If we want to multiply two radical expressions with two terms each, we use the FOIL method. Then we simplify and combine like terms.

Example: Multiply $(\sqrt{5} - \sqrt{2})(\sqrt{5} + 3\sqrt{6})$

　　Recall that the FOIL method is multiplying the First terms, then the Outer terms, the Inner terms and then the Last terms. Another way to think of it is to multiply each term in the first set of parentheses by each term in the second set of parentheses.

$(\sqrt{5} \cdot \sqrt{5}) + (\sqrt{5} \cdot 3\sqrt{6}) + (- \sqrt{2} \cdot \sqrt{5}) + (- \sqrt{2} \cdot 3\sqrt{6})$

　　F　　　　O　　　　　I　　　　　L

$5 + 3\sqrt{30} - \sqrt{10} - 3\sqrt{12}$

$5 + 3\sqrt{30} - \sqrt{10} - 3(\sqrt{4} \cdot \sqrt{3})$

$5 + 3\sqrt{30} - \sqrt{10} - 3(2 \cdot \sqrt{3})$
$5 + 3\sqrt{30} - \sqrt{10} - 6\sqrt{3}$

Example: Multiply and assume that $y > 0$. $[\sqrt{(7y)} + \sqrt{2}][\sqrt{(2y)} + \sqrt{3}]$

$[\sqrt{(7y)} \cdot \sqrt{(2y)}] + [\sqrt{(7y)} \cdot \sqrt{3}] + [\sqrt{2} \cdot \sqrt{(2y)}] + (\sqrt{2} \cdot \sqrt{3})$

　　　F　　　　　　　O　　　　　I　　　　　L

$\sqrt{(14y^2)} + \sqrt{(21y)} + \sqrt{(4y)} + \sqrt{6}$

$\sqrt{14} \cdot \sqrt{(y^2)} + \sqrt{(21y)} + (\sqrt{4} \cdot \sqrt{y}) + \sqrt{6}$

$y\sqrt{14} + \sqrt{(21y)} + 2\sqrt{y} + \sqrt{6}$.

Example: Multiply $(\sqrt{10} - \sqrt{6})(\sqrt{10} + \sqrt{6})$

•Note that $(x - y)(x + y) = x^2 - y^2$. Knowing this fact makes multiplying such a problem much easier. There is no need to use FOIL. We can simply remove the radicals and subtract 6 from 10 to get 4.

To check by using the FOIL method, we get

$\sqrt{10} \cdot \sqrt{10} + \sqrt{10} \cdot \sqrt{6} + (-\sqrt{6}) \cdot \sqrt{10} + (-\sqrt{6}) \cdot \sqrt{6}$

$\sqrt{100} + \sqrt{60} - \sqrt{60} - \sqrt{36}$

$10 - 6 = 4$.

Dividing

We now focus on the division of radicals. The important aspect with division of radicals is to make sure there are no radicals in the denominator of a fraction. We remove radicals from the denominator by what is known as **rationalizing the denominator**. What this means is that we replace the radical in the denominator by a rational number. For example, if you want to divide $\sqrt{6}$ by $\sqrt{2}$, first write this as a fraction.

$\dfrac{\sqrt{6}}{\sqrt{2}}$ To eliminate $\sqrt{2}$ from the denominator, we need to multiply the numerator and the denominator by something that will make the number under the radical a perfect square. In this case we know that 4 is a perfect square, so multiply the numerator and denominator by $\sqrt{2}$ to get

$$\dfrac{\sqrt{6} \cdot \sqrt{2}}{\sqrt{2} \cdot \sqrt{2}} = \dfrac{\sqrt{12}}{\sqrt{4}} = \dfrac{\sqrt{4} \cdot \sqrt{3}}{\sqrt{4}} = \sqrt{3}.$$

•Note that when you need to rationalize the denominator that has a square root, multiply the numerator and denominator by the denominator. The result of the denominator is the term under the radical. For example, if the denominator is $\sqrt{(6x)}$, multiply the numerator and denominator by $\sqrt{(6x)}$ and the denominator becomes $6x$. Knowing this fact will make the process easier by cutting out the step of multiplying $\sqrt{(6x)}$ by $\sqrt{(6x)}$ to get $\sqrt{(36x)^2}$ and then simplifying to get $6x$.

Examples: Rationalize each denominator.

1. $\sqrt{(10/3)}$
   Begin by writing this as a fraction of two radicals and multiply the numerator and denominator by $\sqrt{3}$.
   $$\dfrac{\sqrt{10}}{\sqrt{3}} = \dfrac{\sqrt{10} \cdot \sqrt{3}}{\sqrt{3} \cdot \sqrt{3}} = \dfrac{\sqrt{30}}{\sqrt{9}} = \dfrac{\sqrt{30}}{3}$$

2. $6\sqrt{3} / (5\sqrt{2})$
   Begin by writing this as a fraction of two radicals and then multiply the numerator and denominator by $\sqrt{2}$.
   $$\dfrac{6\sqrt{3} \cdot \sqrt{2}}{5\sqrt{2} \cdot \sqrt{2}} = \dfrac{6\sqrt{6}}{5(2)} = \dfrac{6\sqrt{6}}{10} = \dfrac{3\sqrt{6}}{5}$$

3. $\dfrac{\sqrt{(3xy^2)}}{\sqrt{(2x)}}$

   Multiply the numerator and denominator by $\sqrt{(2x)}$ because $2x \cdot 2x = 4x^2$ which is a perfect square.

$$\frac{\sqrt{(3xy^2)} \cdot \sqrt{(2x)}}{\sqrt{(2x)} \cdot \sqrt{(2x)}} = \frac{\sqrt{(6x^2y^2)}}{\sqrt{(4x^2)}} = \frac{xy\sqrt{6}}{2x} = \frac{y\sqrt{6}}{2}$$

In the previous examples, we learned how to rationalize radical expressions where the denominators are square roots. Suppose the denominator is a cube root. To rationalize a cube root, we need to multiply the denominator by something that will make what's under the radical a perfect cube. For example, suppose the denominator of a radical expression is $\sqrt[3]{9}$. To rationalize this, we must multiply the numerator and denominator by $\sqrt[3]{3}$ because $\sqrt[3]{9} \cdot \sqrt[3]{3} = \sqrt[3]{27} = 3$.

•Note that the first 10 prefect cubes are 1, 8, 27, 64, 125, 216, 343, 512, 729 and 1000. This will help you to rationalize denominators that are cube root.

Examples: Rationalize each denominator.

1. $\dfrac{\sqrt[3]{2}}{\sqrt[3]{(4x^2)}}$

To get a perfect cube in the denominator we need to multiply both numerator and denominator by $\sqrt[3]{(16x)}$ because $4 \cdot 16 = 64$ and $x^2 \cdot x = x^3$, which are both perfect cubes.

$$\frac{\sqrt[3]{2} \cdot \sqrt[3]{(16x)}}{\sqrt[3]{(4x^2)} \cdot \sqrt[3]{(16x)}} = \frac{\sqrt[3]{(32x)}}{\sqrt[3]{(64x^3)}} = \frac{\sqrt[3]{x} \cdot \sqrt[3]{8} \cdot \sqrt[3]{4}}{4x} = \frac{2 \cdot \sqrt[3]{(4x)}}{4x} = \frac{\sqrt[3]{(4x)}}{2x}$$

2. $\sqrt[3]{(1/16y^3)}$

Write this as a fraction of two radicals.

$$\frac{\sqrt[3]{1}}{\sqrt[3]{(16y^3)}}$$

Now we can multiply to get a perfect cube in the denominator, or we can simplify first before rationalizing the denominator. I suggest simplifying as much as possible first.

$$\frac{1}{\sqrt[3]{(8y^3)} \cdot \sqrt[3]{2}}$$ ($\sqrt[3]{1} = 1$, since $1^3 = 1$)
(the reason to break it down this way is because $8y^3$ is a perfect cube since $(2y)^3 = 8y^3$

Therefore,

$$\frac{1}{\sqrt[3]{(8y^3)} \cdot \sqrt[3]{2}} = \frac{1}{2y \cdot \sqrt[3]{2}}$$

Now we can rationalize the denominator by multiplying the numerator and denominator by $\sqrt[3]{4}$ because we know 8 is a perfect cube and $2 \cdot 4 = 8$.

$$\frac{1 \cdot \sqrt[3]{4}}{2y \cdot \sqrt[3]{2} \cdot \sqrt[3]{4}} = \frac{\sqrt[3]{4}}{2y \cdot \sqrt[3]{8}} = \frac{\sqrt[3]{4}}{2y \cdot 2} = \frac{\sqrt[3]{4}}{4y}$$

Review Problems: Set 3

Simplify and combine like radicals.

1. $\sqrt{8} - \sqrt{2}$
2. $\sqrt{48} + \sqrt{27} - \sqrt{75}$
3. $\sqrt[3]{16} - \sqrt[3]{250}$
4. $\sqrt[3]{(24y)} + \sqrt[3]{(3y)}$
5. $\sqrt{(72x^2)} + \sqrt{(32x^2)} - \sqrt{(4x^2)}$

6. $5 \cdot \sqrt[3]{125} + 8 \cdot \sqrt[3]{27}$
7. $\sqrt{(288x)} + \sqrt{(128x)} - \sqrt{(80x)}$
8. $\sqrt{(36x^2y^2)} - \sqrt{(9x^2y^2)}$
9. $\sqrt[3]{(8x^3)} + \sqrt[3]{(125x^6)} - \sqrt[3]{(64x^6)}$

Multiply and simply each of following radicals.

10. $\sqrt{12} \cdot \sqrt{10}$
11. $\sqrt{7} \cdot \sqrt{14}$
12. $(3 \cdot \sqrt[3]{4})(5 \cdot \sqrt[3]{16})$
13. $(- \sqrt[3]{5})(10 \cdot \sqrt[3]{25})$
14. $\sqrt{(32x^2)} \cdot \sqrt{(108y^2)}$
15. $\sqrt[3]{27} \cdot \sqrt[3]{(-64)}$
16. $4\sqrt{3}(5\sqrt{2} - 6\sqrt{6})$
17. $(\sqrt{7} + \sqrt{2})(\sqrt{7} + \sqrt{5})$
18. $(\sqrt{10} - 1)(\sqrt{10} + 3)$

Divide and simplify each of the following radicals.

19. $\sqrt{(5/3)}$
20. $\sqrt{(8/2)}$
21. $\dfrac{\sqrt{3}}{\sqrt{50}}$
22. $\sqrt[3]{(2/9)}$
23. $\dfrac{\sqrt[3]{9}}{\sqrt[3]{25}}$

Radical Equations

In previous chapters, we learned how to solve linear equations and quadratic equations. Now we will learn how to solve radical equations. To solve equations involving radicals, we must use what is known as the **power rule**, which states that if x, y and n are real numbers and $x = y$, then $x^n = tn$. This is important because to solve radical equations we have to remove the radical. In order to remove the radical, we must raise the radical to the index of the radical. For example, if we have $\sqrt[3]{(x+3)}$, we raise $\sqrt[3]{(x+3)}$ to the 3rd power to remove the radical. To remove a radical involving a square root, we raise it to the 2nd power and so on.

Sometimes when we raise both sides of an equation to the same power, we will get equations that are not equivalent. The reason for this is that their solution sets are different.

For example, if $x = 4$, the solution set is {4}. Now if we raise both sides to the 4th power, we get $x^4 = 256$, with a solution set of {4, -4}. Notice the solution sets are different. The first equation is not satisfied by $x = -4$, as it is in the second equation. Therefore, we must always check each solution in the original equation to make sure it satisfies the equation. Any solution that doesn't satisfy the equation is discarded. Those discarded solutions are also known as **extraneous solutions**.

A **radical equation** is an equation with a radical expression. Some examples of radical equations are

$\sqrt{(x - 3)} = 8, \quad \sqrt{(2x + 5)} = \sqrt{(x + 2)}, \quad \sqrt[3]{(8x)} = 9, \quad \sqrt[3]{(3x + 4)} = \sqrt[3]{(x^2)}$

The first step in solving a radical equation is the same as for solving a linear equation. We want to isolate the radical expression to one side of the equation. Next, we raise both sides of the equation to the power that equals the index of the radical. Then we solve the equation for the variable and check all solutions to make sure they satisfy the original equation. Eliminate those solutions which don't satisfy the equation.

Example: Solve $\sqrt{(2x + 7)} = 7$.

First step is to isolate the radical to one side. The problem is set up with it already isolated. Next step is to square both sides to remove the radical.

$[\sqrt{(2x + 7)}]^2 = (7)^2$

$2x + 7 = 49$

Now solve for x.

$2x = 42$

$x = 21$.

Check to make sure 21 satisfies the original equation.

$\sqrt{(2x + 7)} = 7$

$\sqrt{(2 \cdot 21 + 7)} = 7$

$\sqrt{(42 + 7)} = 7$

$\sqrt{49} = 7$

$7 = 7$. Therefore 21 is the solution to the equation.

Example: Solve $\sqrt{(4x - 11)} + 4 = x$.

First isolate the radical.

$\sqrt{(4x - 11)} + 4 = x$

$\sqrt{(4x - 11)} + 4 - 4 = x - 4$

$\sqrt{(4x - 11)} = x - 4$

Next, square both sides of the equation to remove the radical.

$[\sqrt{(4x - 11)}]^2 = (x - 4)^2$
$4x - 11 = (x - 4)^2$

Now we solve the equation for x.

$4x - 11 = x^2 - 8x + 16$ (by the FOIL method $(x - 4)(x - 4)$)

$-11 = x^2 - 12x + 16$

$0 = x^2 - 12x + 27$

Factor to get

$0 = (x - 3)(x - 9)$ $(-9 \cdot (-3) = 27$ and $-9 + (-3) = -12)$

$0 = (x - 3)$ or $0 = (x - 9)$. therefore $x = 3, 9$
Check both answers to make sure they satisfy the original equation.

For $x = 3$, $\sqrt{(4 \cdot 3 - 11)} + 4 = 3$ For $x = 9$, $\sqrt{(4 \cdot 9 - 11)} + 4 = 9$

$\sqrt{1} + 4 = 3$ $\sqrt{25} + 4 = 9$

$5 \neq 3$ $9 = 9$

Therefore 9 is a solution to the equation, but 3 is not a solution.

Example: Solve $\sqrt[3]{(x^3 + 8)} = x + 2$.

The radical is already isolated on the left side of the equation, so now we have to raise both sides to the 3rd power to remove the radical.

•Note that in this problem we raise to the 3rd power because the index is 3. The previous examples were square roots and thus we raised each side to the 2nd power.

$$[\sqrt[3]{(x^3 + 8)}]^3 = (x + 2)^3$$

$$x^3 + 8 = (x + 2)(x + 2)(x + 2)$$

$$x^3 + 8 = (x^2 + 4x + 4)(x + 2)$$

$$x^3 + 8 = x^3 + 6x^2 + 12x + 8$$

$$8 = 6x^2 + 12x + 8$$

$$0 = 6x^2 + 12x$$

$$0 = 6x(x + 2)$$

$$0 = 6x \qquad \text{or} \qquad 0 = x + 2$$

$$x = 0, -2$$

Check solutions in original equation.

For $x = 0$, $\sqrt[3]{(0^3 + 8)} = 0 + 2$ For $x = -2$ $\sqrt[3]{((-2)^3 + 8)} = -2 + 2$
                          $2 = 2$ $0 = 0$

Therefore, 0 and -2 are both solutions to the equation.

     In the previous examples we showed how to solve radical equations with one radical. Now we will learn how to solve radical equations with two radicals. In some cases we can solve them using the square root property once, but other times we must rearrange the terms and use the square root property twice.

Example: Solve $\sqrt{(5x - 8)} = 2\sqrt{(x + 4)}$.

Square both sides of the equation to remove the radicals.

$$[\sqrt{(5x - 8)}]^2 = [2\sqrt{(x + 4)}]^2$$

$$5x - 8 = 4(x + 4)$$

Isolate x on one side of the equation and solve.

$$5x - 8 = 4x + 16$$
$$5x = 4x + 24$$

$$5x - 4x = 24$$

$$x = 24$$

Check to see if 24 is a solution by substituting back into the original equation for x.

$$\sqrt{(5 \cdot 24 - 8)} = 2\sqrt{(24 + 4)}$$

$\sqrt{112} = 2\sqrt{28}$

$\sqrt{4} \cdot \sqrt{28} = 2\sqrt{28}$

$2\sqrt{28} = 2\sqrt{28}$.   Therefore, 24 is a solution to the equation.

•Note that 2√28 is not in simplest form. Since we are just checking a solution we showed the two quantities to be 2√28. So there is no need to simplify.

Example: Solve $\sqrt{(2x + 1)} + \sqrt{x} = 5$.

First we have to isolate a radical on one side. Subtract $\sqrt{x}$ from both sides of the equation.

$\sqrt{(2x + 1)} = 5 - \sqrt{x}$

Now square both sides to remove the radical from the left side of the equation.

$[\sqrt{(2x + 1)}]^2 = (5 - \sqrt{x})^2$

$2x + 1 = 25 - 10\sqrt{x} + x$ (Note that $(5 - \sqrt{x})^2 = (5 - \sqrt{x})(5 - \sqrt{x}) = 25 - 5\sqrt{x} - 5\sqrt{x} + \sqrt{(x)^2}$)

Since we still have a radical in the equation, we need to isolate the radical again.

$2x + 1 - 25 = -10\sqrt{x} + x$

$2x - 24 = -10\sqrt{x} + x$

$2x - x - 24 = -10\sqrt{x}$

$x - 24 = -10\sqrt{x}$

Now square both sides of the equation to remove the radical

$(x - 24)^2 = (-10\sqrt{x})^2$

$x^2 - 48x + 576 = 100x$ (Notice that $(x - 24)^2 = (x - 24)(x - 24)$ and $(-10\sqrt{x})^2 = (-10)(-10)(\sqrt{x})(\sqrt{x})$)

$x^2 - 148x + 576 = 0$

$(x - 144)(x - 4) = 0$ (Note that you can factor 576 into $2 \cdot 288 = 2 \cdot 2 \cdot 144 = 4 \cdot 144$ and $-4 + (-144) = -148$).

$x - 144 = 0$ or $x - 4 = 0$

$x = 4, 144$

When substituting the values back into the original equation, 144 does not work, but 4 does. Therefore, 4 is a solution to the equation.

Applications of Radical Equations

Suppose we want to determine how long it takes for an object to hit the ground after being dropped from a certain height or we want to know the original cost of equipment that is currently valued at x dollars. These types of scenarios as well as problems in forestry, carpentry, supply and demand and others can be solved using radical equations.

Example: A baseball is hit straight up in the air and takes 4 seconds to hit the ground after reaching it's highest point. What was the height (in feet) of the baseball at its highest point?

The distance an object will fall is given by the formula

$t = \sqrt{(d/16)}$ where t is the time and d is the distance in feet.

Substitute 4 for t and solve for d

$4 = \sqrt{(d/16)}$

Square both sides of the equation to remove the radical.

$4^2 = [\sqrt{(d/16)}]^2$

$16 = d/16$

$d = 256$ feet

Example: Suppose you purchased a car 3 years ago for $15,000. You wish to sell the car and want to know what the car is worth. The rate r at which the car has depreciated is given by the following formula.

$r = 1 - \sqrt[3]{(v/c)}$ where v is the current value and c is the original cost.

What is the value of the car if the rate of depreciation is 8%?

First we convert 8% to 0.08.

Substitute 0.08 for r and $15,000 for c and solve for v.

$0.08 = 1 - \sqrt[3]{(v/15000)}$

Isolate the radical and cube both sides of the equation

$$0.08 - 1 = -\sqrt[3]{(v/15000)}$$
$$-0.92 = -\sqrt[3]{(v/15000)}$$
$$(-0.92)^3 = [-\sqrt[3]{(v/15000)}]^3$$

$-0.7787 = -v/15000$ (-0.92^3 was solved using a calculator)

$11,680.50 = v$

Therefore the value of the car today is $11,680.50.

Example: If the sides of a right triangle are A, B and C, where C is the hypotenuse (side opposite the right angle), then $\sqrt{(A^2 + B^2)} = C$. Suppose we wish to build a 30 foot long wheelchair accessible ramp that reaches the front door that is 5 feet above the ground, as shown on the next page.

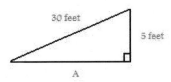

How far from the door should the bottom of the ramp be?

The distance we are looking for in the problem is A.

By the formula above we know $C = 30$ and $B = 5$.

Therefore $\sqrt{(A^2 + 25)} = 30$. Square both sides of the equation to remove the radical.

$[\sqrt{(A^2 + 25)}]^2 = (30)^2$

   $A^2 + 25 = 900$

   $A^2 = 875$

   $A = 29.58$ feet (rounded to 2 decimal places)

Example: Suppose that the number of hammers produced at a given price can be estimated by the formula $S = \sqrt{(8y)}$, where S is the supply (in hundreds) and y is the cost (in dollars). The demand D for the lawn mowers can be estimated by the formula $D = \sqrt{(640 - 2y^2)}$. At what price will the supply equal the demand?

First we have to set $S = D$.

$\sqrt{(8y)} = \sqrt{(640 - 2y^2)}$.

Square both sides of the equation to remove the radicals.

$[\sqrt{(8y)}]^2 = [\sqrt{(640 - 2y^2)}]^2$

   $8y = 640 - 2y^2$

   $0 = -2y^2 - 8y + 640$

   $0 = -2(y^2 + 4y - 320)$

   $0 = -2(y - 16)(y + 20)$

   $y - 16 = 0$ or $y + 20 = 0$

      $y = 16, -20$

   We can eliminate the solution, $y = -20$ because you can't have a negative cost. Substitute 16 into the original equation to check the solution. It does check, therefore 16 is a solution and the cost where supply equals demand is $16.

Example: In a baseball game, a batter hits the ball 250 feet before the right fielder catches it. The fielder throws to third base to try and get a base runner out. The direction the ball was hit, the direction of the throw to third base and the baseline from third base to home plate form a right triangle as seen in the illustration below. How far must the outfielder throw the ball to reach third base?

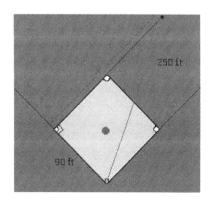

Recall the formula used in a previous example for a right triangle were $\sqrt{(A^2 + B^2)} = C$, where A, B and C are the sides of a right triangle, with C being the hypotenuse (side opposite the right angle). In this case, $C = 250$ and either A or B is 90.

$\sqrt{(90^2 + x^2)} = 250$ (we are using x as the distance between third base and the fielder throwing the ball).

Square both sides of the equation to remove the radical.

$[\sqrt{(90^2 + x^2)}]^2 = (250)^2$

$\quad 8100 + x^2 = 62500$

$\qquad x^2 = 54400$

$\qquad\quad x = 233$ feet (rounded to the nearest whole number. note that the calculation for $\sqrt{54400}$ was done on a calculator)

Review Problems : Set 4

Solve each of the following and eliminate any extraneous solutions.

1. $\sqrt{(2x + 7)} = 5$
2. $\sqrt{(4x + 5)} + 4 = 13$
3. $2\sqrt{(4y + 1)} = \sqrt{(y + 4)}$
4. $\sqrt{[3(x - 6)]} = \sqrt{(5x + 8)}$
5. $\sqrt{(6 - y)} - \sqrt{(2y + 3)} = 0$
6. $\sqrt[3]{(3x + 10)} = 4$
7. $\sqrt[3]{(7y - 3)} = 3$
8. $\sqrt{(3y + 1)} - y = 1$
9. $\sqrt{(2x + 1)} = \sqrt{x} + 1$
10. $\sqrt{(3 + z)} = \sqrt{z} + 1$

Solve the following for the indicated variable.

11. $c = \sqrt{(a^2 + b^2)}$ for b
12. $2ax = \sqrt{(b + 4c)}$ for c
13. $v = \sqrt[3]{(p/0.02)}$ for p

Applications

14. A computer that is now worth $300 originally cost C dollars 4 years ago. The computer depreciated at a rate of 15% per year. The rate, r is defined by the following formula: $r = 1 - \sqrt[3]{(V/C)}$

   What was the original cost of the computer?
15.   The number of screwdrivers that will be produced at a given price can be estimated by the formula $S = \sqrt{(6y)}$, where S is the supply in hundreds and y is the price in dollars. The demand for hammers is estimated by the formula $D = \sqrt{(50 - 4y^2)}$. At what price will the supply equal the demand?

16.   Suppose interstate 55 intersects route 40 and route 201 as seen in the illustration below. Route 40 and route 201 meet at a right angle. The distance from Elm City to Parkville along interstate 55 is 40 miles. The distance from Greentown to Parkville along route 40 is 23 miles. What is the distance from Greentown to Elm City along route 201?

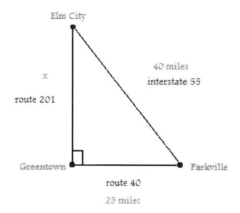

Elm City

40 miles
interstate 55

x
route 201

Greentown
route 40
25 miles

Parkville

Key Terms and Concepts to Review

•Square root
•Principal square root
•Radical symbol
•Radical expression
•Multiplication property of radicals
•Division property of radicals
•Cube root
•Odd and even roots
•Like radicals
•Rationalize the denominator

Answers to Problem Sets

Problem Set 1
Answers and key steps in solution

1. 11 $\sqrt{121} = 11$ because $11 \cdot 11 = 121$
2. 7 $\sqrt{49} = 7$ because $7 \cdot 7 = 49$
3. 15 $\sqrt{225} = 15$ because $15 \cdot 15 = 225$
4. 2/3 $\sqrt{(4/9)} = 2/3$ because $2/3 \cdot 2/3 = 4/9$
5. No real number solution because the product of two positive numbers is always positive.
6. 5 $\sqrt{(-5)^2} = \sqrt{25} = 5$
7. ½ $\sqrt{(16/64)} = 4/8$ since $(4/8)^2 = 16/64$ and $4/8$ simplifies to ½
8. 0.3 $\sqrt{(0.09)} = 0.3$ since $0.3^2 = 0.09$
9. -9 $\sqrt{(81)} = 9$ and apply the - in front to get -9.
10. No real number solution for the square root of a negative number.
11. $5x^2$ $\sqrt{(25x^4)} = 5x^2$ because $\sqrt{25} = 5$ and $\sqrt{x^4} = x^2$
12. $11y$ $\sqrt{(121y^2)} = 11y$ because $\sqrt{121} = 11$ and $\sqrt{y^2} = y$
13. $(x + y)$ $\sqrt{(x + y)^2} = (x + y)$ because the square root of any quantity squared is that quantity
14. $(2y - 7)$ $\sqrt{(2y - 7)^2} = (2y - 7)$ (same reason as in problem 13)
15. $(x - 5)$ $\sqrt{(x^2 - 10x + 25)} = \sqrt{(x - 5)(x - 5)} = \sqrt{(x - 5)^2} = (x - 5)$
16. $(y + 6)$ $\sqrt{(y^2 + 12y + 36)} = \sqrt{(y + 6)(y + 6)} = \sqrt{(y + 6)^2} = (y + 6)$
17. $2\sqrt{6}$ $\sqrt{24} = \sqrt{4} \cdot \sqrt{6} = 2\sqrt{6}$ (note that $\sqrt{4} = 2$)
18. $4\sqrt{3}$ $\sqrt{48} = \sqrt{16} \cdot \sqrt{3} = 4\sqrt{3}$ (note that $\sqrt{16} = 4$)
19. $6\sqrt{2}$ $\sqrt{72} = \sqrt{36} \cdot \sqrt{2} = 6\sqrt{2}$ (note that $\sqrt{36} = 6$)
20. $2x\sqrt{2}$ $\sqrt{(8x^2)} = \sqrt{8} \cdot \sqrt{x^2} = \sqrt{4} \cdot \sqrt{2} \cdot \sqrt{x^2} = 2\sqrt{2} \cdot \sqrt{x^2} = 2\sqrt{2} \cdot x = 2x\sqrt{2}$
21. $2x\sqrt{(7x)}$ $\sqrt{(28x^3)} = \sqrt{4} \cdot \sqrt{7} \cdot \sqrt{x^3} = 2 \cdot \sqrt{7} \cdot \sqrt{x^2} \cdot \sqrt{x} = 2 \cdot \sqrt{7} \cdot x \cdot \sqrt{x} = 2x\sqrt{(7x)}$

22. $6xy^2$ $\sqrt{(36x^2y^4)} = \sqrt{36} \cdot \sqrt{x^2} \cdot \sqrt{y^4} = 6xy^2$

23. $5xy^2\sqrt{(5xy)}$ $\sqrt{(125x^3y^5)} = \sqrt{125} \cdot \sqrt{x^3} \cdot \sqrt{y^5} = \sqrt{25} \cdot \sqrt{5} \cdot \sqrt{x^2} \cdot \sqrt{x} \cdot \sqrt{y^4} \cdot \sqrt{y} = 5\sqrt{5} \cdot x\sqrt{x} \cdot y^2\sqrt{y} =$
         $5xy^2\sqrt{(5xy)}$

24. $7x/5$ $\sqrt{(49x^2/25)} = \sqrt{(49x^2)}/\sqrt{25} = 7x/5$

25. $11/(6y^2)$ $\sqrt{(121/36y^4)} = \sqrt{121}/\sqrt{(36y^4)} = 11/(6y^2)$

26. $5\sqrt{(xy)}$ $\sqrt{(225x^2y^2/5xy)}$ Simplify under the radical sign to get $\sqrt{(25xy)} = \sqrt{25} \cdot \sqrt{(xy)} = 5\sqrt{(xy)}$

27. $2xy$ $\sqrt{(68x^2y^3)}/\sqrt{(17y)} = \sqrt{(68x^2y^3/17y)} = \sqrt{(4x^2y^2)} = 2xy$

28. $5x$ $\sqrt{(50x^2y^3)}/\sqrt{(2y^3)} = \sqrt{(50x^2y^3/2y^3)} = \sqrt{(25x^2)} = 5x$

Problem Set 2
Answers and key steps in solution

1. 4   because $4^3 = 64$
2. -3   because $(-3)^3 = -27$
3. 5   because $5^3 = 125$
4. -6   because $(-6)^3 = -216$
5. 9   because $9^3 = 729$
6. -7   because $(-7)^3 = -343$
7. 3/2   because $(3/2)^3 = 27/8$
8. -4/3   because $(-4/3)^3 = -64/27$
9. 2   because $(-2)^3 = 8$, then apply the – to get -8
10. 5xy   because $(5xy)^3 = 125x^3y^3$
11. $(x – 6)$ from the property of radicals $\sqrt[3]{(x – 6)^3} = (x – 6)$
12. $(7x + 9)$ property of radicals
13. $-(4x + 3)$ property of radicals then apply the -
14. $10y^2$ because $10^3 = 1000$ and $(y^2)^3 = y^6$
15. $6x^2y^3$ because $6^3 = 216$, $(x^2)^3 = x^6$ and $(y^3)^3 = y^9$
16. $2x^3 \cdot \sqrt[3]{(3x^2)}$ $\sqrt[3]{(24x^5)} = \sqrt[3]{24} \cdot \sqrt[3]{(x^5)} = \sqrt[3]{8} \cdot \sqrt[3]{3} \cdot \sqrt[3]{(x^3)} \cdot \sqrt[3]{(x^2)} = 2x^3 \cdot\sqrt[3]{(3x^2)}$
17. $3y \cdot \sqrt[3]{(4y)}$ $\sqrt[3]{(108y^4)} = \sqrt[3]{27} \cdot \sqrt[3]{4} \cdot \sqrt[3]{(y^3)} \cdot \sqrt[3]{y} = 3y \cdot \sqrt[3]{(4y)}$
18. $2 \cdot \sqrt[3]{5}$ $\sqrt[3]{40} = \sqrt[3]{8} \cdot \sqrt[3]{5} = 2 \cdot \sqrt[3]{5}$
19. $3 \cdot \sqrt[3]{2}$ $\sqrt[3]{54} = \sqrt[3]{27} \cdot \sqrt[3]{2} = 3 \cdot \sqrt[3]{2}$
20. $-2 \cdot \sqrt[3]{6}$ $\sqrt[3]{-48} = \sqrt[3]{-8} \cdot \sqrt[3]{6} = -2 \cdot \sqrt[3]{6}$
21. $2xy^2 \cdot \sqrt[3]{10xy}$ $\sqrt[3]{(80x^4y^7)} = \sqrt[3]{10} \cdot \sqrt[3]{8} \cdot \sqrt[3]{(x^3)} \cdot \sqrt[3]{x} \cdot \sqrt[3]{(y^6)} \cdot \sqrt[3]{y} = 2xy^2 \cdot \sqrt[3]{10xy}$
22. $-3x^2 \cdot \sqrt[3]{3}$ $\sqrt[3]{(-81x^6)} = \sqrt[3]{-27} \cdot \sqrt[3]{3} \cdot \sqrt[3]{(x^6)} = -3x^2 \cdot \sqrt[3]{3}$
23. $4x$ $\sqrt[3]{(128x^4/2x)} = \sqrt[3]{(64x^3)} = 4x$
24. $2xy$ $\sqrt[3]{(24x^5y^3/3x^2)} = \sqrt[3]{(8x^3y^3)} = 2xy$
25. $2y^2$ $\sqrt[3]{(48y^6/6)} = \sqrt[3]{(8y^6)} = 2y^2$
26. $3xy$ $\sqrt[3]{(81x^3y^5)} / \sqrt[3]{(3y^2)} = \sqrt[3]{(27x^3y^3)} = 3xy$
27. $-5y^2$ $\sqrt[3]{(-250y^8)} / \sqrt[3]{(2y^2)} = \sqrt[3]{(-125y^6)} = -5y^2$
28. $4xy$ $\sqrt[3]{(256x^7y^3)} / \sqrt[3]{(4x^4)} = \sqrt[3]{(64x^3y^3)} = 4xy$

Problem Set 3
Answers and key steps in solution

1. $\sqrt{2}$ $\sqrt{8} - \sqrt{2} = \sqrt{4} \cdot \sqrt{2} - \sqrt{2} = 2\sqrt{2} - \sqrt{2} = \sqrt{2}$
2. $2\sqrt{3}$ $\sqrt{48} + \sqrt{27} - \sqrt{75} = (\sqrt{16} \cdot \sqrt{3}) + (\sqrt{9} \cdot \sqrt{3}) - (\sqrt{25} \cdot \sqrt{3}) = 4\sqrt{3} + 3\sqrt{3} - 5\sqrt{3} = 2\sqrt{3}$
3. $-3 \cdot \sqrt[3]{2}$ $\sqrt[3]{16} - \sqrt[3]{250} = (\sqrt[3]{8} \cdot \sqrt[3]{2}) - (\sqrt[3]{125} \cdot \sqrt[3]{2}) = 2\cdot\sqrt[3]{2} - 5\cdot\sqrt[3]{2} = -3\cdot\sqrt[3]{2}$
4. $3\cdot\sqrt[3]{(3y)}$ $\sqrt[3]{(24y)} + \sqrt[3]{(3y)} = \sqrt[3]{8} \cdot \sqrt[3]{(3y)} + \sqrt[3]{(3y)} = 2\cdot\sqrt[3]{(3y)} + \sqrt[3]{(3y)} = 3\cdot\sqrt[3]{(3y)}$
5. $2x(5\sqrt{2} - 1)$ $\sqrt{(72x^2)} + \sqrt{(32x^2)} - \sqrt{(4x^2)} = (\sqrt{(36x^2)} \cdot \sqrt{2}) + (\sqrt{(16x^2)} \cdot \sqrt{2}) - \sqrt{(4x^2)} = 6x\sqrt{2} + 4x\sqrt{2} - 2x$
       $= 10x\sqrt{2} - 2x = 2x(5\sqrt{2} - 1)$.
6. 49 $5\cdot\sqrt[3]{125} + 8\cdot\sqrt[3]{27} = 5(5) + 8(3) = 25 + 24 = 49$
7. $4[5\sqrt{(2x)} - \sqrt{(5x)}]$ $\sqrt{(288x)} + \sqrt{(128x)} - \sqrt{(80x)} = (\sqrt{144} \cdot \sqrt{(2x)}) + (\sqrt{64} \cdot \sqrt{(2x)}) - (\sqrt{16} \cdot \sqrt{5}) = 12\sqrt{(2x)} +$
         $8\sqrt{(2x)} - 4\sqrt{5} = 20\sqrt{(2x)} - 4\sqrt{5} = 4(5\sqrt{(2x)} - \sqrt{(5x)})$ Factor out 4 in last step.
8. $3xy$ $\sqrt{(36x^2y^2)} - \sqrt{(9x^2y^2)} = \sqrt{36} \cdot \sqrt{(x^2y^2)} - \sqrt{9} \cdot \sqrt{(x^2y^2)} = 6xy - 3xy = 3xy$
9. $x(2 + x)$ $\sqrt[3]{(8x^3)} + \sqrt[3]{(125x^6)} - \sqrt[3]{(64x^6)} = \sqrt[3]{8} \cdot \sqrt[3]{(x^3)} + \sqrt[3]{125} \cdot \sqrt[3]{(x^6)} - \sqrt[3]{64} \cdot \sqrt[3]{(x^6)} = 2x + 5x^2$
       $- 4x^2 = 2x + x^2 = x(2 + x)$
10. $2\sqrt{30}$ $\sqrt{12} \cdot \sqrt{10} = \sqrt{4} \cdot \sqrt{3} \cdot \sqrt{10} = 2 \cdot \sqrt{3} \cdot \sqrt{10} = 2\sqrt{30}$

11. $7\sqrt{2}$ $\sqrt{7} \cdot \sqrt{14} = \sqrt{7} \cdot \sqrt{7} \cdot \sqrt{2} = 7\sqrt{2}$

12. 60 $(3\cdot\sqrt[3]{4})(5\cdot\sqrt[3]{16}) = 15\cdot\sqrt[3]{64} = 15(4) = 60$

13. -50 $(-\sqrt[3]{5})(10\cdot\sqrt[3]{25}) = -10\cdot\sqrt[3]{125} = -10(5) = -50$

14. $24xy\sqrt{6}$ $\sqrt{(32x^2)} \cdot \sqrt{(108y^2)} = \sqrt{16} \cdot \sqrt{(x^2)} \cdot \sqrt{2} \cdot \sqrt{36} \cdot \sqrt{(y^2)} \cdot \sqrt{3} = 4x\sqrt{2} \cdot (6y)\sqrt{3} = 24xy\sqrt{6}$

15. -12 $\sqrt[3]{27} \cdot \sqrt[3]{(-64)} = 3(-4) = -12$

16. $4(5\sqrt{6} - 18\sqrt{2})$ $4\sqrt{3}(5\sqrt{2} - 6\sqrt{6}) = 4\sqrt{3}(5\sqrt{2}) - 4\sqrt{3}(6\sqrt{6}) = 20\sqrt{6} - 24\sqrt{18} = 20\sqrt{6} - 24(\sqrt{9} \cdot \sqrt{2}) = 20\sqrt{6} -$
      $24(3\sqrt{2}) = 20\sqrt{6} - 72\sqrt{2} = 4(5\sqrt{6} - 18\sqrt{2})$ Factor out a 4 in last step.

17. $7 + \sqrt{35} + \sqrt{14} + \sqrt{10}$ $(\sqrt{7} + \sqrt{2})(\sqrt{7} + \sqrt{5}) = (\sqrt{7})(\sqrt{7}) + (\sqrt{7})(\sqrt{5}) + (\sqrt{2})(\sqrt{7}) + (\sqrt{2})(\sqrt{5})$

18. $7 + 2\sqrt{10}$ $(\sqrt{10} - 1)(\sqrt{10} + 3) = (\sqrt{10})(\sqrt{10}) + (\sqrt{10})(3) + (-1)(\sqrt{10}) + (-1)(3) = 10 + 3\sqrt{10} - \sqrt{10}$
      $- 3 = 7 + 2\sqrt{10}$

19. $\dfrac{\sqrt{15}}{3}$ $\sqrt{(5/3)} = \dfrac{\sqrt{5} \cdot \sqrt{3}}{\sqrt{3} \cdot \sqrt{3}} = \dfrac{\sqrt{15}}{\sqrt{9}} = \dfrac{\sqrt{15}}{3}$

20. 2 $\sqrt{(8/2)} = (\sqrt{4} \cdot \sqrt{2})/\sqrt{2} = \sqrt{4} = 2$

21. $\dfrac{\sqrt{6}}{10}$ $\dfrac{\sqrt{3}}{\sqrt{50}} = \dfrac{\sqrt{3}}{\sqrt{25}\cdot\sqrt{2}} = \dfrac{\sqrt{3} \cdot \sqrt{2}}{5 \cdot\sqrt{2} \cdot \sqrt{2}} = \dfrac{\sqrt{6}}{5\cdot2} = \dfrac{\sqrt{6}}{10}$

22. $\dfrac{\sqrt[3]{6}}{3}$ $\sqrt[3]{(2/9)} = \dfrac{\sqrt[3]{2} \cdot \sqrt[3]{3}}{\sqrt[3]{9} \cdot \sqrt[3]{3}} = \dfrac{\sqrt[3]{6}}{\sqrt[3]{27}} = \dfrac{\sqrt[3]{6}}{3}$

23. $\dfrac{\sqrt[3]{45}}{5}$ $\dfrac{\sqrt[3]{9}}{\sqrt[3]{25}} = \dfrac{\sqrt[3]{9} \cdot \sqrt[3]{5}}{\sqrt[3]{25} \cdot \sqrt[3]{5}} = \dfrac{\sqrt[3]{45}}{\sqrt[3]{125}} = \dfrac{\sqrt[3]{45}}{5}$

Problem Set 4
Answers and key steps in solution.

1. 9, $\sqrt{(2x + 7)} = 5$, square both sides to get $2x + 7 = 25$, $2x = 18$, $x = 9$

2. 19, $\sqrt{(4x + 5)} + 4 = 13$, $\sqrt{(4x + 5)} = 9$, square both sides to get $4x + 5 = 81$, $4x = 76$, $x = 19$

3. 0, $2\sqrt{(4y + 1)} = \sqrt{(y + 4)}$, square both sides to get $4(4y + 1) = y + 4$, $16y + 4 = y + 4$, $15y + 4 =$
      4, $15y = 0$, $y = 0$

4. No real solution, $\sqrt{[3(x - 6)]} = \sqrt{(5x + 8)}$, square both sides to get $3(x - 6) = 5x + 8$, $3x - 18 = 5x + 8$,
      $3x = 5x + 26$, $-2x = 26$, $x = -13$. Substitute -13 into the problem and we get a
      negative value under the square root, which is no real solution.

5. 3, $\sqrt{(6 - y)} - \sqrt{(2y - 3)} = 0$, $\sqrt{(6 - y)} = \sqrt{(2y - 3)}$, $6 - y = 2y - 3$, $6 = 3y - 3$, $9 = 3y$, $3 = y$

6. 18, $\sqrt[3]{(3x + 10)} = 4$, cube both sides to get $3x + 10 = 64$, $3x = 54$, $x = 18$

7. $4\ 2/7$, $\sqrt[3]{(7y - 3)} = 3$, cube both sides to get $7y - 3= 27$, $7y = 30$, $y = 30/7 = 4\ 2/7$

8. 0 and 1, $\sqrt{(3y + 1)} - y = 1$, $\sqrt{(3y + 1)} = 1 + y$, square both sides to get $3y + 1 = y^2 + 2y + 1$, set equal to 0
      to get $0 = y^2 - y$, factor out a y to get $0 = y(y - 1)$, therefore $y = 0$ or $y = 1$, both check so both are
      solutions.

9. 0 and 4, $\sqrt{(2x + 1)} = \sqrt{x} + 1$, square both sides to get $2x + 1 = x + 2\sqrt{x} + 1$, isolate the radical to get $x =$
      $2\sqrt{x}$, square both sides to get $x^2 = 4x$, $x^2 - 4x = 0$, factor out an x to get $x(x - 4) = 0$, therefore $x = 0$ or $x = 4$
      and both solutions satisfy the original equation.

10. 1, $\sqrt{(3 + z)} = \sqrt{z} + 1$, same process as in the previous problem

11. $\sqrt{(c - a)(c + a)}$ $c = \sqrt{(a^2 + b^2)}$, square both sides to get $c^2 = a^2 + b^2$, $c^2 - a^2 = b^2$, take square root of both
      sides to solve for b.

12. $a^2x^2 - (b/4)$, $2ax = \sqrt{(b + 4c)}$, square both sides to get $4a^2x^2 = b + 4c$, $4a^2x^2 - b = 4c$, divide each term
      by 4 to get $(4a^2x^2/4) - (b/4) = a^2x^2 - (b/4)$

13. $0.02v^3$, $v = \sqrt[3]{(p/0.02)}$, cube both sides to get $v^3 = p/(0.02)$, multiply by 0.02 to get $0.02v^3 = p$.

14. $\$488.50$, $.15 = 1 - \sqrt[3]{(300/C)}$, $-0.85 = -\sqrt[3]{(300/C)}$, cube both sides to get $-.614125 = -300/C$, $(-$
      $300/-.614125) = 488.50$

15. $\$10$, $\sqrt{(6y)} = \sqrt{(100 - 4y)}$, square both sides to get $6y = 100 - 4y$, $10y = 100$, $y = 10$

16. 32.7 miles, $40 = \sqrt{(x^2 + 23^2)}$, square both sides to get $1600 = x^2 + 23^2$, $1600 = x^2 + 529$, $1071 = x^2$,
      therefore $x = 32.7$ (rounded to 1 decimal place).

Chapter 6

Rational Expressions and Functions

A **rational expression** is a fraction of two polynomials. Some examples of rational expressions are

$$\frac{4xy^2}{13x}, \qquad \frac{2x + 5}{4x}, \qquad \frac{4x^2 - 3x + 5}{5x - 8} \qquad \text{and} \qquad \frac{12x^3 + 2x^2 - 3x + 7}{3x^2 + 6x + 8}$$

•Note that the denominator of a rational expression cannot equal zero. In the second example above, $5x - 8 \neq 0$, therefore $x \neq 8/5$.

Simplifying Rational Expressions

To simplify rational expressions, factor the numerator and the denominator and divide out the common factors in the numerator and denominator. The **fundamental property of fractions** is used to help simplify rational expressions because it lets us to divide out the common factors.

The following example illustrates this property.

$$\frac{Bx}{Ax} = \frac{B \cdot (x)}{A \cdot (x)} = \frac{B}{A} \cdot 1 = \frac{B}{A}$$

Notice that the x's in the rational expression divide out.

Example: Simplify the following rational expressions.

1. $\dfrac{25x}{75x^3}$

Factor the numerator and the denominator first.

$25x = 5 \cdot 5 \cdot x$

$75x^3 = 5 \cdot 5 \cdot 3 \cdot x \cdot x \cdot x$

$$\frac{25x}{75x^3} = \frac{\mathbf{5 \cdot 5 \cdot x}}{\mathbf{5 \cdot 5} \cdot 3 \cdot \mathbf{x} \cdot x \cdot x}$$

Notice the common factors in bold. Divide out the common factors to get

$$\frac{25x}{75x^3} = \frac{1}{3 \cdot x \cdot x} = \frac{1}{3x^2}$$

2. $\dfrac{6x^2y^3}{9xy^5}$

Factor the numerator and denominator first.

$6x^2y^3 = 3 \cdot 2 \cdot x \cdot x \cdot y \cdot y \cdot y$

$9xy^5 = 3 \cdot 3 \cdot x \cdot y \cdot y \cdot y \cdot y \cdot y$

$$\frac{6x^2y^3}{9xy^5} = \frac{\mathbf{3} \cdot 2 \cdot \mathbf{x} \cdot x \cdot \mathbf{y} \cdot \mathbf{y} \cdot y}{\mathbf{3} \cdot 3 \cdot \mathbf{x} \cdot \mathbf{y} \cdot \mathbf{y} \cdot y \cdot y \cdot y}$$

Notice the common factors in blue. Divide out the common factors to get

$$\frac{6x^2y^3}{9xy^5} = \frac{2 \cdot x}{3 \cdot y \cdot y} = \frac{2x}{3y^2}$$

3. $\dfrac{-16x^3y^2z^6}{24xy^4z^2}$

Factor the numerator and denominator first.

$-16x^3y^2z^6 = -1 \cdot 2 \cdot 2 \cdot 2 \cdot 2 \cdot x \cdot x \cdot x \cdot y \cdot y \cdot z \cdot z \cdot z \cdot z \cdot z \cdot z$

$24xy^4z^2 = 3 \cdot 2 \cdot 2 \cdot 2 \cdot x \cdot y \cdot y \cdot y \cdot y \cdot z \cdot z$

$$\frac{-16x^3y^2z^6}{24xy^4z^2} = \frac{-1 \cdot \mathbf{2 \cdot 2 \cdot 2} \cdot 2 \cdot \mathbf{x} \cdot x \cdot x \cdot \mathbf{y} \cdot \mathbf{y} \cdot \mathbf{z} \cdot \mathbf{z} \cdot z \cdot z \cdot z \cdot z}{3 \cdot \mathbf{2 \cdot 2 \cdot 2} \cdot \mathbf{x} \cdot \mathbf{y} \cdot \mathbf{y} \cdot y \cdot y \cdot \mathbf{z} \cdot \mathbf{z}}$$

Notice the common factors in blue. Divide out the common factors to get

$$\frac{-16x^3y^2z^6}{24xy^4z^2} = \frac{-1 \cdot 2 \cdot x \cdot x \cdot z \cdot z \cdot z \cdot z}{3 \cdot y \cdot y} = \frac{-2x^2z^4}{3y^2}$$

• **Note you can simplify the variables in each of the examples by using the division rule for exponents. For example** $\dfrac{x^3y^2z^6}{xy^4z^2} = x^{(3-1)}y^{(2-4)}z^{(6-2)} = x^2y^{-2}z^4 = \dfrac{x^2z^4}{y^2}$

In the previous examples we simplified rational expressions with monomials in both the numerator and denominator. Now we'll learn how to simply rational expressions with binomials in both the numerator and denominator.

Example: Simplify the following rational expressions.

1. $\dfrac{x + 5}{x^2 - 25}$

Factor the numerator and denominator first.

The numerator is in simplest form.

Recall that $x^2 - 25 = (x - 5)(x + 5)$

Therefore $\dfrac{x + 5}{x^2 - 25} = \dfrac{x + 5}{(x - 5)(x + 5)}$

Notice the common factor of $x + 5$. Divide that out to get $\dfrac{1}{x - 5}$.

2. $\dfrac{2x + 6}{3x^3 - 27x}$

Factor the numerator and denominator first.

$2x + 6 = 2(x + 3)$

$3x^3 - 27x = 3x(x^2 - 9)$ (notice that $x^2 - 9$ is a difference of squares, therefore $x^2 - 9 = (x - 3)(x + 3)$.

$$\frac{2x + 6}{3x^3 - 27x} = \frac{2(x + 3)}{3(x - 3)(x + 3)}$$

Notice the common factor is $(x + 3)$. Divide that out to get $\frac{2}{3(x - 3)}$.

   Just as we simplified rational expressions with binomials in the numerator and denominator, we can also simplify rational expressions with trinomials in both the numerator and denominator. Likewise, we can simplify rational expressions with a different number of terms in the numerator and denominator. For example, we can simplify a rational expression with a binomial in the numerator and trinomial in the denominator. Be careful when dividing out common factors. The factors must be common to the entire numerator and entire denominator.

   For example, $(4 + 9)/4$. You cannot divide out the 4 in the numerator with the 4 in the denominator. In order to simplify, you must be able to divide out the 4 with both terms in the numerator and 4 does not divide into 9 evenly.

Example: Simplify the following rational expressions.

1. $\dfrac{4x + 8}{x^2 + 6x + 8}$

Factor the numerator and denominator first.

$4x + 8 = 4(x + 2)$

$x^2 + 6x + 8 = (x + 2)(x + 4)$

$$\frac{4x + 8}{x^2 + 6x + 8} = \frac{4(x + 2)}{(x + 2)(x + 4)}$$

Notice the common factor of $(x + 2)$. Divide that out to get $\dfrac{4}{x + 4}$.

2. $\dfrac{3x^2 - 13x - 10}{6x^2 + 13x + 6}$

Factor the numerator and denominator first.

$3x^2 - 13x - 10 = (3x + 2)(x - 5)$

$6x^2 + 13x + 6 = (2x + 3)(3x + 2)$

$$\frac{3x^2 - 13x - 10}{6x^2 + 13x + 6} = \frac{(3x + 2)(x - 5)}{(2x + 3)(3x +2)}$$

Notice the common factor of $(3x + 2)$. Divide that out to get $\dfrac{(x - 5)}{(2x + 3)}$.

3. $\dfrac{2x^2 - 3xy - 9y^2}{3y^2 - xy}$

Factor the numerator and denominator first.

$2x^2 - 3xy - 9y^2 = (2x + 3y)(x - 3y)$

$3y^2 - xy = y(3y - x)$

$$\frac{2x^2 - 3xy - 9y^2}{3y^2 - xy} = \frac{(2x + 3y)(x - 3y)}{y(3y - x)}$$

Notice the binomials $x - 3y$ and $3y - x$. They have the same terms with opposite signs. Therefore when we divide the binomials, the result is 1.

$$\frac{(x - 3y)}{(3y - x)} = \frac{-1(-x + 3y)}{(3y - x)} = \frac{-1(3y - x)}{(3y - x)} = -1.$$

Notice how we factored out a -1 in the numerator. That enables us to divide out the common factor of $(3y - x)$.

Therefore $\dfrac{2x^2 - 3xy - 9y^2}{3y^2 - xy} = \dfrac{-1(2x + 3y)}{y} = \dfrac{-(2x + 3y)}{y}$.

•Note that sometimes rational expressions are already in simplest form.

Example: Simplify the following rational expression, if possible.

$$\frac{Ax + By + Bx + Ay}{A - B}$$

Factor the numerator to get $x(A + B) + y(A + B) = (A + B)(x + y)$ (factored by grouping $(Ax + Bx) + (Ay + By)$)

The denominator is already in simplest form.

$$\frac{Ax + By + Bx + Ay}{A - B} = \frac{(A + B)(x + y)}{A - B}$$

There are no common factors, therefore $\dfrac{Ax + By + Bx + Ay}{A - B}$ is already in simplest form.

Review Problems: Set 1

Simplify each rational expression, if possible.

1. $\dfrac{15x^2}{5x}$

2. $\dfrac{4x^2 y^6}{18x^4 y^2}$

3. $\dfrac{25xy^3 z^5}{50xyz^7}$

4. $\dfrac{6x + 18}{x + 3}$

5. $\dfrac{x^2 - y^2}{x + y}$

6. $\dfrac{7x - 14}{x^2 + 4x - 12}$

7. $\dfrac{2x^2 - 9x - 5}{3x^2 - 13x - 10}$

8. $\dfrac{x - xy}{xy - y}$

9. $\dfrac{4y^2 + 8y + 3}{-2y^2 + y + 6}$

10. $\dfrac{2x^2 + 7x - 15}{2x^2 + 13x + 15}$

11. $\dfrac{xy - x + y - 1}{x - y}$

12. $\dfrac{5x^3 - 125x}{6x + 30}$

Adding and Subtracting Rational Expressions

When adding and subtracting rational expressions, we use the same rules that apply to adding and subtracting simple fractions. Recall when adding simple fractions, if the denominators are the same, add the numerators and keep the denominators the same.

For example, $\qquad \dfrac{1}{3} + \dfrac{4}{3} = \dfrac{5}{3}$.

The same concept applies to adding and subtracting rational expressions.

Examples: Add the following rational expressions.

1. $\dfrac{5}{4y} + \dfrac{11}{4y}$

   $\dfrac{(5 + 11)}{4y}$ (Add the numerators since the expressions have common denominators)

   $\dfrac{16}{4y} = \dfrac{4}{y}$ (Simplify whenever possible)

2. $\dfrac{xy}{y^2} - \dfrac{4xy}{y^2}$

   $\dfrac{(xy - 4xy)}{y^2}$ (Subtract the numerators since the expressions have common denominators)

   $\dfrac{-3xy}{y^2} = \dfrac{-3x}{y}$

3. $\dfrac{x^3}{x^2 - 1} - \dfrac{x^2}{x^2 - 1}$

   $\dfrac{x^3 - x^2}{x^2 - 1}$

   Factor the numerator and the denominator first.

   $\dfrac{x^2(x - 1)}{(x - 1)(x + 1)}$ (Notice the common factor of $(x - 1)$ will divide out)

   $\dfrac{x^2}{(x + 1)}$

The order in which we add or subtract more than two rational expressions will not affect the answer. It's the same concept when adding or subtracting real numbers. For example, in the problem 2 + 4 - 5, we can perform the addition first to get 6 and then subtract 5 to get 1. We can subtract 5 from 4 first to get -1 and add 2 and still get 1.

Example: Perform the operations in the following expression.

$$\frac{7}{3x} + \frac{13}{3x} - \frac{6}{3x}$$

Adding first and then subtracting.

$$\frac{(7 + 13) - 6}{3x} = \frac{20 - 6}{3x} = \frac{14}{3x}$$

Subtracting first and then adding.

$$\frac{7 + (13 - 6)}{3x} = \frac{7 + 7}{3x} = \frac{14}{3x}$$

Notice that the result is the same. The associative property of addition allows the regrouping the terms without affecting the result.

Adding and subtracting rational expressions is a bit more complex with unlike denominators. Before adding, we have to get a common denominator. We should try to get the **lowest common denominator**, (LCD) before adding or subtracting. Any common denominator would enable us to add or subtract, but if it's not the LCD, simplifying may become more difficult.

For example, add the following fractions.

$$\frac{2}{6} + \frac{10}{12}$$

We could pick 24 as the common denominator since 6 and 12 both divide evenly into 24. But by doing that we get

$$\frac{2}{6} \cdot \frac{(4)}{(4)} + \frac{10}{12} \cdot \frac{(2)}{(2)} = \frac{8}{24} + \frac{20}{24} = \frac{28}{24} = \frac{7}{6}$$

Notice that we multiplied the numerator and denominator of the first fraction by 4. In order to get the denominator to equal 24, we had to multiply 6 by 4. You must multiply the numerator by 4 also. We are changing the fraction to an equivalent fraction with a denominator of 24. Essentially we are multiplying the fraction by 1 because $\frac{4}{4} = 1$. Therefore, the equivalent fraction of $\frac{2}{6} = \frac{8}{24}$.

We multiplied the numerator and the denominator of the second fraction by 2 to change $\frac{10}{12}$ to an equivalent fraction with a denominator of 24.

But the lowest common denominator is not 24. To find the LCD, get the prime factorization of each denominator and take the highest power of each factor and multiply them together.

$$6 = 2 \cdot 3$$

$$24 = 2 \cdot 2 \cdot 2 \cdot 3$$

The highest power of each factor multiplied together gives us $2 \cdot 2 \cdot 3 = 12$. Therefore the LCD is 12. This will make simplifying the fraction easier.

Examples: Find the lowest common denominator (LCD) of the following.

1. $\dfrac{6}{xy}$, $\dfrac{12x}{5y^2}$

Factor each denominator.

First term denominator: $xy = x \cdot y$
Second term denominator: $5y^2 = 5 \cdot y \cdot y$
The highest power of each factor multiplied together gives us $5 \cdot x \cdot y \cdot y = 5xy^2$. Therefore, the LCD is $5xy^2$.

2. $\dfrac{16y}{4x^3z^4}$, $\dfrac{32}{14x^4z}$

Factor each denominator

First: $4x^3z^4 = \mathbf{2 \cdot 2} \cdot x \cdot x \cdot x \cdot \mathbf{z \cdot z \cdot z \cdot z}$
Second: $14x^4z = 2 \cdot \mathbf{7} \cdot x \cdot x \cdot \mathbf{x \cdot x} \cdot z$
The highest power of each factor (noted in blue) multiplied together gives us $2 \cdot 2 \cdot 7 \cdot x \cdot x \cdot x \cdot x \cdot z \cdot z \cdot z \cdot z = 28x^4z^4$.

3. $\dfrac{5}{x^2 + 6x + 9}$, $\dfrac{2 - x}{5x + 15}$

Factor each denominator.

First term denominator: $x^2 + 6x + 9 = (x + 3)(x + 3) = \mathbf{(x + 3)^2}$
Second term denominator: $5x + 15 = \mathbf{5}(x + 3)$

The highest power of each factor (noted in bold) multiplied together gives us a LCD of $5(x + 3)^2$.

4. $\dfrac{3}{12xy}$, $\dfrac{5}{36x^3y^4}$, $\dfrac{7}{42xy^5}$

Factor each denominator.

First term denominator: $12xy = \mathbf{2 \cdot 2} \cdot 3 \cdot x \cdot y$
Second term denominator: $36x^3y^4 = 2 \cdot 2 \cdot \mathbf{3 \cdot 3} \cdot \mathbf{x \cdot x \cdot x} \cdot y \cdot y \cdot y \cdot y$
Third term denominator: $42xy^5 = 2 \cdot 3 \cdot \mathbf{7} \cdot x \cdot \mathbf{y \cdot y \cdot y \cdot y \cdot y}$

The highest power of each factor (noted in bold) multiplied together gives us a LCD of $2 \cdot 2 \cdot 3 \cdot 3 \cdot 7 \cdot x \cdot x \cdot x \cdot y \cdot y \cdot y \cdot y \cdot y = 252x^3y^5$.

Example: Add $\dfrac{8}{5xy^2}$ + $\dfrac{9}{14x^3}$.

Find the LCD

$5xy^2 = 5 \cdot x \cdot y \cdot y$
$14x^3 = 2 \cdot 7 \cdot x \cdot x \cdot x$

The LCD is $2 \cdot 5 \cdot 7 \cdot x \cdot x \cdot x \cdot y \cdot y = 70x^3y^2$.

Multiply each numerator and denominator by whatever it takes to get $70x^3y^2$. An easy way to do that is to compare the factorization of each term with the factorization of the LCD.

First term denominator: $5 \cdot x \cdot y \cdot y$
LCD: $2 \cdot 5 \cdot 7 \cdot x \cdot x \cdot x \cdot y \cdot y$
Match the term factorization to the LCD factorization. Notice the first term needs $2 \cdot 7 \cdot x \cdot x$ to match the LCD.

Therefore, multiply the numerator and denominator of the first term by $14x^2$.

Second term denominator: $2 \cdot 7 \cdot x \cdot x \cdot x$
LCD: $2 \cdot 5 \cdot 7 \cdot x \cdot x \cdot x \cdot y \cdot y$

    The second term needs $5 \cdot y \cdot y$ to match the LCD. Therefore multiply the numerator and denominator of the second term by $5y^2$.

Putting it all together gives us

$$\frac{8}{5xy^2} \cdot \frac{(14x^2)}{(14x^2)} + \frac{9}{14x^3} \cdot \frac{(5y^2)}{(5y^2)} = \frac{112x^2 + 45y^2}{70x^3y^2}$$

Example: Subtract $\dfrac{y}{y^2 - 7y + 6} - \dfrac{4}{y + 5}$

The denominator of the second expression is in simplest form, so the only factor is $(y + 5)$.
Factor the denominator of the first expression: $y^2 - 7y + 6 = (y - 1)(y - 6)$

$$\frac{y}{(y - 1)(y - 6)} - \frac{4}{y + 5}.$$

The LCD is the product of the 3 factors: $(y - 1)(y - 6)(y + 5)$

    We must multiply the numerator and denominator of the first expression by $(y + 5)$. Next multiply the numerator and denominator of the second expression by $(y - 1)(y - 6)$. Remember we must do this to get the common denominator of $(y - 1)(y - 6)(y + 5)$.

$$\frac{y(y + 5)}{(y - 1)(y - 6)(y + 5)} - \frac{4(y - 1)(y - 6)}{(y - 1)(y - 6)(y + 5)}$$

Simplify the numerators of each term: $\quad \dfrac{y^2 + 5y}{(y - 1)(y - 6)(y + 5)} - \dfrac{4y^2 - 28y + 24}{(y - 1)(y - 6)(y + 5)}$

Combine like terms in the numerator:

$$\frac{-3y^2 + 33y - 24}{(y - 1)(y - 6)(y + 5)}$$

    Notice there is a common factor of 3 in the numerator. Factor out -3 to remove the negative from the squared term. Generally, we want the squared term to be positive (example, x^2 as opposed to $-x^2$).

Therefore the answer is $\quad \dfrac{-3(y^2 - 11y + 8)}{(y - 1)(y - 6)(y + 5)}$.

Example: Combine $\quad \dfrac{6}{x^2 - 16} + \dfrac{11}{x + 4} - \dfrac{5}{x}.$

Factor the denominator of each rational expression.

Denominator of first expression: $x^2 - 16 = (x - 4)(x + 4)$
Second expression is in simplest form, so the only factor is $(x + 4)$.
Denominator of third expression is in simplest form, so the only factor is x.

The LCD is $x(x - 4)(x + 4)$.

The factored form of the expression is $\quad \dfrac{6}{(x - 4)(x + 4)} + \dfrac{11}{x + 4} - \dfrac{5}{x}.$

To get the LCD of $x(x - 4)(x + 4)$, we must multiply the numerator and denominator of the first expression by x, the second expression by $x(x - 4)$ and the third expression by $(x - 4)(x + 4)$.

The result is $\dfrac{6x}{x(x-4)(x+4)} + \dfrac{11x(x-4)}{x(x-4)(x+4)} - \dfrac{5(x+4)(x-4)}{x(x+4)(x-4)}$

Multiply and add like terms in the the numerators: $\dfrac{6x}{x(x-4)(x+4)} + \dfrac{11x^2 - 44x}{x(x-4)(x+4)} - \dfrac{5x^2 - 80}{x(x-4)(x+4)}$

Combine like terms: $\dfrac{6x^2 - 38x + 80}{x(x-4)(x+4)}$.

Factor a 2 out of the numerator: $\dfrac{2(3x^2 - 19x + 40)}{x(x-4)(x+4)}$

Multiplying and Dividing Rational Expressions

When multiplying rational expressions, we use the same procedure as multiplying fractions. Multiply the numerators and multiply the denominators and simplify. Sometimes simplification can be done before multiplying. Generally, if you can simply first, do so because the multiplication will be easier. Another advantage of simplifying first is that the simplification may become more difficult if waiting until after multiplying.

For example, suppose we want to multiply $\dfrac{x^2 + 10x + 25}{x} \cdot \dfrac{x^4}{x+5}$

If we multiply first, we get $\dfrac{x^6 + 10x^5 + 25x^4}{x^2 + 5x}$

Now divide out the common factor of x: $\dfrac{x^5 + 10x^4 + 25x^3}{x+5}$

But notice that the numerator is not completely simplified. There is a common factor of x^3 that can be factored out.

$\dfrac{x^3(x^2 + 10x + 25)}{x+5}$, Notice that $x^2 + 10x + 25$ can be factored.

$\dfrac{x^3(x+5)(x+5)}{x+5}$

Now the $(x+5)$ factors in bold can divide out to get $\dfrac{x^3}{(x+5)}$

Suppose we simplify first, then multiply.

$\dfrac{x^2 + 10x + 25}{x} \cdot \dfrac{x^4}{x+5} = \dfrac{(x+5)(x+5)}{x} \cdot \dfrac{x^4}{x+5}$

Now the simplification is easy. The $(x+5)$ terms in bold will divide out and $\dfrac{x^4}{x} = x^3$

Therefore the answer is $\dfrac{x^3}{x+5}$

Notice how the problem was easier by simplifying first and then multiplying.

In the following example, the variable part is easy to simplify whether multiplying first or simplifying first, but the numerical part is much more difficult to simplify if multiplying first.

$\dfrac{72xy}{13} \cdot \dfrac{52}{216x}$

If we multiply first we get $\dfrac{3744xy}{2808x}$, and simplifying this to lowest terms may be a bit difficult.

If we simplify first, the problem is quite easy because 72 divides evenly into 216 and 13 divides evenly into 52. The x's will also divide out.

Therefore, $\dfrac{72xy}{13} \cdot \dfrac{52}{216x} = \dfrac{y}{1} \cdot \dfrac{4}{3x} = \dfrac{4y}{3x}$

Example: Multiply $\dfrac{x^2 + 8x + 15}{x^2 - 9} \cdot \dfrac{x - 3}{x^2 - 3x - 40}$

Factor the numerator and denominator of each rational expression, if possible.

Numerator of first expression: $x^2 + 8x + 15 = (x + 3)(x + 5)$
Denominator of first expression: $x^2 - 9 = (x + 3)(x - 3)$
Numerator of second expression is already in simplest form: $x - 3$
Denominator of second expression: $x^2 - 3x - 40 = (x + 5)(x - 8)$

Rewrite the problem in factored form. $\dfrac{(x + 3)(x + 5)}{(x + 3)(x - 3)} \cdot \dfrac{x - 3}{(x + 5)(x - 8)}$

Notice $(x + 3)$, $(x - 3)$ and $(x + 5)$ will all divide out. Therefore the answer is $\dfrac{1}{x - 8}$.

Example: Multiply $\dfrac{6x^2 + x - 1}{3x^2 + 8x - 3} \cdot \dfrac{x^2 + x - 20}{2x^2 + 11x + 5}$

Factor the numerator and denominator of each expression, if possible.

Numerator of first expression: $6x^2 + x - 1 = (2x + 1)(3x - 1)$
Denominator of first expression: $3x^2 + 8x - 3 = (3x - 1)(x + 3)$
Numerator of first expression: $x^2 + x - 20 = (x - 4)(x + 5)$
Denominator of second expression: $2x^2 + 11x + 5 = (2x + 1)(x + 5)$

Rewrite the problem in factored form. $\dfrac{(2x + 1)(3x - 1)}{(3x - 1)(x + 3)} \cdot \dfrac{(x - 4)(x + 5)}{(2x + 1)(x + 5)}$

Notice $(3x - 1)$, $(2x + 1)$ and $(x + 5)$ will all divide out. Therefore the answer is $\dfrac{x - 4}{x + 3}$.

Example: Multiply $\dfrac{x^2 - 4}{x^2 + x - 2} \cdot \dfrac{x^2 + 3x - 4}{x^2 + 2x - 8}$

Factor the numerator and denominator of each expression, if possible.

Numerator of first expression: $x^2 - 4 = (x - 2)(x + 2)$
Denominator of first expression: $x^2 + x - 2 = (x + 2)(x - 1)$
Numerator of second expression: $x^2 + 3x - 4 = (x + 4)(x - 1)$
Denominator of second expression: $x^2 + 2x - 8 = (x - 2)(x + 4)$

Rewrite the problem in factored form. $\dfrac{(x - 2)(x + 2)}{(x + 2)(x - 1)} \cdot \dfrac{(x + 4)(x - 1)}{(x - 2)(x + 4)}$

Notice all the factors divide out. When all of the factors divide out, the answer is 1 and not 0.

Dividing Rational Expressions

Recall when dividing fractions, we multiply the first fraction by the reciprocal of the second fraction. The same is true when dividing rational expressions. Essentially there is nothing new to learn in this section. We just have to remember to take the reciprocal of the second expression before multiplying.

Example: Divide: $\dfrac{2}{x} \div \dfrac{xy}{5}$

Take the reciprocal of the second expression and multiply.

$$\dfrac{2}{x} \cdot \dfrac{5}{xy} = \dfrac{10}{x^2 y}$$

Example: Divide: $\dfrac{3x^2 y^3 z}{10} \div \dfrac{8xz^4}{25}$

Take the reciprocal of the second expression and multiply.

$$\dfrac{3x^2 y^3 z}{10} \cdot \dfrac{25}{8xz^4}$$

Simplify to get $\quad \dfrac{3xy^3}{2} \cdot \dfrac{5}{8z^3}$

Multiply to get $\quad \dfrac{15xy^3}{16z^3}$

Example: Divide: $\dfrac{x^3 - 4x^2}{x + 3} \div (x - 4)$

Take the reciprocal of the second expression and multiply.

•Note that $(x - 4)$ is the same as $\dfrac{x - 4}{1}$. So the reciprocal of $(x - 4)$ is $\dfrac{1}{x - 4}$.

$$\dfrac{x^3 - 4x^2}{x + 3} \cdot \dfrac{1}{x - 4} = \dfrac{x^2(x - 4)}{x + 3} \cdot \dfrac{1}{x - 4} = \dfrac{x^2}{x + 3}.$$

Notice the $(x - 4)$ in red divide out.

Some problems combine multiplication and division of rational expressions. In such problems, follow the order of operations that require multiplication and division to be performed in order from left to right.

Example: Simplify $\dfrac{6}{x^2 + 10x + 16} \cdot \dfrac{4x^2 - 16}{8} \div \dfrac{3x}{x^2 + 3x - 28}.$

Factor the numerator and denominator of each expression.

Numerator of first expression, denominator of second expression and numerator of third expression are in simplest form.

Numerator of second expression: $4x^2 - 16 = 4(x^2 - 4) = 4(x - 2)(x + 2)$
Denominator of third expression: $x^2 + 3x - 28 = (x + 7)(x - 4)$

Multiply the first two rational expressions in factored form.
$$\dfrac{6}{(x + 8)(x + 2)} \cdot \dfrac{4(x - 2)(x + 2)}{8} = \dfrac{24(x - 2)(x + 2)}{8(x + 8)(x + 2)} = \dfrac{3(x - 2)}{x + 8}$$

$$\dfrac{3(x - 2)}{x + 8} \div \dfrac{3x}{(x + 7)(x - 4)}$$

Take the reciprocal of the second expression and multiply it by the first.

$$\frac{3(x-2)}{x+8} \cdot \frac{(x+7)(x-4)}{3x} = \frac{(x-2)(x+7)(x-4)}{x(x+8)}$$

Review Problems: Set 2

Simplify the following.

1. $\frac{4}{2x} + \frac{7}{2x}$ **2.** $\frac{5}{3y} - \frac{8}{3y}$ **3.** $\frac{2x}{5y-1} -- \frac{6x}{5y-1}$

Find the lowest common denominator (LCD) of the denominators listed.

4. $6xy,\ 20x^2y^3$
5. $3xz^3,\ 10xy^2,\ 30x^2yz$
6. $x^4 + 4x,\ x^2 - 16$
7. $x^2 + 4x + 4,\ x^2 - 10x - 24,\ x^2 - 12x$

Simplify the following.

8. $\frac{2}{3x} + \frac{7}{2x}$ **9.** $\frac{5}{x+3} + \frac{6}{x+4}$ **10.** $\frac{7}{x-2} - \frac{4}{x-5}$ **11.** $\frac{x-14}{x-3} - \frac{x+3}{x+5}$

12. $\frac{4y}{y^2 - 5y + 4} + \frac{7}{y^2 - 2y - 8}$ **13.** $\frac{3x-1}{2x^2 - 5x + 2} -- \frac{2x}{6x^2 + x - 2}$

14. $\frac{2}{5xy} - \frac{7}{2x} + \frac{8}{14y^3}$

Multiply the following.

15. $\frac{a^2}{6b^3} \cdot \frac{4b^4}{5a}$ **16.** $\frac{x^2}{y^3} \cdot \frac{y^2}{x^3y^3}$ **17.** $\frac{x^2 - 5x + 6}{x^3} \cdot \frac{x^2}{x^2 + 3x - 10}$

18. $\frac{5y - 30}{7y + 28} \cdot \frac{y^2 - 16}{y^2 - 12y + 36}$

Divide the following.

19. $\frac{3}{2x} \div \frac{9}{4x}$ **20.** $\frac{8x^2y^3}{5} \div \frac{32xy}{15}$ **21.** $\frac{y^2 - 9}{y^2 - 16} \div \frac{y - 3}{y + 4}$

Simplify the following.

22. $\frac{A^2 - 36}{3} \div (A^2 + 4A - 12) \cdot \frac{A + 2}{4A + 28}$

Complex Fractions

     A **complex fraction** or **complex rational expression** is a rational expression which contains a rational expression in the numerator, the denominator or both. It can also be thought of as a fraction divided by a fraction. For example,

$\dfrac{\frac{3}{x}}{\frac{14}{y}}$, is a complex fraction. The numerator is the rational expression $\dfrac{3}{x}$ and the denominator is the rational expression $\dfrac{14}{y}$.

To simplify a complex fraction means to write the complex fraction as a single fraction. To do this think of a complex fraction in terms of a division problem.

Just as $\dfrac{\frac{1}{3}}{14}$ is the same as 1 divided 3, the rational expression above can be thought of as $\dfrac{3}{x}$ divided by $\dfrac{14}{y}$.

We can solve this division problem by the same method as we did in the previous section.

$$\dfrac{3}{x} \div \dfrac{14}{y} = \dfrac{3}{x} \cdot \dfrac{y}{14} = \dfrac{3y}{14x}.$$

An alternate method to simplify a complex fraction is to multiply the fraction by one in the form of LCD divided by LCD. For example, the LCD in the problem above is xy, so we could multiply both the numerator and the denominator by xy.

$$\dfrac{\frac{3}{x} \cdot (xy)}{\frac{14}{y} \cdot (xy)} = \dfrac{3y}{14x}$$

•**Note that when it's difficult to determine the LCD, it's easier to use the first method to simplify complex fractions.**

Example: Simplify $\dfrac{\frac{3}{x} + 2}{5 + x}$

Rewrite the numerator with the LCD of x, $\dfrac{3 + 2x}{x}$

Rewrite the complex fraction as $\dfrac{3 + 2x}{x} \div 5 + x$

Multiply the first complex fraction by the reciprocal of the second. $\dfrac{3 + 2x}{x} \cdot \dfrac{1}{5 + x} = \dfrac{3 + 2x}{x(5 + x)}.$

Example: Simplify $\dfrac{\frac{2}{x} - \frac{3}{y}}{\frac{2}{x} + \frac{3}{y}}$

In this example, we'll use the second method to simplify. Notice the LCD is xy, so multiply the numerator and denominator of the complex fraction by xy.

Multiply the numerator by xy to get

$$\dfrac{2}{x}(xy) - \dfrac{3}{y}(xy) = 2y - 3x$$

Multiply the denominator by xy to get
$$\dfrac{2}{x}(xy) + \dfrac{3}{y}(xy) = 2y + 3x$$

Therefore the complex fraction is now simplified to $\dfrac{2y - 3x}{2y + 3x}$.

Example: Simplify $\dfrac{\dfrac{3}{x^2 - 7x + 12}}{\dfrac{5}{(x - 4)} + \dfrac{4}{(x - 3)}}$

Start by factoring the rational expression in the numerator.

$$\frac{3}{x^2 - 7x + 12} = \frac{3}{(x - 4)(x - 3)}$$

Get the LCD of the rational expression in the denominator and rewrite the complex fraction.

$$\frac{5}{(x - 4)} + \frac{4}{(x - 3)} = \frac{5(x - 3) + 4(x - 4)}{(x - 4)(x - 3)} = \frac{5x - 15 + 4x - 16}{(x - 4)(x - 3)} = \frac{9x - 31}{(x - 4)(x - 3)}$$

Rewrite the complex fraction as a division problem.

$$\frac{3}{(x - 4)(x - 3)} \div \frac{9x - 31}{(x - 4)(x - 3)}$$

When multiplying by the reciprocal, $(x - 4)(x - 3)$ divides out.

$$\frac{3}{\boldsymbol{(x - 4)(x - 3)}} \cdot \frac{\boldsymbol{(x - 4)(x - 3)}}{9x - 31} = \frac{3}{9x - 31}.$$

Example: Simplify $\dfrac{\dfrac{1}{y^2} + \dfrac{1}{x^2}}{\dfrac{1}{x} - \dfrac{1}{y}}$

Get the LCD of the rational expression in the numerator of the complex fraction and rewrite.

$$\frac{1(x^2) + 1(y^2)}{x^2 y^2} = \frac{x^2 + y^2}{x^2 y^2}$$

Get the LCD of the rational expression in the denominator of the complex fraction and rewrite.

$$\frac{1(y) - 1(x)}{xy} = \frac{y - x}{xy}$$

Rewrite the complex fraction as a division problem.

$$\frac{x^2 + y^2}{x^2 y^2} \div \frac{y - x}{xy}$$

When multiplying by the reciprocal an xy term will divide into $x^2 y^2$.

$$\frac{x^2 + y^2}{\boldsymbol{x^2 y^2}} \cdot \frac{\boldsymbol{xy}}{y - x} = \frac{x^2 + y^2}{xy(y - x)}$$

Solving Rational Equations

Equations involving rational expressions are called **rational equations.** To solve rational equations, we want to multiply both sides of the equation by the LCD. This process will eliminate the denominators in all the expressions and make solving for the variable easier.

Example: Solve $\dfrac{1}{4} + \dfrac{8}{x + 5} = \dfrac{3}{2}$.

•Note that $x \neq -5$ because that would result in a 0 in the denominator.

The LCD is $4(2)(x + 5)$. Multiply both sides of the equation by $8(x + 5)$.

$\dfrac{1}{4} \cdot 8(x + 5) + \dfrac{8}{x + 5} \cdot 8(x +5) = \dfrac{3}{2} \cdot 8(x + 5) = 2(x + 5) + 8(8) = 3(4)(x + 5)$

Multiply and then combine like terms on each side of the equation.

$$2(x + 5) + 8(8) = 3(4)(x + 5)$$
$$2x + 10 + 64 = 12(x + 5)$$
$$2x + 74 = 12x + 60$$

Solve for x.

$$2x + 74 = 12x + 60$$
$$74 = 12x - 2x + 60$$
$$74 = 10x + 60$$
$$74 - 60 = 10x$$
$$14 = 10x$$
$$\dfrac{14}{10} = x$$

$$\dfrac{7}{5} = x$$

•Note that you can check the answer by substituting back into the equation.

Example: Solve $\dfrac{3A}{A^2 - 4} + \dfrac{A}{A - 2} = \dfrac{4A + 2}{A + 2}$.

•Note that $A \neq 2$ or -2 because it will make the denominator 0.

Factor the denominator of the first expression to get $(A - 2)(A + 2)$ and then get the LCD of the rational expressions, which is $(A - 2)(A + 2)$. Multiply both sides of the equation by the LCD.

$\dfrac{3A}{(A - 2)(A + 2)} \cdot (A - 2)(A + 2) + \dfrac{A}{A - 2} \cdot (A - 2)(A + 2) = \dfrac{4A +2}{A + 2} \cdot (A - 2)(A + 2)$

Multiply and then combine like terms on each side of the equation.

$3A + A(A + 2) = (4A + 2)(A - 2)$

$3A + A^2 + 2A = 4A^2 - 8A + 2A - 4$

$A^2 + 5A = 4A^2 - 6A - 4$

Solve for A.

$5A = 4A^2 - A^2 - 6A - 4$
$0 = 4A^2 - A^2 - 6A - 5A - 4$

$0 = 3A^2 - 11A - 4$

$0 = (3A + 1)(A - 4)$

$3A + 1 = 0$ or $A - 4 = 0$

$A = -1/3$ or $A = 4$

Example: Solve $5 - \dfrac{C + 4}{3} = \dfrac{6}{C}$

•Note that $C \neq 0$ since it will give a 0 in the denominator.

The LCD is $3C$, so multiply each side of the equation by $3C$ to clear the denominators.

$5\,(3C) - \dfrac{(C + 4)}{3} \cdot (3C) = \dfrac{6}{C} \cdot (3C)$

Solve for C.

$15C - (C + 4)C = 6(3)$
$15C - C^2 - 4C = 18$
$0 = 18 - 15C + C^2 + 4C$
$0 = C^2 - 11C + 18$
$0 = (C - 2)(C - 9)$

$C - 2 = 0$ or $C - 9 = 0$

$C = 2$ or $C = 9$

Check the answers to make sure they satisfy the equation because sometimes solving the equations yields false solutions.

Example: Solve $\dfrac{2B + 3}{B - 5} = \dfrac{B + 8}{B - 5}$.

•Note that $B \neq 5$ since it will give a 0 in the denominator.

Multiply both sides of the equation by $(B - 5)$ to clear the denominator.

$\dfrac{2B + 3}{B - 5} \cdot (B - 5) = \dfrac{B + 8}{B - 5} \cdot (B - 5)$

Solve for B.

$2B + 3 = B + 8$
$2B = B + 5$
$B = 5$

Notice the restriction that $B \neq 5$, therefore 5 is an extraneous solution and there is no solution to this problem. Sometimes we use formulas in math that involve rational expressions. We can solve these formulas for specified variables.

Example: The area of a trapezoid is given by the formula $A = \dfrac{(b_1 + b_2)h}{2}$

Solve for h.

Multiply both sides of the equation by 2 to clear the denominator.

$2A = (b_1 + b_2)h$

Divide both sides by ($b_1 + b_2$).

$$\frac{2A}{b_1 + b_2} = h$$

Example: In physics, the Doppler effect is the relationship between the observed frequency of a wave f and the emitted frequency f_o. The observed frequency is given by the formula

$$f = \frac{v}{v + v_s} \cdot f_o$$, where v is the velocity of the wave and v_s is the velocity of the source.

Solve the formula for the emitted frequency f_o.

Multiply both sides by $(v + v_s)$ to clear the denominator.

$$f(v + v_s) = v(f_o)$$

Divide both sides by v.

$$\frac{f(v + v_s)}{v} = f_o$$

Example: In chemistry, Boyle's Law states that the volume of gas is inversely proportional to pressure at a constant temperature. Charle's Law states that the volume of gas is directly proportional to Kelvin temperature at a constant pressure. The law that combines the two which relates initial and final pressure, temperature and volume is given by the formula

$$\frac{P_i V_i}{T_i} = \frac{P_f V_f}{T_f}$$

Suppose we want to solve for the final pressure, P_f. We can start by multiplying both sides of the equation by the LCD, $T_i T_f$.

$$\frac{P_i V_i}{T_i} \cdot (T_i T_f) = \frac{P_f V_f}{T_f} \cdot (T_i T_f)$$

$$P_i V_i T_f = P_f V_f T_i$$

Divide both sides by $V_f T_i$ to solve for P_f.

$$\frac{P_i V_i T_f}{V_f T_i} = P_f$$

Review Problems: Set 3

Simplify the following.

1. $\dfrac{\dfrac{3y}{x}}{\dfrac{12x^2 z}{y}}$

2. $\dfrac{\dfrac{10xz^3}{y}}{\dfrac{5z^2}{4y}}$

3. $\dfrac{\dfrac{x^2 + 2x - 8}{6y}}{\dfrac{x^2 + 4x - 12}{9y}}$

4. $\dfrac{3}{y} - \dfrac{3}{x}$ over xy

5. $\dfrac{\dfrac{x}{y} - \dfrac{y}{x}}{\dfrac{1}{x} + \dfrac{1}{y}}$

6. $\dfrac{x}{x^2 + 10x + 16} + \dfrac{2}{x + 8} + \dfrac{x}{x + 2}$

7. $\dfrac{x^2 - 16}{x^2 + 5x + 4} \cdot \dfrac{x - 4}{x + 1}$

Solve the following.

8. $\dfrac{3}{4} + \dfrac{8}{x} = 1$ **9.** $\dfrac{6}{5y} + \dfrac{4}{y} = 12$ **10.** $\dfrac{5x + 3}{x - 1} = \dfrac{x + 2}{x - 4}$ **11.** $\dfrac{4x - 7}{x - 2} = \dfrac{3x - 5}{x - 2}$

12. $\dfrac{2 - 5x}{x^2 - 4} + \dfrac{3 + 2x}{x^2 + 5x + 6} = \dfrac{2 - 3x}{x^2 + x - 6}$

Solve for the indicated variable.

13. $\dfrac{1}{R} = \dfrac{1}{R_1} + \dfrac{1}{R_2}$, for R_1

Rational Functions

When a function is defined in terms of a rational expression in one variable, it is known as a **rational function**. The value of the denominator in the expression cannot be zero. Some examples of rational functions are as follows:

$$f(x) = \dfrac{5x + 6}{2x} \ , \quad g(x) = \dfrac{0.45x - 7}{x} \ , \quad h(x) = \dfrac{9 - 13x}{3x + 5}$$

Suppose the cost of renting a car is $50 for the first day and $25 for each additional day. The average cost per day for renting the car is given by the equation

$$C = \dfrac{50 + 25d}{d + 1}$$, where d is the number of days after the first day.

The function that gives the average daily cost can be written as

$$C(d) = \dfrac{50 + 25d}{d + 1}$$

Example: Using the function $C(d)$ above, find the average cost when renting a car for 4 days and for renting a car for 7 days.

To find the average cost of the rental per day for 4 days, substitute 3 for d and solve.

$$C(3) = \dfrac{50 + 25(3)}{4} = \dfrac{50 + 75}{4} = \dfrac{125}{4} = \$31.25$$

The average cost per day for a 7 day rental is

$$C(6) = \dfrac{50 + 25(6)}{7} = \dfrac{50 + 150}{7} = \dfrac{200}{7} = \$28.57$$

To graph the function, set up a table and choose values for d and solve for C(d) and plot the points on the graph.

d	C(d)	(d, C(d))
2	33.33	(2, 33.33)
4	30	(4, 30.00)
6	28.57	(6, 28.57)
8	28.13	(8, 28.13)
10	27.5	(10, 27.50)

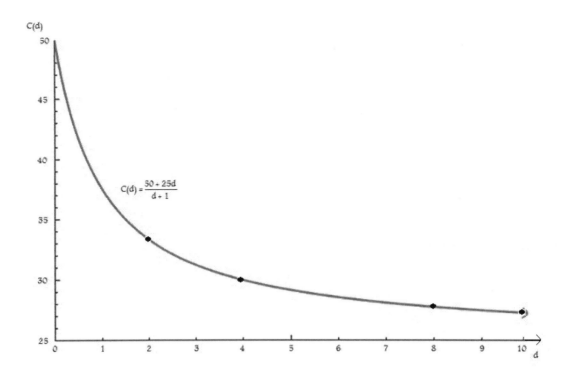

Notice on the graph how C(d) approaches 25 as d gets larger. Also notice how C(d) approaches 50 as d gets smaller. When a graph approaches a line, the line it approaches is called an **asymptote**. The line d = 25 is called the **horizontal asymptote**. If C(d) = y, then the line y = 50 is called the **vertical asymptote**.

Example: The time (in hours) it takes for an airplane to travel 3,000 miles is given by the function $r(t) = \dfrac{3,000}{t}$
Solve for time t given the following values for rate r.

r = 550 mph

$550 = \dfrac{3,000}{t}$, 550t = 3,000, t = 5.45 hours

r = 475 mph

$475 = \dfrac{3,000}{t}$, 475t = 3,000, t = 6.32 hours

r = 625 mph

$625 = \dfrac{3,000}{t}$, 625t = 3,000, t = 4.8 hours

Example: Given the graph of the function below, find the following values

f(1), f(2) and f(4)

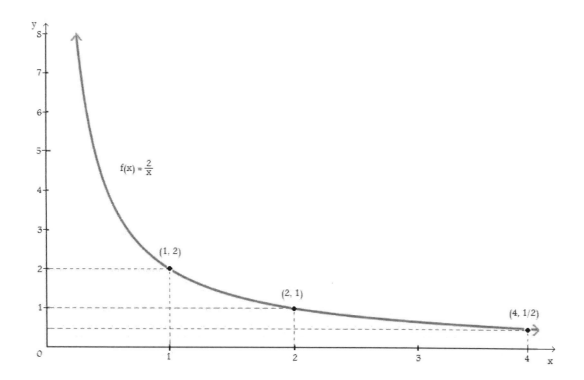

To find *f(1)* move over 1 on the x axis and up on the *f(x)* axis until you hit the graph. Notice the value of *f*(1) = 2. Likewise, for *f*(2), move over 2 on the x axis from the origin and move up until you hit the graph. The value of *f*(2) = 1 and similarly the value of *f*(4) = ½. You could also substitute the values for x into the function to get *f*(1) = 2/1 = 2, *f*(2) = 2/2 = 1 and *f*(4) = 2/4 = ½. The horizontal asymptote is the line x = 0 and the vertical asymptote is the line y = 0.

Domain of Rational Functions

Recall that the denominator of a fraction or rational expression is undefined when it equals zero. To find the domain of a rational function, set the denominator equal to zero and solve for the variable. The value or values you obtain are excluded from the domain and all other values are included in the domain.

Example: Find the domain of $f(x) = \dfrac{10}{2x + 6}$.

Set the denominator equal to 0 and solve for x.

$2x + 6 = 0$

$\quad 2x = -6$

$\quad x = -3$

Therefore the domain is all real numbers except for -3. In interval notation, the domain is (-∞, -3) U (-3, ∞).

Example: Find the domain of $f(x) = \dfrac{3x - 7}{x^2 - 11x + 18}$.

Set the denominator equal to 0 and solve for x.

$x^2 - 11x + 18 = 0$

$(x - 2)(x - 9) = 0$

$x - 2 = 0$ or $x - 9 = 0$

$x = 2$ or $x = 9$

Therefore 2 and 9 are not part of the domain and the domain is all real numbers except for 2 and 9. In interval notation, the domain is $(-\infty, 2) \cup (2, 9) \cup (9, \infty)$.

Review Problems: Set 4

Given the following rational functions, find the value of f(1), f(-1) and f(2) .

1. $f(x) = \dfrac{2x - 3}{4x}$ **2.** $f(x) = \dfrac{x + 6}{x^2 - 3x + 2}$ **3.** $f(x) = \dfrac{7x}{x^2 - 4}$ **4.** $f(x) = \dfrac{9 - x}{5x - 3}$

Complete the following tables for the rational function given.

5. $f(x) = \dfrac{12}{x + 3}$

x	f(x)
1	
2	
3	
4	
5	

6. $f(x) = \dfrac{x + 12}{x}$

x	f(x)
1	
2	
5	
8	
12	

7.   Suppose a long distance phone plan costs 15 cents for the first minute and 7 cents for each additional minute. The function for the average cost per minute for a phone call is given by the following

$C(n) = \dfrac{.15 + .07n}{n}$, where n is the number of minutes after the first minute.

What is the average cost per minute of a phone call that is 45 minutes long? What is the average cost per minute of a phone call that is 200 minutes long?

Find the domain of each of the following rational functions

8. $f(x) = \dfrac{3x^2 - 5x + 5}{x - 9}$,   **9.** $f(x) = \dfrac{6x + 11}{4x^2 - 100}$,   **10.** $f(x) = \dfrac{2}{3x^2 - 11x + 4}$

Key Terms and Concepts to Review

- Rational expression
- Fundamental property of fractions
- Adding, subtracting and multiplying rational expressions
- Lowest common denominator (LCD)
- Complex fraction (complex rational expression)
- Rational equation
- Rational function
- Graphing rational functions
- Domain and range of rational functions

Answers to Problem Sets

Problem Set 1
Answers and key steps in solution

1. $3x$,　　　　$\dfrac{15x^2}{5x}$, $\dfrac{15}{5} = \mathbf{3}$, $\dfrac{x^2}{x} = \boldsymbol{x}$ (simplified and multiplied terms in bold to get $3x$)

2. $\dfrac{2y^4}{9x^2}$,　　　$\dfrac{4x^2y^6}{18x^4y^2} = \dfrac{4}{18} = \dfrac{\mathbf{2}}{\mathbf{9}}$, $\dfrac{x^2}{x^4} = x^{-2} = \dfrac{\mathbf{1}}{\boldsymbol{x^2}}$, $\dfrac{y^6}{y^2} = \boldsymbol{y^4}$ (simplify and multiply)

3. $\dfrac{y^2}{2z^2}$,　　　$\dfrac{25xy^3z^5}{50xyz^7} = \dfrac{25}{50} = \dfrac{\mathbf{1}}{\mathbf{2}}$, (the x terms divide out), $\dfrac{y^3}{y} = \boldsymbol{y^2}$, $\dfrac{z^5}{z^7} = \dfrac{\mathbf{1}}{\boldsymbol{z^2}}$

4. 6,　　　　$\dfrac{6x + 18}{x + 3} = \dfrac{6\boldsymbol{(x + 3)}}{\boldsymbol{x + 3}}$, common factor of $(x + 3)$ divides out.

5. $x - y$,　　　$\dfrac{x^2 - y^2}{x + y} = \dfrac{(x - y)\boldsymbol{(x + y)}}{\boldsymbol{x + y}}$, common factor of $(x + y)$ divides out.

6. $\dfrac{7}{x + 6}$,　　$\dfrac{7x - 14}{x^2 + 4x - 12} = \dfrac{7\boldsymbol{(x - 2)}}{(x + 6)\boldsymbol{(x - 2)}}$, common factor of $(x - 2)$ divides out.

7. $\dfrac{2x + 1}{3x + 2}$,　　$\dfrac{2x^2 - 9x - 5}{3x^2 - 13x - 10} = \dfrac{(2x + 1)\boldsymbol{(x - 5)}}{(3x + 2)\boldsymbol{(x - 5)}}$, common factor of $(x - 5)$ divides out.

8. $\dfrac{x(1 - y)}{y(x - 1)}$　　$\dfrac{x - xy}{xy - y} = \dfrac{x(1 - y)}{y(x - 1)}$, notice there are no common factors, cannot be simplified further.

9. $\dfrac{-(2y + 1)}{y - 2}$,　$\dfrac{4y^2 + 8y + 3}{-2y^2 + y + 6} = \dfrac{(2y + 1)\boldsymbol{(2y + 3)}}{-1\boldsymbol{(2y + 3)}(y - 2)}$, common factor of $(2y + 3)$ divides out.

10. $\dfrac{2x - 3}{2x + 3}$,　$\dfrac{2x^2 + 7x - 15}{2x^2 + 13x + 15} = \dfrac{(2x - 3)\boldsymbol{(x + 5)}}{(2x + 3)\boldsymbol{(x + 5)}}$, common factor of $(x + 5)$ divides out.

11. $\dfrac{(y - 1)(x + 1)}{x - y}$　　$\dfrac{xy - x + y - 1}{x - y} = \dfrac{(xy + y) + (-x - 1)}{x - y} = \dfrac{y(x + 1) - 1(x + 1)}{x - y} = \dfrac{(y - 1)(x + 1)}{x - y}$

12. $\dfrac{5x(x - 5)}{6}$,　$\dfrac{5x^3 - 125x}{6x + 30} = \dfrac{5x(x^2 - 25)}{6(x + 5)} = \dfrac{5x(x - 5)\boldsymbol{(x + 5)}}{6\boldsymbol{(x + 5)}}$, common factor of $(x + 5)$ divides out.

Problem Set 2
Answers and key steps in solution

1. $\dfrac{11}{2x}$, add numerators (4 + 7 = 11)

2. $\dfrac{-1}{y}$, subtract numerators (5 - 8 = -3), then simplify (3's divide out)

3. $\dfrac{3x}{5y - 1}$, $2x - 6x + 7x = 3x$

4. $60x^2y^3$, $6xy = 2 \cdot \mathbf{3} \cdot x \cdot x$, $20x^2y^3 = \mathbf{2 \cdot 2 \cdot 5} \cdot x \cdot x \cdot \mathbf{y \cdot y \cdot y}$, multiply highest power of factors

5. $30x^2y^2z^3$, $3xz^3 = 3 \cdot x \cdot \mathbf{z \cdot z \cdot z}$, $10xy^2 = 2 \cdot 5 \cdot x \cdot \mathbf{y \cdot y}$, $30x^2yz = \mathbf{2 \cdot 5 \cdot 3} \cdot \mathbf{x \cdot x} \cdot y \cdot z$, multiply highest power of factors.

6. $x(x - 4)(x + 4)$, $x^2 + 4x = \mathbf{x(x + 4)}$, $x^2 - 16 = \mathbf{(x - 4)}(x + 4)$, multiply highest power of factors.

7. $x(x + 2)^2(x - 12)$, $x^2 + 4x + 4 = \mathbf{(x + 2)^2}$, $x^2 - 10x - 24 = (x + 2)\mathbf{(x - 12)}$, $x^2 - 12x = \mathbf{x}(x - 12)$, multiply the highest power of factors.

8. $\dfrac{25}{6x}$, $\dfrac{2}{3x} + \dfrac{7}{2x}$ Multiply numerator and denominator of first expression by 2 and second expression by 3 to get LCD of 6x, then add numerators.

9. $\dfrac{11x + 38}{(x + 4)(x + 3)}$, $\dfrac{5}{x + 3} + \dfrac{6}{x + 4}$, Multiply numerator and denominator of first expression by (x + 4) and second expression by (x + 3) to get LCD of (x + 4)(x + 3). The terms in the numerator are 5(x + 4) and 6(x + 3). Expand these to get 5x + 20 and 6x + 18 and combine like terms.

10. $\dfrac{3(x - 9)}{(x - 2)(x - 5)}$, $\dfrac{7}{x - 2} - \dfrac{4}{x - 5}$, Multiply numerator and denominator of first expression by (x - 5) and second expression by (x - 2) to get LCD of (x - 2)(x - 5). The terms in the numerator are 7(x - 5) and 4(x - 2). Expand these to get 7x - 35 and 4x - 8. Apply the negative to 4x - 8 to get -4x + 8 and combine like terms.

11. $\dfrac{-9x - 61}{(x - 3)(x + 5)}$, $\dfrac{x - 14}{x - 3} - \dfrac{x + 3}{x + 5}$, Multiply numerator and denominator of first expression by (x + 5) and second expression by (x - 3) to get LCD of (x - 3)(x + 5). The terms in the numerator are (x - 14)(x + 5) and (x + 3)(x - 3). Expand these to get x^2 - 9x - 70 and x^2 - 9. Apply the negative to x^2 - 9 to get -x^2 + 9 and combine like terms.

12. $\dfrac{4y^2 + 15y - 7}{(y - 4)(y - 1)(y + 2)}$, $\dfrac{4y}{y^2 - 5y + 4} + \dfrac{7}{y^2 - 2y - 8}$ Factor denominator of first expression to get (y - 4)(y - 1) and denominator of second expression to get (y - 4)(y + 2). Next multiply numerator and denominator of first expression by (y + 2) and second expression by (y - 1) to get the LCD of (y - 4)(y - 1)(y + 2). The terms in the numerator are 4y(y + 2) and 7(y - 1). Expand these and combine like terms.

13. $\dfrac{7x^2 + 7x - 2}{(x - 2)(2x - 1)(3x + 2)}$, $\dfrac{3x - 1}{2x^2 - 5x + 2} - \dfrac{2x}{6x^2 + x - 2}$, Factor denominator of first expression to get (x - 2)(2x - 1) and denominator of second

expression to get $(3x + 2)(2x - 1)$. Next multiply numerator and denominator of first expression by $(3x + 2)$ and second expression by $(x - 2)$ to get LCD of $(3x + 2)(2x - 1)(x - 2)$. The terms in the numerator are $(3x - 1)(3x + 2)$ and $2x(x - 2)$. Expand these and combine like terms.

14. $\dfrac{-245y^3 + 28y^2 + 40x}{70xy^3}$, $\quad \dfrac{2}{5xy} - \dfrac{7}{2x} + \dfrac{8}{14y^3}$, $\quad$ Multiply numerator and denominator of first expression by $14y^2$, the second expression by $35y^3$ and third expression by $5x$. The numerator becomes $2(14y^2) - 7(35y^3) + 8(5x)$. Simplify the numerator.

15. $\dfrac{2ab}{15}$, $\quad \dfrac{a^2}{6b^3} \cdot \dfrac{4b^4}{5a}$ $\quad$ Simplify the a's and simplify the b's, using rules for exponents, then multiply.

16. $\dfrac{x}{y^4}$, $\quad \dfrac{x^2}{y^3} \cdot \dfrac{y^2}{x^3y^3}$ $\quad$ Simplify the x's and the y's using rule for exponents, then multiply.

17. $\dfrac{x - 3}{x(x + 5)}$, $\quad \dfrac{x^2 - 5x + 6}{x^3} \cdot \dfrac{x^2}{x^2 + 3x - 10}$, $\quad$ Factor numerator of first expression to get $(x - 3)(x - 2)$ and denominator of second expression to get $(x - 2)(x + 5)$. Simplify the x's using rule for exponents and $(x - 2)$ in numerator and denominator divide out.

18. $\dfrac{5(y - 4)}{7(y - 6)}$, $\quad \dfrac{5y - 30}{7y + 28} \cdot \dfrac{y^2 - 16}{y^2 - 12y + 36}$ $\quad$ Factor numerators to get $5(y - 6)$ and $(y - 4)(y +4)$ and each denominator to get $7(y + 4)$ and $(y - 6)(y - 6)$ then divide out common factors.

19. $\dfrac{2}{3}$, $\quad \dfrac{3}{2x} \div \dfrac{9}{4x}$ $\quad$ Multiply first expression by reciprocal of second expression and divide out common factors.

20. $\dfrac{3xy^2}{4}$, $\quad \dfrac{8x^2y^3}{5} \div \dfrac{32xy}{15}$ $\quad$ Multiply first expression by reciprocal of second expression and divide out common factors.

21. $\dfrac{y + 3}{y - 4}$, $\quad \dfrac{y^2 - 9}{y^2 - 16} \div \dfrac{y - 3}{y + 4}$ $\quad$ Factor numerator of first expression to get $(y - 3)(y +3)$ and denominator to get $(y - 4)(y + 4)$, then multiply by reciprocal of second expression and divide out common factors.

22. $\dfrac{A + 3}{12(A + 7)}$, $\quad \dfrac{A^2 - 36}{3} \div (A^2 + 4A - 12) \cdot \dfrac{A + 2}{4A + 28}$ $\quad$ Factor numerator of first term to get $(A - 6)(A + 6)$ and the second to get $(A - 6)(A + 2)$ and denominator of the third to get $4(A + 7)$. Take the reciprocal of the second and then multiply and divide out common factors.

Problem Set 3
Answers and key steps in solution

1. $\dfrac{y^2}{4x^3z}$, $\quad$ Multiply $\dfrac{3y}{x}$ by the reciprocal of $\dfrac{12x^2z}{y}$ and then simplify.

2. $8xz$, $\quad$ Multiply $\dfrac{10xz^3}{y}$ by the reciprocal of $\dfrac{5z^2}{4y}$ and then simplify.

3. $\dfrac{3(x + 4)}{2(x + 6)}$, Factor the numerator of the rational expression in the numerator to $(x + 4)(x - 2)$ and in the rational expression in the denominator to $(x - 2)(x + 6)$. Then multiply rational expression in the numerator by the reciprocal of the rational expression in the denominator and simplify. The $(x - 2)$ and the y divide out and the 6 can simplify with the 9.

4. $\dfrac{3(x - y)}{x^2 y^2}$, Multiply the rational expression in the numerator and denominator by xy to get $\dfrac{\dfrac{3x - 3y}{xy}}{\dfrac{xy}{xy}}$.

Then factor $3x - 3y$ to $3(x - y)$ and multiply $\dfrac{3(x - y)}{xy}$ by the reciprocal of xy and simplify.

5. $x - y$, Multiply the rational expression in the numerator and denominator by xy.

This gives you $\dfrac{x^2 - y^2}{x + y}$. Factor the numerator to $(x - y)(x + y)$ and notice the $(x + y)$ divides out.

6. $\dfrac{x}{x^2 + 10x + 4}$, Factor the denominator of the rational expression in the numerator to $(x + 8)(x + 2)$. Get the LCD of $(x + 8)(x + 2)$ for the rational expression in the denominator. Then multiply both rational expressions by $(x + 8)(x + 2)$. That removes the denominators. Then simplify.

7. 1, Factor the rational expression in the numerator to get $\dfrac{(x - 4)(x + 4)}{(x + 1)(x + 4)}$. The $(x + 4)$ terms divide out. Notice that both rational expressions remaining are the same, so they divide out to get an answer of 1.

8. 32, Multiply both sides of the equation by $4x$ to get $3x + 32 = 4x$, solve for x to get $x = 32$.

9. 13/30, Multiply both sides of the equation by $5y$ to get $6 + 20 = 60y$, $26 = 60y$, solve for y to get $y = 26/60$, which simplifies to 13/30.

10. -1/2, 5, Multiply both sides of the equation by the LCD of $(x - 1)(x - 4)$. That leaves you with $(5x + 3)(x - 4) = (x - 1)(x + 2)$. Multiply out to get $5x^2 - 17x - 12 = x^2 + x - 2$. Therefore $4x^2 - 18x - 10 = 0$, $2(2x^2 - 9x - 5) = 0$. Factor to get $(2x + 1)(x - 5) = 0$. Set each factor equal to 0 and solve for x.

11. No solution, Note the restriction that $x \neq 2$ because it will give a 2 in the denominator. When multiplying both sides of the equation by $(x - 2)$ to clear the denominator, we get $4x - 7 = 3x - 5$. Solve for x. $x = 2$. We know from the restriction that $x \neq 2$, therefore there is no solution.

12. - 2/5, Factor the denominator in each rational expression to get $(x - 2)(x + 2)$, $(x + 3)(x + 2)$ and $(x - 2)(x + 3)$, respectively. Multiply both sides of the equation by the LCD of $(x - 2)(x + 2)(x + 3)$ to get $(2 - 5x)(x + 3) + (3 + 2x)(x - 2) = (2 - 3x)(x + 2)$. Multiply and combine like terms to get $-3x^2 - 14x = -3x^2 - 4x + 4$. Isolate x to get $-10x = 4$, therefore $x = -4/10 = -2/5$.

13. $\dfrac{R_2 R}{R_2 - R}$, Multiply both sides of the equation by the LCD of $R_1 R_2$ to get $R_1 R_2 = R_2 R + R_1 R$. Subtract $R_1 R$ from both sides of the equation to get $R_1 R_2 - R_1 R = R_2 R$. Factor left side of the equation to get $R_1(R_2 - R) = R_2 R$. Divide both sides by $(R_2 - R)$.

Problem Set 4
Answers and key steps in solution

1. f(1) = -1/4, f(-1) = 3/2, f(2) =1/8, $f(1) = \dfrac{2(1) - 3}{4(1)}$, $f(-1) = \dfrac{2(-1) - 3}{4(-1)}$, $f(2) = \dfrac{2(2) - 3}{4(2)}$

2. f(1) = undefined, f(-1) = 5/6, f(2) = undefined, $f(1) = \dfrac{1+6}{1^2 - 3(1) + 2}$, $f(-1) = \dfrac{-1+6}{(-1)^2 - 3(-1) + 2}$

$f(2) = \dfrac{2+6}{2^2 - 3(2) + 2}$

3. f(1) = -7/3, f(-1) = 7/3, f(2) = undefined, $f(1) = \dfrac{7(1)}{1^2 - 4}$, $f(-1) = \dfrac{7(-1)}{(-1)^2 - 4}$, $f(2) = \dfrac{7(2)}{2^2 - 4}$

4. f(1) = 4,   f(-1) = -5/4, f(2) = 1, $f(1) = \dfrac{9-1}{5(1) - 3}$, $f(-1) = \dfrac{9 - (-1)}{5(-1) - 3}$, $f(2) = \dfrac{9-2}{5(2) - 3}$

For problems 5 and 6, substitute the values for x into the function and solve.
For example, in problem 5, $f(1) = \dfrac{12}{(1+3)} = 3$

5.

x	f(x)
1	3
2	$\frac{12}{5}$
3	2
4	$\frac{12}{7}$
5	$\frac{3}{2}$

6.

x	f(x)
1	13
2	7
5	$\frac{17}{5}$
8	$\frac{5}{2}$
12	2

7. 7.34 cents per minute for 45 minutes,   7.08 cents per minute for 200 minutes.   Substitute 44 in for *n* in the function for the first part and 199 in for *n* in the second part.

8. All real numbers except for 9 (-∞, 9) U (9, ∞). Set the denominator equal to 0 and solve for x.   x - 9 = 0, x = 9, therefore the domain is all real numbers except for 9.

9. All real numbers except for 5 and -5 (-∞, -5) U (-5, 5) U (5, ∞). $4x^2$ - 100 = 0, $4(x^2 - 25)$ = 0, x^2 - 25 = 0, (x + 5)(x - 5) = 0, x = 5 or -5. Domain is all real numbers except for 5 and -5.

10. All real numbers except for -1/3 and 4 (-∞, -1/3) U (-1/3, 4) U (4, ∞). $3x^2$ - 11x + 4 = 0, (3x + 1)(x - 4) = 0. 3x + 1 = 0 or x - 4 = 0, x = -1/3 or x = 4. Domain is all real numbers except for -1/3 and 4.

Chapter 7

Radical Functions and Variation

Radical Functions

In the chapter 5 we learned about radical expressions and simplifying radicals. We will now learn about **radical functions**, their graphs and domains and ranges. A radical function is a function that contains roots. Examples of radical functions are $f(x) = \sqrt{x}$, $g(y) = \sqrt[3]{(2y + 3)}$ and $h(z) = \sqrt{(3z - 5)}$.

Square Root Function

One of the most common radical functions is the **square root function**. We will start with the most basic square root function, $f(x) = \sqrt{x}$. We are interested its graph and its domain and range. First, we'll find the domain of the function. Recall that only values for $x \geq 0$ satisfy $\sqrt{x}$. If $x < 0$, we will not get a real number solution for $\sqrt{x}$. (The square root of a negative number is a complex number, which is a more advanced topic in algebra and beyond the scope of this book).

To graph $f(x) = \sqrt{x}$, we'll set up a table of values.
For $x = 1$, $f(1) = \sqrt{1} = 1$

$x = 4$, $f(4) = \sqrt{4} = 2$

$x = 9$, $f(9) = \sqrt{9} = 3$

$x = 16$, $f(16) = \sqrt{16} = 4$

x	$f(x)$	$(x, f(x))$
1	1	(1, 1)
4	2	(4, 2)
9	3	(9, 3)
16	4	(16, 4)

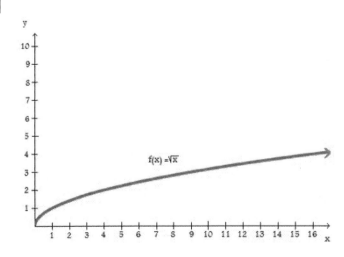

Notice we used values for x that are perfect squares. They are much easier to graph.

•Note that we only used the principal square root for the values of *f(x)*. The reason for this will be noted after the graph.

Recall that the square root has both positive and negative values (ie, √4 = 2 and -2). But the reason we did not use the negative values on the graph is because we are assuring that it is a function.   The graph below shows what happens if we include the negative values. Notice the vertical line shows that it would not pass the vertical line test and would not be a function. Therefore the graph of the function *f(x)* = √x are only the values in the first quadrant.

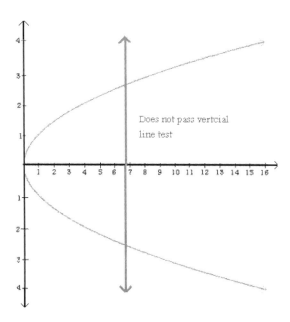

Knowing the graph of the basic square root function, *f(x)* = √x, will help us graph many other radical functions. If *h* > 0, then *f(x)* = √(x +h) and *f(x)* = √(x - h) are the graphs of *f(x)* = √x moved to the left and right *h* units, respectively.

Example: Graph *f(x)* = √(x + 1)

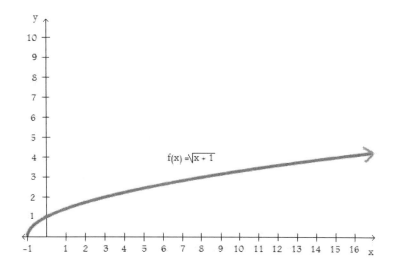

Notice when *x* = -1, *f(x)* = 0. The x-intercept is (-1, 0). When *x* = 0, *f(x)* = 1. The domain is *x* ≥ -1 because *x* <

-1 will yield a negative under the radical and the square root of a negative is not a real number. You can plot several other points that makes $\sqrt{(x + 1)}$ a perfect square. Notice this graph is the graph of $f(x) = \sqrt{x}$ moved 1 unit to the left. It is said to be **translated** 1 unit to the left.

Example: Graph $f(x) = \sqrt{(x - 1)}$.

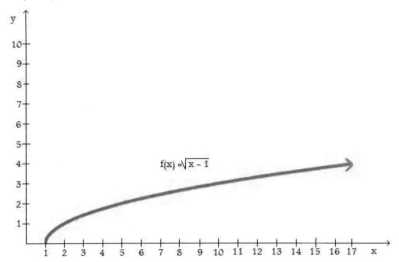

Notice when $x = 1$, $f(x) = 0$. The x-intercept is (1, 0) There is no y-intercept. The domain is $x \geq 1$ because if $x < 1$ we'll have a negative under the radical and the square root of a negative is not a real number. We could continue to plot more points that makes $\sqrt{(x - 1)}$ a perfect square. Compare the graph to the graph of $f(x) = \sqrt{x}$ and notice that this graph is translated 1 unit to the right.

We learned how to graph radical functions that are translations left and right of the square root function, $f(x) = \sqrt{x}$. Now we will learn how to graph radical functions that are that translations up and down of the square root function $f(x) = \sqrt{x}$. If $k > 0$, then $f(x) = \sqrt{x} - k$ and $f(x) = \sqrt{x} + k$ are the graphs of $f(x)$ moved down k units and up k units, respectively.

Example: Graph $f(x) = \sqrt{x} + 3$.

Following the definition above, $f(x) = \sqrt{x} + k$ is the graph of $f(x) = \sqrt{x}$ translated k units up. In this problem, $k = 3$, therefore the graph is as follows.

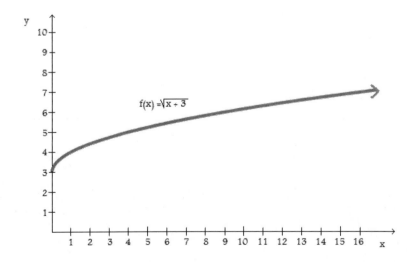

Notice that the y- intercept is (0,3), which is 3 units up from the y- intercept of (0, 0) for the graph of $f(x) = \sqrt{x}$. There is no x- intercept because for the square root function with only an upward translation, the graph is entirely in the first quadrant (where both x and $f(x)$ are positive)

Example: Graph $f(x) = \sqrt{x} - 3$.

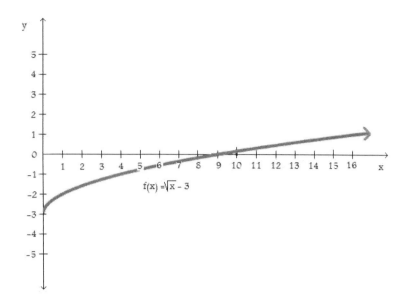

The graph of this function is translated 3 units down from the graph of $f(x) = \sqrt{x}$. Therefore the graph crosses the $f(x)$ axis at (0, -3). The x- intercept is (9, 0). Notice this graph is in both the first and fourth quadrants (where both x and $f(x)$ are positive and where x is positive and $f(x)$ is negative).

Example: Graph $f(x) = \sqrt{(x - 2)} + 1$.

Notice in this problem there are two translations. There is a translation up 1 unit and 2 units to the right.

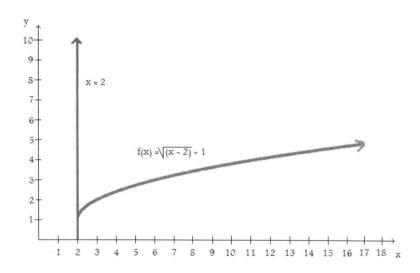

Notice the vertical line through $x = 2$. The domain of the function is $x \geq 2$. This shows that there are no points on the graph to the left of 2 on the x axis. The graph is in the first quadrant where both x and $f(x)$ are positive.

Cube Root Function

The **cube root function** is a radical function defined as $f(x) = \sqrt[3]{x}$. To graph the function we want to choose values for x that are a perfect cube. For example 1 is a perfect cube because 1(1)(1) = 1 and 8 is a perfect cube because (2)(2)(2) = 8. A list of many perfect cubes was given in Chapter 4.

To graph $f(x) = \sqrt[3]{x}$, we'll set up a table of values.
Fox $x = 1$, $f(1) = \sqrt[3]{(1)} = 1$

$\qquad x = -1$, $f(-1) = \sqrt[3]{(-1)} = -1$

$\qquad x = 8$, $f(8) = \sqrt[3]{(8)} = 2$

$\qquad x = -8$, $f(-8) = \sqrt[3]{(-8)} = -2$

$\qquad x = 27$, $f(27) = \sqrt[3]{(27)} = 3$

$\qquad x = -27$, $f(-27) = \sqrt[3]{(-27)} = -3$

x	f(x)	(x, f(x))
1	1	(1, 1)
-1	-1	(-1,-1)
8	2	(8, 2)
-8	-2	(-8, -2)
27	3	(27, 3)
-27	-3	(27, -3)

Notice the graph of $f(x) = \sqrt[3]{x}$ below.

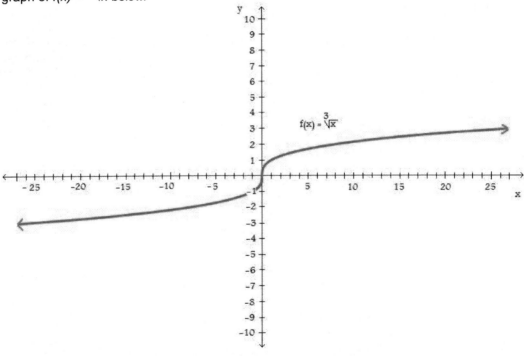

The function contains values in the first and third quadrants and no values in the second and fourth quadrants. As with the square root function, there are translations with the cube root function. The next couple graphs show translations of the cube root function.

Example: Graph $f(x) = \sqrt[3]{x} - 3$

We can substitute perfect cube values in the function for x as in the previous or we can notice the -3 after the radical. Since $f(x) = \sqrt[3]{x}$ is the cube root function, the graph of this function is the same the previous graph translated down 3 units.

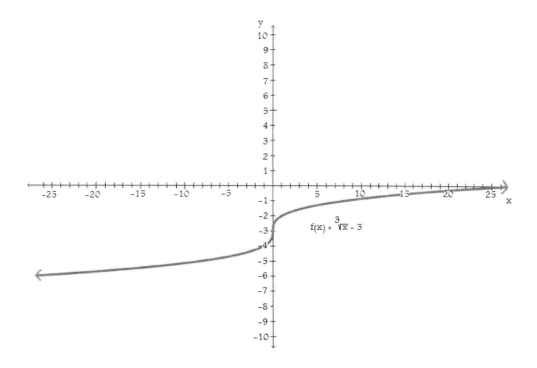

Example: Graph $f(x) = \sqrt[3]{(x + 2)} - 3$.

Notice that this is the cube root function and very similar to the previous example with the exception of the +2 under the radical. This graph is the same as the previous except it is translated 2 units to the left. If this is difficult to see, choose perfect cube values for x and substitute in for $f(x)$ and make a table and plot the points.

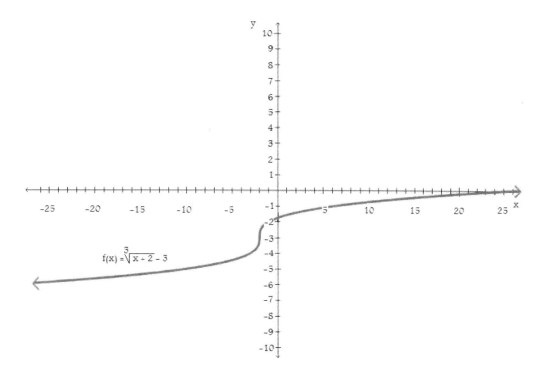

Review Problems: Set 1

Complete the tables for the following functions.

1. $f(x) = \sqrt{x}$

x	f(x)	(x, f(x))
4		
	3	
		(16, 4)
	5	

2. $f(x) = \sqrt{x} + 2$

x	f(x)	(x, f(x))
4		
9		
	6	
	7	

3. $f(x) = \sqrt{(x + 3)}$

x	f(x)	(x, f(x))
1		(1,)
6		(6,)
	4	(, 4)
22		(22,)

4. $f(x) = \sqrt[3]{x}$

x	f(x)	(x, f(x))
1		(1,)
	2	
	-3	
64		(64,)
	5	

5. $f(x) = \sqrt[3]{(x + 1)} + 2$

x	f(x)	(x, f(x))
0		
7		
-2		
-9		
26		

State the translations of the following square root and cube root functions.

6. $f(x) = \sqrt{(x - 1)}$

7. $f(x) = \sqrt{x} + 5$
8. $f(x) = \sqrt{(x + 2)} - 3$
9. $f(x) = \sqrt[3]{(x + 7)}$
10. $f(x) = \sqrt[3]{x} - 4$
11. $f(x) = \sqrt[3]{(x - 3)} + 2$

Graph the following functions.

12. $f(x) = \sqrt{(x + 3)}$
13. $f(x) = \sqrt{x} + 2$
14. $f(x) = \sqrt[3]{(x - 1)}$
15. $f(x) = \sqrt[3]{x} + 4$

Variation

Variation problems involve formulas which show the relationship between two or more **variables.** The types of variation we will learn about in the upcoming sections are direct, inverse, joint and combined.

Direct Variation

Direct variation is represented as a linear equation with one variable found by multiplying the other by a constant. For example, the formula for circumference of a circle is $C = 2\pi R$. Notice that C is always found by multiplying R by the constant 2π. In terms of variation, we say that C **varies directly** with R or C is **directly proportional** to R. In general, if y varies directly with x, then $y = kx$ for some constant k, $(k \neq 0)$. The constant k is known as the **constant of variation.**

There is a step by step process to solve problems involving variation. First translate the verbal model into an equation. Substitute the values given into the equation and solve for the constant k. Put the value of k back into the equation and all other remaining values. Then solve for the unknown variable.

Example: y varies directly with x. When y is 10, x is 4. What is y when $x = 7$?

Step 1: Write the equation.

Since y varies directly with x, $y = kx$.

Step 2: Substitute the values in for x and y and solve for k.

$10 = k(4)$

$10 = 4k$

$5/2 = k$

Step 3: Substitute k back into the original equation as well as 7 for x and solve for y.

$y = (5/2)(7)$

$y = 35/2$

Example: y varies directly with x. When $y = 4$, $x = 11$. What is x when $y = 9$?

The equation is $y = kx$, now substitute 4 for y and 11 for x into the equation.

$4 = 11(k)$
$4 = 11k$, solve for k to get
$4/11 = k$
Now substitute 4/11 in for k and 9 for y into the original equation and solve for x.

$9 = (4/11)x$

$99/4 = x$ (divided 9 by 4/11 which is the same as multiplying 9 by 11/4)

Example: Suppose you are interested in converting US dollars to Philippine pesos. The number of pesos received is directly proportional to the number of dollars to be exchanged. If 21 US dollars equals 894 pesos, how many pesos will you receive for $1,400 dollars?

Let y = number of pesos and x = number of US dollars and k = constant of variation.

The equation for this problem is $894 = k(21)$

$894 = 21k$

$42.57 = k$

To find out how many pesos you will receive for $1,400, substitute 42.57 for k and $1,400 for x.

$y = 42.57(1,400)$

$y = 59,598$

•**Note the the equation for direct variation, $y = kx$, is linear. The graph of this is a straight line through the origin with a slope of k. The graph below is for a value of $k > 0$.**

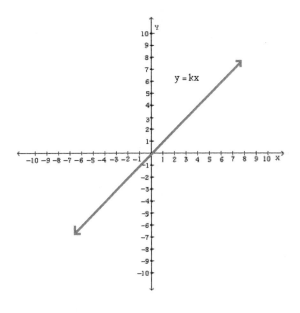

Inverse Variation

In some formulas, when one value increases, another value decreases. An example of such a formula is $h = 20/b$. In such cases, we say that h **varies inversely** with b or h is **inversely proportional** to b. In general, if y varies inversely with x then $y = k/x$ for some value of k, $k \neq 0$.

Example: Suppose y varies inversely with x. If $y = 5$ when $x = 14$, what is x when $y = 8$?

Set up the equation for inverse variation and solve for k.
$y = k/x$

$5 = k/14$

$70 = k$

Substitute 70 for k and 8 for y into the original equation and solve for x.

$8 = 70/x$

$8x = 70$

$x = 70/8$

$x = 35/4$

Example: If y varies inversely with x and $y = 6$ when $x = 5$, what is y when $x = 12$?

$y = k/x$

$6 = k/5$

$30 = k$

Substitute 30 for k and 12 for x in the original equation and solve for y.

$y = 30/12$

$y = 5/2$

Example: On a dance floor, the amount of floor space per person is inversely proportional to the number of people. If n represents the number of people and s represents the amount of square feet of floor space per person, then

$s = k/n$ represents the relationship between s and n.

If there are 12 people on the dance floor and each of them have 11 square feet of floor space, how much floor space will each person have if there are 20 people on the dance floor?

Substitute 12 for n and 11 for s and solve for k.

$11 = k/12$
$132 = k$

Now substitute 132 for k and 20 for n and solve for s.

$s = 132/20$

$s = 6.4$ feet^2

Example: If y varies inversely with the square of x and y is 6 when x is 4, what is y when x is 10 ?

The equation for this is $y = k/x^2$ (notice the difference from $y = k/x$ since the variation is with the **square** of x) Substitute the value for y and x and solve for k.

$6 = k/(4^2)$

$6 = k/16$

$96 = k$

Now substitute 16 for k and 10 for x in the original equation and solve for y.

$y = 96/(10^2)$

$y = 96/100$

$y= 24/25$ or 0.96

Joint Variation

A relationship between variables is called **joint variation** when one variable varies directly with the product of two or more variables.   An example of joint variation is the formula for the area of a triangle. Recall that the area of a triangle is ½ the base times the height. $(A = (1/2)bh)$

In general, if y varies jointly with x and z, then $y = kxz$, where k is the constant of variation and $k > 0$.

Example: Suppose y varies jointly with x and z and y is 12 when x is 3 and z is 2. What is the value of y when x is 8 and z is 5 ?

Start with the equation $y = kxz$ and substitute 12 for y, 3 for x and 2 for z and solve for k.

$12 = k(3)(2)$

$12 = 6k$

$2 = k$

Now substitute 2 for k, 8 for x and 5 for z in the original equation and solve for y.

$y = (2)(8)(5)$

$y = 16(5)$

$y = 80$

Example: Suppose the costs incurred by a lumber hauling company varies jointly with the number of trucks used to haul the lumber and the number of hours each truck is used. The cost is $3,400 when 6 trucks are used for 5 hours each. What are the costs when 8 trucks are used for 7 hours each ?

Let c = costs, n = number of trucks and h = hours each truck is used. Therefore the equation used is

$c = khn$. Substitute $3,400 for c, 5 for h and 6 for n. Then solve for k.

$3,400 = k(5)(6)$

$3,400 = 30k$

$113\ 1/3 = k$

Now substitute 113 1/3 for k, 7 for h and 6 for n in the original equation and solve for c.

$c = (113\ 1/3)(7)(6)$

$c = (113\ 1/3)(42)$

$c = \$4,\ 760$ (multiply on a calculator or change 113 1/3 to 340/3 and multiply by 42 to get $(340/3)(42) = 340(14)$ = $4,760)

Example: The cost of concrete used to pave a sidewalk varies jointly with the length, width and depth of each rectangular piece. If a piece costs $300 for a piece 5 feet long, 3 feet wide and 6 inches thick, how much would it cost for a piece 12 feet long, 4 feet wide and 6 inches thick ?

Let C = cost, l = length, w = width and d = depth. Use k for the constant of variation.

$C = klwd$

Substitute the values for C, l, w and d and solve for k.

$300 = k(5)(3)(1/2)$

•**Note when the dimensions are in different units, we must convert to the same unit. Therefore converting 6 inches to feet, we use ½ for d.**

$300 = (15/2)k$

$40 = k$

Now substitute 40 for k, 12 for l, 4 for w and ½ for d into the original equation and solve for C.

$C = 40(12)(4)(1/2)$

$C = \$960$

Another method to solve a problem like this is to get the volume of each piece and calculate how many times larger the one piece is. Then multiply that value by $300.

The volume of the second piece is $(12)(4)(1/2) = 24$ feet^3
The volume of the first piece is $(5)(3)(1/2) = 7.5$ feet^3

The volume of the second one is $24/(7.5) = 3.2$ times the volume of the first, so the cost is 3.2 times the cost of the first. Therefore $300(3.2) = \$960$.

Essentially, the problem was solved by setting up a proportion.

Think of the proportion as

Cost 1/Volume 1 = Cost 2/Volume 2

$300/(15/2) = C/24$

$40 = C/24$

$C = 960$.

Another example of a proportion:

$$\frac{3x}{5} = \frac{14}{9}$$

Multiply the numerator of the first fraction by the denominator of the second fraction.

$3x(9) = 27x$

Multiply the denominator of the first fraction by the numerator of the second fraction.

$5(14) = 70$

Set the quantities equal to each other and solve for x.

$27x = 70$

$x = 70/27$

•**Note that all proportions can be solve by the basic method shown in the previous example. The process of multiplying shown above is known as "cross multiplication".**

Combined Variation

Many problems combine direct and inverse variation. This is known as **combined variation**. In general, if y varies directly with x and inversely with z then $y = kx/z$, where $k \neq 0$. If the problem stated that y *is directly proportional to x,* the equation would be $y = kx$. Notice the inverse variation has z in the denominator. If the problem stated that *y varies inversely with z*, the equation would be $y = k/z$. Combining the two gives us $y = kx/z$.

Example: Suppose that y varies directly with x and inversely with z^2. If $y = 6$, when $x = 4$ and $z = 3$, what is the value of y when $x = 2$ and $z = 4$?
The equation for *y varies directly with x* is $y = kx$. The equation for *y varies inversely with z^2* is $y = k/z^2$.
Therefore the equation for the combined variation is $y = kx/z^2$.

Substitute the values for x, y and z in the original equation and solve for k.

$6 = k(4)/(3^2)$

$6 = 4k/9$

$54 = 4k$

$13 \tfrac{1}{2} = k$

Now substitute 13 ½ for k, 2 for x and 4 for z in the original equation and solve for y.

$y = (13\ 1/2)(2)/(4)^2$

$y = 27/16$

Example: The time it takes to mow a rectangular area of grass varies directly with the length and width of the area to be mowed and inversely with the number of workers. If it takes 10 hours for 5 workers to mow a rectangular area of land 1000 feet long and 450 feet wide, how long will it take 8 workers to mow an area of grass 2000 feet long and 345 feet wide?

Let t = mowing time, l = length, w = width and n = number of workers.

The equation is $t = klw/n$ ($t = klw$ is direct variation, $t = k/n$ is the inverse variation)

Substitute the values in for t, l, w and n and solve for k.

$10 = k(1000)(450)/5$

$10 = 450000k/5$

$k = 1/9000$

Now substitute 1/9000 for k, 2000 for l, 340 for w, 8 for n and solve for t.

$t = (1/9000)(2000)(340)/8$

$t = 9.4$ hours (multiplied and divided on a calculator)

Review Problems: Set 2

Convert each verbal model into symbols.

1. x varies directly with y.
2. y varies directly with the square of z.
3. z varies inversely with the cube of y.
4. q varies directly with s and inversely with t
5. a varies directly with the square of b and the cube of c.
6. C varies inversely with h and w.
7. V varies directly with l and w and inversely with p.
8. x varies jointly with y and z.
9. y varies jointly with the square of w and z.
10. y varies jointly with the square of x and z and inversely with w.

Describe each variation in words. The constant of variation in each is k.

11. $A = kbh$
12. $B = kx/y$
13. $C = kx^2y/z$
14. $D = kxyz$
15. $E = k/r$
16. $F = ka^2b^2c^3$
17. $G = k/h^3j^2$

Solve each of the following.

18. If y varies directly with x and $y = 5$ when $x = 14$, what is y when $x = 8$?
19. If y varies inversely with x and $y = 10$ when $x = 7$, what is x when $y = 4$?
20. If y varies directly with x and inversely with z and $y = 6$ when $x = 4$ and $z = 3$, what is y when $x = 6$ and $z = 2$?
21. If x varies jointly with w and z and $x = 4$ when $y = 4$ and $z = 8$, what is the x when $y = 9$ and $z = 3$?

Applications

22. The external work on a spring when stretched, known as it's elastic potential energy, is given by the formula $PE = (\frac{1}{2})kL^2$, where L is the length that the spring is stretched. If the elastic potential energy is 400 when the length of the stretched spring is 15 cm, what is the elastic potential energy when the spring is stretched 10 cm ?

23. The distance that a car goes is directly proportional to the number of gallons of gasoline the car uses. If a car goes 375 miles on 18 gallons of gasoline, how many gallons are used to travel 252 miles?

24. The volume a gas occupies varies inversely with the pressure applied (assuming a constant temperature). If the gas occupies a volume of 40 cubic centimeters under a pressure of 3 pounds per square centimeter, how much is the volume of gas when it is under a pressure of 5 pounds per square centimeter?

25. The value of a same make of car is inversely proportional to the age of the car. If a 5 year old car is worth $12,400, how much is a 3 year old car worth?

Key Terms and Concepts to Review

•Radical functions
•Square root function
•Translation
•Cube root function
•Variation
•Direct variation, varies directly, directly proportional
•Constant of variation
•Varies inversely, inversely proportional

•Joint variation
•Combined variation

Answers to Problem Sets

Problem Set 1
Answers and key steps in solution

1. $f(x) = \sqrt{x}$

x	f(x)	(x, f(x))
4	2	(4, 2)
9	3	(9, 3)
16	4	(16, 4)
25	5	(25, 5)

If given x, substitute for x in $\sqrt{x}$. So for $x = 4$, $\sqrt{4} = 2$. If given the value for $f(x)$, square it to get x. So for $f(x) = 3$, $x = 3^2 = 9$.

2. $f(x) = \sqrt{x} + 2$

x	f(x)	(x, f(x))
4	4	(4, 4)
9	5	(9, 5)
16	6	(16, 6)
25	7	(25, 7)

Notice that this is the square root function translated 2 units up, therefore each value for $f(x)$ will be 2 greater than in the square root function. We can also find $f(x)$ by substituting x into the function, $f(4) = \sqrt{4} + 2 = 4$, etc. If given $f(x)$, substitute the number in and solve for x. For example, $f(x) = 6$, therefore $6 = \sqrt{x} + 2$, $4 = \sqrt{x}$, $16 = x$.

3. $f(x) = \sqrt{(x + 3)}$

x	f(x)	(x, f(x))
1	2	(1, 2)
6	3	(6, 3)
13	4	(13, 4)
22	5	(22, 5)

Notice that this is the square root function translated 3 units to the left. Therefore you know $f(x) = 2$ when $x = 4$, translated 3 units to the left is 1. $f(x) = 3$ when $x = 9$, so translated 3 units to the left is 6 and so on. You can also get the answers by substitution. For example, when $x = 22$, $f(x) = \sqrt{(22 + 3)} = \sqrt{25} = 5$. When $f(x) = 4$, $4 = \sqrt{(x + 3)}$. Square both sides to get $16 = x + 3$, therefore $x = 13$.

4. $f(x) = \sqrt[3]{x}$

x	f(x)	(x, f(x))
1	1	(1, 1)
8	2	(8, 2)
-8	-3	(-8, 3)
64	4	(64, 4)
125	5	(125, 5)

This is the cube root function. If given x, substitute in for x and get the cube root, so for $x = 1$, $\sqrt[3]{1} = 1$. If given f(x), substitute in and cube to get x. Therefore if $f(x) = -2$, $-2 = \sqrt[3]{x}$. Cube both sides to get $-8 = x$.

5. $f(x) = \sqrt[3]{(x + 1)} + 2$

x	f(x)	(x, f(x))
0	3	(0, 3)
7	4	(7, 4)
-2	1	(-2, 1)
-9	0	(-9, 0)
26	5	(26, 5)

This is the cube root function translated 1 unit to the left and 2 units up. An easy way to get the values for f(x) is to substitute x into f(x). For $x = 7$, $\sqrt[3]{(x + 1)} + 2 = \sqrt[3]{(7 + 1)} + 2 = 2 + 2 = 4$.

6. Translated 1 unit to the right
7. Translated 5 units up
8. Translated 2 units left and 3 units down
9. Translated 7 units left
10. Translated 4 units down
11. Translated 3 units right and 2 units up.

For the graphs, note that they are all translations of the basic square root and cube root functions. Refer to the examples in the text on how to graph radical functions with translations. The graphs for 12 through 15 are on the two pages.

12.

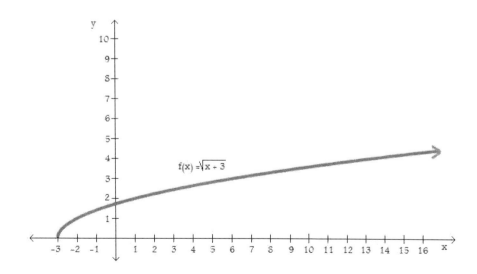

13.

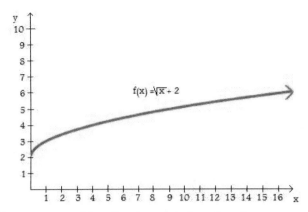

Problem 13 is the graph of the square root function translated up 2 units.

14.

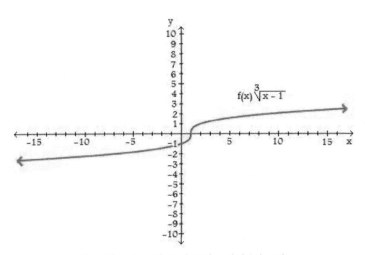

Notice that problem 14 is the cube root function translated to the right 1 unit.

15.

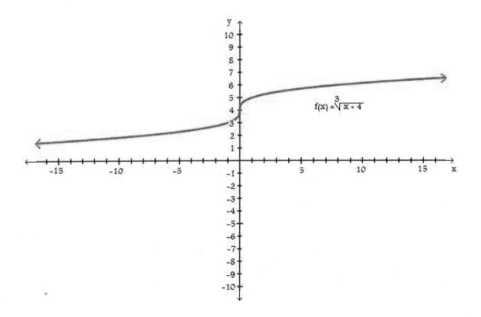

Problem 15 is the cube root function translated up 4 units.

Problem Set 2
Answers and key steps in solution

1. $x = ky$
2. $y = kz^2$
3. $z = k/y^3$
4. $q = ks/t$
5. $a = kb^2/c^3$
6. $c = k/hw$
7. $v = klw/p$
8. $x = kyz$
9. $y = kw^2z$
10. $y = kx^2z/w$

In the 10 problems above, the key to remember is direct variation is in the form $y = kx$, joint variation is in the form $y = kxz$ (for 2 variables), inverse variation is in the form $y = k/x$ and combined variation is a mixture of the others. If you are having difficulty getting these answers, refer to the example problems in the text.

11. A varies directly with b and h.
12. B varies directly with x and inversely with y.
13. C varies directly with the square of x and y and inversely with z.
14. D varies jointly with x, y and z.
15. E varies inversely with r.
16. F varies jointly with the square of a, the square of b and the cube of c.
17. G varies inversely with the cube of h and the square of j.
18. 20/7 $y = kx$, $5 = 14k$, $k = 5/14$, therefore $y = (5/14)(8) = 40/14 = 20/7$
19. 17 ½ $y = k/x$, $10 = k/7$, $k = 70$, therefore $4 = 70/x$, $4x = 70$, $x = 70/4 = 35/2 = 17$ ½
20. 27/2 $y = kx/z$, $6 = 4k/3$, $18 = 4k$, 4 ½ $= k$, therefore $y = (4\ 1/2)(6)/2 = 27/2$
21. 27/8 $x = kwz$, $4 = k(4)(8)$, $4 = 32k$, $1/8 = k$, therefore $x = (1/8)(9)(3) = 27/8$
22. 178 $PE = (1/2)kL^2$, $400 = (1/2)k(15^2)$, $400 = (225/2)k$, $3.56 = k$, therefore $PE = (1/2)(3.56)(10^2) = 178$
23. 12.1 $d = kg$, $375 = k(18)$, $20.8 = k$, therefore $252 = 20.8g$, $g = 12.1$
24. 24 $v = k/p$, $40 = k/3$, $120 = k$, therefore $v = 120/5$, $v = 24$
25. $20,666.67 $v = k/a$, $12,400 = k/5$, $62,000 = k$, therefore $v = 62,000/3 = 20,666.67$

Appendix

Additional Practice With Word Problems

The length of the sides of a trapezoid are 4.5 inches. The length of the parallel bases are 10 inches and 14 inches. Find the perimeter of the trapezoid.

Solution:

The perimeter is found by adding the lengths of all the sides of the trapezoid. Therefore, the perimeter is 4.5 + 4.5 + 10 + 14 = 33 inches.

Suppose you are looking for someone to paint your back porch. You have narrowed your choices down to 2 painters. One charges $40 per hour plus $30 for supplies and the other charges $35 per hour and $20 for supplies. The first person estimates the job to take 2 1/2 hours and the second says he can complete the job in 3 hours. Which person should you hire and how much money will you save?

Solution:

Cost of hiring first person: $40t + 30$ where t is the time to complete the job. $40(2.5) + 30 = \$130$.

Cost of hiring second person: $35t + 20$, $35(3) + 20 = \$125$.

You should hire the second person and save $5.

The distance a tire rolls in one revolution is found by taking the circumference of the tire. If a tire has a diameter or 24 inches, how many revolutions must the tired make to cover a distance of 57 feet?

Solution:

The circumference of a circle is given by the formula $C = \pi d$, where d is the diameter of the circle. We need to get the units the same, so convert 24 inches to 2 feet.

$C = \pi(2)$, using 3.14 as an approximation for π, C is approximately 6.28 feet.

To calculate the number of revolutions in 57 feet, take $57/(6.28) = 9.07$. (rounded to 2 decimal places)

The diameter of a baseball is approximately 7.37 cm. A hockey puck is cylindrical with a thickness of 2.54 cm and a diameter of 7.6 cm. Which has the greatest volume?

Solution:

A baseball is spherical and the volume of a sphere is $(4/3)\pi r^3$. The radius of the sphere is half the diameter, so $r = 3.685$ cm. Using 3.14 for π, the volume of the baseball is $(4/3)(3.14)(3.685)^3 = 209.5$ cm^3. (rounded to one decimal place)

The volume of a cylinder is $\pi r^2 h$. The radius of the hockey puck is 3.8 cm, the height is 2.54 cm. Therefore the volume of the hockey puck is $(3.14)(3.8)^2(2.54) = 115.2$ cm^3. (rounded to one decimal place)

The volume of a baseball is nearly double the volume of a hockey puck.

Suppose you have a metal cone shaped container and a plastic container in the shape of a shoe box. The cone shaped container is 14 inches high with a diameter of 10 inches. The plastic container is 12 inches long, 6 inches wide and 4 inches high. You want to fill up one container with water. Which container will hold the most water?
Solution:

The volume of a cone is $(1/3)\ \pi r^2 h$.

Therefore, the volume of the cone shaped container is $(1/3)(3.14)(5)^2(14) = 366.3$ inches^3 (rounded to one decimal place)

The volume of a rectangular solid is length times width times height, therefore the volume of the plastic container is $(12)(6)(4) = 288$ inches^3.

The metal cone shaped container will hold the most water.

The directions on a cake recipe say to bake the cake at 204 degrees Celsius, but your oven only has units in Fahrenheit. What must you set your oven at in degrees Fahrenheit? Note that $C = (5/9)(F - 32)$.

Solution:

We can substitute 204 in for C first and then solve for F or solve for F first and then substitute.

Solve for F first.   Multiply the entire equation by $(9/5)$ to remove the fraction.

$(9/5)C = (9/5)(5/9)(F - 32)$
$(9/5)C = F - 32$
$F = (9/5)C + 32$
$F = (9/5)(204) + 32$
$F = 399.2$, which is approximately 400. Set the oven to 400 degrees F.

Steve and Bill are stamp collectors. Together, they have 6,590 stamps. Steve has 200 more than twice the number that Bill has. How many stamps do each of them have?

Solution:

Let x = number of stamps that Bill has.

$200 + 2x$ = number of stamps that Steve has.

Number of stamps Bill has plus the number of stamps Steve has equals 6,590, therefore

$x + 200 + 2x = 6,590$
$3x + 200 = 6,590$
$3x = 6,390$
$x = 2,130.$

Bill has 2,130 stamps

Substitute 2,130 in for x in $2x + 200$ to find the number of stamps that Steve has.

Steve has $2(2,130) + 200 = 4,460$ stamps.

A carpenter cuts a board that is 60 feet long into 3 pieces. He needs one piece to be 2 feet longer than the shortest piece. The longest piece must be twice as long as the middle piece. How long is each piece?

Solution:

Let x = length of shortest piece

$x + 2$ = length of middle piece

$2(x + 2)$ = length of longest piece

The sum of the lengths of all pieces must equal 60 feet.

Therefore, $x + x + 2 + 2(x + 2) = 60$

$$x + x + 2x + 4 = 60$$
$$4x + 4 = 60$$
$$4x = 54$$
$$x = 13.5$$

The lengths of the pieces are 13.5, 15.5 and 31 feet.

Suppose you wish to buy a mixture of peanuts and cashews at the store. Peanuts for $2.50 per pound and cashews sell for $4.00 per pound. You want 15 pounds of peanuts. How many pounds of cashews must you buy for the mixture to cost $3.00 per pound?

Solution:

For this kind of problem, it's easier to solve by setting up a table.

	Pounds	Price Per Pound	Total Cost
Peanuts	15	2.5	(15)(2.5)
Cashews	p	4	$4p$
Mixture	$15 + p$	3	$(15 + p)(3)$

Cost of peanuts plus the cost of the cashews equals the cost of the mixture.

Therefore $(15)(2.5)+ 4p = (15 + p)(3)$
$$37.5 + 4p = 45 + 3p$$
$$4p = 45 - 37.5 + 3p$$
$$4p = 7.5 + 3p$$
$$p = 7.5$$

You must buy 7.5 pounds of cashews for the total mixture to cost $3 per pound.

A car purchased for $30,000 is expected to depreciate (lose value) according to the equation $y = 30,000 - 1,750x$, where y is the value of the car and x is the number of years after purchase. What is the value of the car 6 years after the purchase?

Solution:

$x = 6$, substitute 6 into the equation for x to get

$y = 30,000 - 1,750(6)$

$y = 30,000 - 10,500$

$y = \$19, 500$

After how many years will the car be with $6,000?

This time we solve for x so we substitute $6,000 for y to get

$6,000 = 30,000 - 1,750x$

$-24,000 = -1,750x$

$x = 13.7$ (rounded to 1 decimal place)

The number of computers produced depends on the price. The lower the price, the fewer produced and the higher the price, the more produced. Supposed the equation that relates the price and number of computers produced is given by $p = (1/20)n + 100$, where p is the price and n is the number produced. How many computers will be produced if the price is $600?

Solution:

Since $p = 600$, we substitute 600 into the equation and solve for n

$600 = (1/20)n + 100$

$600 - 100 = (1/20)n$

$500 = (1/20)n$

$(20)(500) = n$

$10,000 = n$

Suppose the total cost of attending a prestigious university was $14,000 per year in 1990. In 2011, the cost has increased to $50,000 per year. Assuming the increase per year is linear, what is the average increase in cost per year? (Hint, use slope formula)

Solution:

We can think of the years as the x variable and the cost as the y variable.

$(x_1 , y_1) = (1990, 14,000)$

$(x_2 , y_2) = (2011, 50,000)$

Slope (average rate of change) $= \dfrac{(y_2 - y_1)}{(x_2 - x_1)} = \dfrac{(50,000 - 14,000)}{(2011 - 1990)} = \dfrac{36,000}{21} = 1,714.29$ (rounded to 2 decimal places)

Therefore the average increase in cost per year for attending the university is $1,714.29.

The height of a ball shot from the ground straight upward is given by the function $f(t) = -16t^2 + 256t$, where t is the time in seconds after the ball is shot. What is the height of the ball after 7 seconds? What is the height of the ball after 10 seconds? Interpret the results for the height after 10 seconds.

Solution:

The height of the ball after 7 seconds is $f(7) = -16(7)^2 + 256(7) = 1008$ feet.

The height of the ball after 10 seconds is $f(10) = -16(10)^2 + 256(10) = 960$ feet.
The height of the ball after 10 seconds is lower than the height after 7 seconds because the ball is already on the way back down. In fact, the ball reaches its maximum height 8 seconds after being shot.

Assume the function is in the form $f(t) = at^2 + bt$, then
the maximum height is reached at $t = -b/2a = -256/(-32) = 8$ seconds.

The flight of two planes is being tracked on a rectangular coordinate system. The flight of the first plane is defined by the equation $3x + 4y = 12$ and the flight of the second plane is defined by the equation $y = -(3/4)x + 10$. If the planes continue along the same paths, is there any danger of them colliding? (Assume the planes are flying at the same altitude)

Solution:

To determine if the planes will collide, we need to find the point of intersection of the two lines.

Substitute $-(3/4)x + 10$ for y in the first equation and solve for y.

$3x + 4[-(3/4)x + 10] = 12$

$3x - 3x + 40 = 12$

$40 = 12$ is a false statement. Therefore, there is no solution. There is no chance of the two planes colliding if they keep flying along the same paths.

Another way to solve this is to get the slope of each line. If the slopes are the same without the same y – intercept, then the lines are parallel and therefore the planes cannot collide.

$3x + 4y = 12$

$4y = 12 - 3x$

$y = 4 - (3/4)x$. Notice the slope of both lines is -3/4. The y – intercepts are different. Therefore there is no chance of the planes colliding if they continue along their same path.

Tom leaves at noon and drives west at 50 miles per hour. John leaves from the same location one hour later and travels along the same route as Tom at 65 miles per hour. At what time will John catch up to Tom?

Solution:

Set up a table for rate, distance and time.
Let t = time that John is driving. Since Tom left one hour earlier, Tom's time is $t + 1$.

	Rate	Time	Distance
Tom	50	$t + 1$	$50(t + 1)$
John	65	t	$65t$

Since we want to know when John catches up to Tom, we set their distances equal and solve for t.

$50(t + 1) = 65t$

$50t + 50 = 65t$

$50 = 15t$

$t = 3.\overline{33}$, John catches Tom after John has been driving for 3 hours and 20 minutes, which is at 4:20PM.

Tickets for admission to an amusement park are $20 for children and $25 for adults. If 100 tickets were sold for a total cost of $2,200, how many of each ticket were sold?

Solution:

Let x = Number of adult tickets
     y = Number of children tickets

Number of adult tickets plus number of children tickets equals 100.

$x + y = 100$

Cost of adult tickets sold plus costs of children tickets sold equals $2,200.

$25x + 20y = 2,200$

We can solve this graphically, by substitution or by elimination. Let's eliminate the x variable by multiplying the first equation by 25 and subtract the second equation from it.

$25(x + y = 100)$

$25x + 25y = 2,500$
$-(25x + 20y = 2,200)$

$5y = 300$

  $y = 60,$

Therefore $x + 60 = 100$, $x = 40$.

There were 60 children tickets and 40 adult tickets sold.

The sum of three positive integers is 16. If the first integer is doubled, the sum is 22. If the third integer is tripled, the sum is 20. What are the 3 integers?

Solution:

Let x = First integer
     y = Second integer
     z = Third integer

 $x + y + z = 16$ (Sum of the integers is 16)
$2x + y + z = 22$ (Double the first integer and the sum is 22)
$x + y + 3z = 20$ (Triple the third integer and the sum is 20)

We can eliminate both the y and z variable by subtracting the second equation from the first, therefore

$x + y + z = 16$
$-(2x + y + z = 22)$

$-x = -6$, $x = 6$

Subtract third equation from the first equation to eliminate the x and y variable, therefore

$x + y + z = 16$
$-(x + y + 3z = 20)$

$-2z = -4, z = 2$

Now substitute 6 for x and 2 for z in the first equation and solve for y.

$6 + y + 2 = 16$
$8 + y = 16$

$y = 8$

The three integers are 6, 8 and 2.

A student needs to get an average of 90 or higher for an A in the class. He has test scores of 93, 85, 87, 90 and 89. What does he need on the next test to achieve an A for the marking period?

Solution:

To obtain the average, we add up all the scores and divide by number of scores.

Let x = score on the next test.

$$\frac{(93 + 85 + 87 + 90 + 89 + x)}{6} =$$ Average of the 6 test scores.

$$\frac{444 + x}{6} = 90$$

$444 + x = 540$

$x = 96$

•Note that we set up the problem as an addition problem by multiplying the score desired by the number of scores to know what the sum of the test scores must be.

Michael has a budget of $1200 for the golf season. The course he plays costs $40 for a round of golf. He also wants to takes lessons which costs $70 each. He wants to play twice as many rounds as lessons taken. How many rounds of golf can Michael play for the season? How many lessons can he have?

Solution:

Let x = Number of rounds played
    $x/2$ = Number of lessons

Total cost of rounds played plus total number of lessons must be less than or equal to $1,200.

$40x$ = Total cost of rounds played
$70(x/2) = 35x$ = Total cost of lessons taken

$40x + 35x \leq 1,200$

$75x \leq 1,200$

$x \leq 16$. Therefore, Michael can play 16 times and take 8 lessons for the season.

The temperatures on a day in January satisfy the inequality $|t - 30| \leq 12$. The temperatures on a day in August satisfy the equation $|t - 70| \leq 16$. What are the temperature ranges for January and August and which month has the widest range of temperatures?

Solution:

Solve each inequality.

$|t - 30| \leq 12$

Recall for absolute value there is a positive case and a negative case.

The positive case is $t - 30 \leq 12$ and the negative case is $-12 \leq t - 30$.

$t - 30 \leq 12$, $-12 \leq t - 30$
      $t \leq 42$ $18 \leq t$

Therefore, the temperature ranges from 18 to 42 in January.

$|t - 70| \leq 16$

$t - 70 \leq 16$, $-16 \leq t - 70$
      $t \leq 86$ $54 \leq t$

Therefore, the temperature ranges from 54 to 86 in August.
The range for January temperatures is 24. (42 - 18 = 24)
The range for August temperatures is 32. (86 - 54 = 32)

Suppose you buy a condominium and a townhouse for investment purposes. You want to keep both properties for 4 years and then sell them. The townhouse was purchased for $145,000 and the condominium was purchased for $250,000. Their value after x years is given by the following functions:

$T(x) = 145,000 + 1,400x$
$C(x) = 250,000 + 3,000x$

How much is the townhouse worth after 4 years? How much is the condominium worth after 4 years? How much has the combined value increased after 4 years?

Solution:

$T(4) = 145,000 + 1,400(4) = \$150,600$
$C(4) = 250,000 + 3,000(4) = \$262,000$

Combined value is $150,000 + $262,000 = $412,600

Purchased value was $145,000 + $250,000 = $395, 000

Therefore, their combined value has increased by $17,600.

Suppose a swimming pool that is 4500 cm long, 2200 cm wide and 400 cm deep is completely filled with water. What is the volume of the water in the pool? Write your answer in scientific notation.

Solution:

The volume of a rectangular sold is lwh, where l is the length, w is the width and h is the height of the solid.

Convert each number to scientific notation first and then multiply or multiply and then write in scientific notation.
When multiplying first we get
(4500)(2200)(400) = 3,960,000,000.
Converting to scientific notation gives us 3.96×10^7 cm^3.

If we choose to convert first then we have
$(4.5 \times 10^3)(2.2 \times 10^3)(4 \times 10^2) = (4.5)(2.2)(4)(10^3)(10^3)(10^2) = 39.6 \times 10^8 = 3.96 \times 10^7$ cm^3.

If James can paint a room in 4 hours and Alan can paint a room in 3 hours, how long will it take them to paint a room if they work together?

Solution:

Set up a table for rate, time worked and total work done. Think of rate as the amount of the job done in 1 hour. Since James can finish the entire job in 4 hours, he completes ¼ of the job in an hour, so his rate is ¼. Time is the total time to complete the job, which is unknown so we label that as t. Total work done is the rate times the time.

	Rate	Time Worked	Total Work Done
James	¼	t	$t/4$
Alan	⅓	t	$t/3$

Since James and Alan complete the job, total work done is equal to one. If they completed half of the painting, total work done would equal ½ and so on.

Therefore,

$t/4 + t/3 = 1$.

Multiply the equation by the common denominator of 12 to clear the fractions

$12(t/4 + t/3 = 1)$

$3t + 4t = 12$

$7t = 12$

$t = 12/7 \approx 1.7$ hours

A rectangular pool x feet wide and $x + 20$ feet long is surrounded by a uniform walkway 10 feet in width. If the total area is 6,300 ft^2, what is the area of the pool?

Solution:

The area of the pool plus the area of the walkway equals the total area.
Since the pool is rectangular, the area is represented by length times width, which is $(x + 40)x$.
The walkway adds an additional 20 feet to both the length and the width since 10 feet is added to all 4 sides of the pool. The dimensions of the pool and the walkway is $x + 40$ by $x + 20$.

Therefore, $(x + 40)(x + 20) = 6,300$

$x^2 + 60x + 800 = 6,300$

$x^2 + 60x - 5500 = 0$

$(x - 50)(x + 110) = 0$

$x = 50$ or $x = -110$. Since x represents the width of the pool, it cannot be -110. Therefore $x = 50$ and the area of the pool is $(50 + 40)(50) = 90(50) = 4,500$ ft².

A truck driver delivering lumber has three stops to make over the course of the day. The truck travels x_1 miles at s_1 miles per hour, x_2 miles at s_2 miles per hour and x_3 miles at s_3 miles per hour. The average speed of the truck is given by

$$A = \dfrac{x_1 + x_1 + x_3}{\dfrac{x_1}{s_1} + \dfrac{x_2}{s_2} + \dfrac{x_3}{s_3}}$$

Simplify the equation, determine the average speed and total time driving if $x_1 = 70$, $x_2 = 100$, $x_3 = 250$, $s_1 = 55$, $s_2 = 60$ and $s_3 = 65$.

Solution:

Multiply the numerator and denominator of the rational expression by the LCD of $s_1 s_2 s_3$ to get

$$A = \dfrac{s_1 s_2 s_3 (x_1 + x_2 + x_3)}{s_2 s_3 x_1 + s_1 s_3 x_2 + s_1 s_2 x_3}$$

Substitute the values given to get the average speed.

$$A = \dfrac{(55)(60)(65)(70 + 100 + 250)}{(60)(65)(70) + (55)(65)(100) + (55)(60)(250)}$$

$A = 61.89$ mph (rounded to 2 decimal places)

Total time driving is the sum of the times at each speed. Therefore, total time driving is

$$\dfrac{x_1}{s_1} + \dfrac{x_2}{s_2} + \dfrac{x_3}{s_3} = \dfrac{70}{55} + \dfrac{100}{60} + \dfrac{250}{65} \approx 1.27 + 1.67 + 3.85 = 6.79 \text{ hours}$$

A plane travels 3,000 miles from New York to Los Angeles in clear weather with no significant wind. The return flight is in stormy weather and the plane's average speed is 50 mph less due to the conditions. The return flight is 2 hours longer. How fast did the plane fly in either direction?

Solution:

Set up a table with rate, distance and time for the flight to and from Los Angeles. Denote rate as r and note that distance equals rate multiplied by time.

	Rate	Time	Distance
To Los Angeles	r	$3000/r$	3000
From Los Angeles	$r - 50$	$3000/(r - 50)$	3000

Time to travel to LosAngles plus 2 equals time it takes to travel from Los Angeles, therefore

$$\dfrac{3000}{r} + 2 = \dfrac{3000}{r - 50}$$

Multiply both sides of the equation by the LCD of $r(r - 50)$ to clear the fractions.

The r's divide out in the first term and $(r - 50)$'s divide out in the last term. That leaves us with

$(r - 50)(3000) + 2r(r - 50) = 3000r$

$3000r - 150000 + 2r^2 - 100r = 3000r$

$2r^2 - 100r - 150000 = 0$

$2(r^2 - 50r - 75000) = 0$

$2(r - 300)(r + 250) = 0$

$r = 300$ or $r = -250$. Since r is the speed of the plane, it cannot be -250. Therefore $r = 300$. The plane flew 300 mph to Los Angeles and 250 mph from Los Angeles.

The instructions on a can of paint read that a half gallon of paint will cover approximately 175 square feet. How many half gallon cans of paint must be purchased to apply 2 coats of paint to cover 600 square feet per coat?

Solution:

We can think of this problems in terms of direct variation. The amount of paint needed is directly proportional to the area that needs to be painted.

Let y = amount of paint in gallons
    x = area to be painted in square foot.

Therefore, we use the equation for direction variation, $y = kx$.

Substitute ½ for y and 175 for x and solve for k.

½ = $k(175)$ (Divide both sides by 175)

$1/350 = k$

To apply 2 coats over 600 square feet means we need enough paint to cover 1,200 square feet, therefore

$y = (1/350)(1200)$

$y = 3.42$ gallons.

We need to purchase 7 cans of paint because $7(1/2) = 3.5$.

The time it takes a home building company to build a new home is directly proportional to the size of the home and inversely proportional to the number of people on the building crew. If it takes 10 workers 4 weeks to build a 2,000 square foot home, how long will it take 6 workers to build the home?

Solution:

Let t = time it takes to build a home
    w = number of workers
    s = size of home

The joint variation between these variables can be represented by

$t = ks/w$

Substitute 4 for t, 2000 for s and 10 for w and solve for k.

4 = k(2000)/10

Multiply both sides by 10 to clear the denominator.

40 = k(2000)

Divide by 2000 to get
40/2000 = 1/50 = k.

Now substitute 6 for w, 2000 for s and 1/50 for k and solve for t.

t = (1/50)(2000/6)

t = 2000/300, t = 6.$\overline{66}$.   Therefore, it takes 6 workers 6 2/3 weeks to build a 2,000 square foot home.

The time in seconds t it takes an object to fall d feet is given by the formula

$$t = \frac{\sqrt{d}}{4}$$

The Empire State Building in New York is 1,250 feet high. How long will it take for a penny dropped off the top of the building to reach the ground? If it takes an object 12 seconds to reach the ground, from what height was it dropped from?

Solution:

Substitute 1,250 for d and solve for t.

$t = \frac{\sqrt{1250}}{4}$, $t \approx 8.84$ seconds. (calculations were done on a calculator)

If an object takes 12 seconds to reach the ground, we can calculate the height it was dropped. Substitute 12 for t and solve for d.

$12 = \frac{\sqrt{d}}{4}$

48 = $\sqrt{d}$

$(48)^2 = (\sqrt{d})^2$

2,304 feet = d

Mary and Janet start at the same location and go for a walk. Mary walks north at 5 miles per hour and Janet walks east at 4 miles per hour. How far apart are they after 2 hours?

Solution:

After 2 hours Mary walks 10 miles and Janet walks 8 miles.

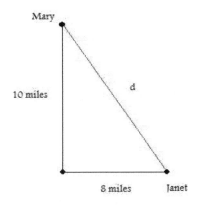

The graph shows their relative locations after 2 hours. The distance d can be found by using the fact that in a right triangle $a^2 + b^2 = c^2$, where c is the hypotenuse (side opposite the right angle) of the triangle.

Therefore,

$d^2 = 10^2 + 8^2$

$d^2 = 100 + 64$

$d^2 = 164$

$d \approx 12.8$ miles

We can also solve the above by using the **distance formula**, which states for any two points (x_1, y_1) and (x_2, y_2),

$d = \sqrt{[(x_2 - x_1)^2 + (y_2 - y_1)^2]}$

Think of Mary's location as (x_1, y_1) and Janet's location as (x_2, y_2). We label their starting location as the origin, $(0, 0)$. Then Mary's location is $(0, 10)$ and Janet's location is $(8, 0)$.

$d = \sqrt{[(10 - 0)^2 + (0 - 8)^2]} = \sqrt{164} \approx 12.8$ miles

Glossary

Absolute value – The absolute value of a number is the distance between that number and zero on a number line. For example, the absolute value of 3, noted as |3| = 3 and |-3| = 3. Absolute value is always positive or zero since distance is not measured as a negative number. In general, if $x \geq 0$, $|x| = x$. If $x < 0$, $|x| = -x$.

Absolute value function – A function that is defined by $f(x) = |x|$. The domain of the function is all real numbers and the range is all real numbers greater than or equal to zero.

Algebraic expression – An algebraic expression is a combination of numbers and/or variables mixed with mathematical operations such as addition, subtraction, multiplication, division, radicals and raising to exponents. Examples of algebraic expressions are $3x + 10$, $\sqrt{(x - 3)}$ and $5x^2 - 2x + 6$.

Algebraic term – An algebraic term is a number, variable or multiplication of numbers and variables raised to a exponent. Examples of algebraic terms are 14, $12xy$, $-3x^2y^3$ and $(1/2)xyz^3$.

Associative property of addition – The associative property of addition allows the grouping of numbers in an addition problem in any way without changing the result. If x, y and z are real numbers, then $(x + y) + z = x + (y + z)$.

Associative property of multiplication - The associative property of multiplication allows the grouping of numbers in a multiplication problem in any way without changing the result. If x, y and z are real numbers, then $(xy)z = x(yz)$.

Asymptote – When a graph approaches a line and never crosses it, the line the graph approaches is called an asymptote.

Base - The base of an exponential expression is the number or variable being raised to a certain power. For example, in an exponential expression in the form of x^n, x is the base.

Binomial – A binomial is a polynomial with 2 terms. Examples of binomials are $3x - 8$, $2x^2 + 17$ and $5x^2y^2z^4 + 16xyz^3$.

Coefficient – A coefficient is the number that is multiplied by the variable. It always appears to the left of the variable. In the expression $x^3 + 3x^2 - 15x + 30$, the coefficients are 1, 3, -15 and 30. Note that 30 can be thought of as $30x^0$ since $x^0 = 1$, so the coefficient of $30x^0$ is 30.

Combined variation – A combination of direct and inverse variation . For example, suppose y is directly proportional to z and inversely proportional to x. Then $y = kz/x$.

Combining like terms – Adding and subtracting algebraic terms that have the same variables raised to the same power. When combining like terms, keep the variables and exponents the same while adding the coefficients.

Commutative property of addition – The commutative property of addition allows adding real numbers in any order without affecting the result. In general, for real numbers x and y, $x + y = y + x$.

Commutative property of multiplication - The commutative property of multiplication allows the multiplication of real numbers in any order without affecting the result. In general, for real numbers x and y, $xy = yx$.

Common denominator – A common denominator is when two or more fractions have the same denominator. When adding and subtracting fractions, they must have a common denominator.

Common factor - A common factor is a factor that is common in two or more terms. For example, a common factor of 4, 18 and $36xy$ is 2 since 2 is a factor of each term.

Complex fraction - Also known as a complex rational expression, a complex fraction is a fraction whose numerator and denominator contain rational expressions. Examples of complex fractions are

$$\frac{\frac{3xy}{x}}{\frac{4}{7y}}, \qquad \frac{\frac{2x-5}{4y}}{\frac{7x+1}{9y}}, \qquad \frac{\frac{4x^2+9x-11}{x+8}}{\frac{6x+11}{x^2y^3}}$$

Composite number – A number that is greater than 1 that is not a prime number is known as a composite number. A composite number can also be thought of as any number that has more than 2 factors. For example, 4 is a composite number because the factors of 4 are 1, 2 and 4.

Compound inequality – A statement of two inequalities joined with the word *and*. Examples of compound inequalities are $x > 6$ and $x < -2$, $3x - 1 \geq 4$ and $x < -6$, $6x - 1 > 2$ and $5x + 3 \leq 9$.

Consistent system - A system of equations that has a solution. An example of a consistent system is

$$x + y = 5$$
$$y = 4$$

In this system, $y = 4$ and $x = 1$.

Constant - A number in an equation that remains the same no matter what the change is in the variable. In the equation $Ax + By = C$, A, B and C are constants and x and y are the variables. In an equation $x + 3y + 2 = 0$, 3 and 2 are constants.

Constant of variation – In direct variation ($y = kx$), inverse variation ($y = k/x$), and joint variation ($y = kxz$), $k > 0$, k is known as the constant of variation.

Coordinate(s) – A number or numbers representing a point on a number line or a point on a rectangular coordinate system. For example, a point located on a rectangular coordinate system at $x = 4$ and $y = 5$ is represented as (4, 5). The coordinates are 4 and 5.

Cross multiplication – Also known as cross product. In a proportion, the numerator of the first fraction multiplied by the denominator of the second fraction equals the denominator of the first fraction multiplied by the numerator of the second fraction. In the following proportion

$\frac{a}{b} = \frac{c}{d}$, $\quad ad = bc$. Using cross multiplication is useful to help in solving proportions. For example,

$\frac{3}{x} = \frac{7}{9}$. $\quad 7(x) = 3(9)$, $\quad 7x = 27$ and $x = \frac{27}{7}$.

Cube root – The cube root of number x is any number when multiplied by itself 3 times equals x. For example, the cube root of 8 is 2 because $2(2)(2) = 8$ or $2^3 = 8$. In general, the cube root of x is denoted as $^3\sqrt{x}$. It's defined as $^3\sqrt{x} = y$, if $y^3 = x$.

Cube root function - A function defined by the equation $f(x) = {}^3\sqrt{x}$. It is a member of a larger group of functions called radical functions. The cube root function may be translated k units up or down. The function is then defined by the equation $f(x) = {}^3\sqrt{x} + k$ or $f(x) = {}^3\sqrt{x} - k$. The function may be translated h units left and right. It is then defined by the equation $f(x) = {}^3\sqrt{(x+h)}$ or $f(x) = {}^3\sqrt{(x-h)}$.

Cubing function - A function that is defined as $f(x) = x^3$. The domain and range of the cubing function is all real numbers.

Degree of a polynomial – The degree of a polynomial is the degree of the term in the polynomial with the highest degree. The degree is determined by the sum of the highest power of each variable. For example, the degree of $3x^3y^2$ is 5 because the sum of the exponents of x and y is 5.

Denominator – The number, term or expression under the bar in a fraction or rational expression.

Dependent equations – Two equations with the same graph. The equations will also be the same when simplified. For example, $2y + 4x = 10$ and $6y + 12x = 30$ are dependent equations. Each can be simplified to $y + 2x = 5$.

Difference of two cubes – If x and y are both perfect cubes, then $x^3 - y^3 = (x - y)(x^2 + xy + y^2)$.

Difference of two squares – If x and y are both perfect squares, the $x^2 - y^2 = (x - y)(x + y)$.

Direct variation – If $y = kx$, where k is a nonzero constant, then y is said vary directly with x or y is directly proportional to x.

Distance formula – The distance between any two ordered pairs (x_1, y_1) and (x_2, y_2) is given by the formula $d= \sqrt{[(x_2 - x_1)^2 + (y_2 - y_1)^2]}$.

Distributive property of multiplication - If x, y and z are real numbers then $x(y + z) = xy + xz$. The distributive property allows us to remove parentheses when an expression is multiplied. Basically, the quantity outside the parentheses is multiplied by each term inside the parentheses.

Division property by one - For any real number n, n divided by 1 equals n.

Division property by itself – For any real number n, n divided by n equals 1.

Division property of radicals - Division of a radical expression is the same as dividing the radical in the numerator in the expression by the radical in the denominator of the expression.

In other words, if $\sqrt[n]{x}$ and $\sqrt[n]{y}$ are real numbers, then

$$\sqrt[n]{(x/y)} = \frac{\sqrt[n]{x}}{\sqrt[n]{y}}.$$

Domain of a function – All the possible input values of a function. The domain is all real numbers for non-rational and non-radical functions. For rational functions, the domain is all values for where the denominator is defined. The domain of a rational function is found by setting the denominator equal to zero and solve for the variable. The domain is all values except where the denominator equals zero. For radical functions, the domain is all real numbers if the radical has an odd index. If the radical has an even index, the domain is all values for which the expression under the radical is greater than or equal to zero.

Double inequality – An inequality with two inequality symbols. Examples of double inequalities are $-4 < 3x \le 8$ and $10 \le 5x + 2 < 20$.

Elimination method – Also known as the addition method, it is used to solve systems of equations. In the elimination method, the equations or multiples of the equations in the system are added together to eliminate one of the variables.

Equation – A mathematical sentence with an = sign. Equations show that the relationship between quantities are equal. Types of equations include dependent, exponential, independent, linear, radical and rational, among others.

Even integers – Integers that are divisible by 2. The set of even integers is {....., -8, -6, -4, -2, 0, 2, 4, 6, 8, ...}.

Even root – When n is an even number greater than 0 and x is greater than 0, then $\sqrt[n]{x}$ is an even root. For example the 4th root of 16 is an even root noted as $\sqrt[4]{16}$.

Exponents – They make writing products of repeated numbers, variables or terms simpler and in a more compact form. If n is a real number, then x^n equals n factors of x multiplied together and n is referred to as the exponent. For example, $x^4 = x \cdot x \cdot x \cdot x$. The exponent is 4.

Exponential expression – If x is a variable and n is an exponent, then x^n is an exponential expression. The exponential expression is read as "x to the nth power" or "x raised to the nth power".

Extraneous solution – False solutions that occur when multiplying an equation by a variable or term to eliminate a denominator. For example,

$$\frac{x + 5}{x - 2} = \frac{3x + 1}{x - 2}$$

Notice that $x \neq 2$ because it will give a 0 in the denominator. When multiplying the equation by $(x - 2)$ to clear the denominators, we get $x + 5 = 3x + 1$. Solving for x, we get $x = 2$. But we know $x \neq 2$, therefore it is an extraneous solution.

Factor – A factor is a number, term or polynomial that divides evenly into another number, term or polynomial. For example 2 is a factor of 6 since 2 times 3 equals 6. A factor of $x^2 y$ is y since y divides evenly into the term. A factor of $x^2 - 4$ is $(x + 2)$ since it divides evenly into $x^2 - 4$.

Factoring – Methods by which polynomials can broken down into a product in simplest form. For example, the polynomial $x^2 + 5x + 6$ can be factored into $(x + 3)(x + 2)$.

Factor by grouping - A method of factoring where terms in a polynomial are grouped according to terms that have a common factor. Generally factoring by grouping is used when there are 4 terms and there are no terms in common among all 4 terms. If we wish to factor $x + ax + y + ay$, group $(x + ax)$ and $(y + by)$ and factor each separately. Therefore $x(1 + a) + y(1 + a) = (x + y)(1 + a)$ is the result of factoring by grouping.

First degree equations – Also known as linear equations, first degree equations are equations in which the highest exponent of the variable is 1. For example, $3x + 10 = 18$ is a first degree equation.

FOIL method – A method used to multiply two binomials. FOIL stands for First, Outer, Inner and Last. It is the order in which we multiply terms. For example, multiply $(2x + 5)(x + 4)$ by the FOIL method:
First terms = $2x(x)$
Outer terms = $2x(4)$
Inner terms = $5(x)$
Last terms = $5(4)$

Then add like terms to simplify.

Fraction – A fraction indicates part of a whole. To represent 1 part out of 4, it can be written in terms of the fraction ¼. The top part of the fraction is known as the numerator and the bottom part of the fraction is known as the denominator.

Fundamental property of fractions – If x, y and a are real numbers where $y \neq 0$ and $a \neq 0$, then

$$\frac{x}{y} = \frac{x \cdot a}{y \cdot a}.$$

The property shows that common factors, in this case a, can be divided out. This is useful for simplifying rational expressions.

Function – An association between a set of input values known as the domain and a set of output values known as the range. Exactly one output value in the range is assigned to each input value in the domain. For example, if the domain is the x variable and the range is the y variable, then the following table represents a function.

x	y
1	3
2	5
3	6

The following would not represent a function because there are 2 different y values for the x value of 2.

x	y
2	4
3	6
2	-2
5	9

General form of equation of a line - The general form is a linear equation written in the form $Ax + By = C$, where x and y are variables and A, B and C are numbers known as constants. This is also known as standard form.

Greatest common factor (GCF) – The largest number or monomial that divides evenly into a number or monomial. For example, the greatest common factor of 12, 24 and 36 is 12 since 12 is the largest number that divides evenly into all 3 numbers. The greatest common factor of $4x^2y$, $8x$ and $36xy$ is $4x$ since $4x$ is the largest monomial that divides evenly into all 3 monomials.

Horizontal asymptote - When a graph approaches a horizontal line, the line is called a horizontal asymptote. For example, in a rectangular coordinate system with an x-axis and y-axis, if a graph approaches the line $y = 2.5$, then $y = 2.5$ is a horizontal asymptote.

Horizontal axis – In a rectangular coordinate system, the horizontal axis is the line the passes left and right through the center of the graph. If the points on the graph are in the form (x, y) then the horizontal axis is also known as the x- axis.

Hypotenuse – In a right triangle, the hypotenuse is the side opposite the right angle. It's always the longest side of a right triangle.

Identity property of addition - Also known as *additive identity*, states that the sum of any number and 0 is the number itself. If n is a number, then $n + 0 = n$.

Identity property of multiplication – Also known as *multiplicative identity*, states that the product of any number and 1 is the number itself. If n is a number, then $n \cdot 1 = n$.

Improper fraction – A fraction in which the numerator is larger than the denominator. Examples of improper fractions are 11/8, 6/5 and 8/3.

Inconsistent system – A system of equations that has no solution. This occurs when the lines in a single plane are parallel because parallel lines do not intersect.

Independent equations – Equations that have different graphs. The only equations that will not have different graphs are those that are identical.

Inequality – A statement which related two quantities that are not equal. Examples of inequalities include $x < 6$, $y > 4$, $2x \le 11$, $5y \ge -15$, $x \ne 7$.

Index - The small number in the upper left hand corner on the outside of the radical sign. If n is a real number in the radical $\sqrt[n]{x}$, then n is the index of the radical and is called the *nth root of x*.

Inequality symbols – The symbols used to show that two quantities are not equal. The inequality symbols are
$\ne$ meaning not equal
$>$ meaning greater than
$<$ meaning less than
$\le$ meaning less than or equal to
$\ge$ meaning greater than or equal to

Infinity – Refers to an indefinite quantity. The symbol used for infinity is ∞.

Integer – A whole number or negative whole number. The set of integers is {....,-4, -3, -2, -1, 0, 1, 2, 3, 4, ...}.

Intercept – Where a line intersects an axis. The x-intercept is where a line intersects the x-axis and the y-intercept is where a line intersects the y-axis.

Intersection – The intersection of two sets are the elements that are found in both sets. Intersection is noted by the symbol ∩. For example, if set A = {1, 2, 3} and set B = {2, 4,6} then $A \cap B$ = {2}.

Interval – The graph of a set of real numbers that is part of a number line. Intervals can be bounded or unbounded. An unbounded interval extends to infinity or negative infinity. A bounded interval does not include infinity or negative infinity. Closed intervals contain both endpoints are represented as [a, b]. Open intervals do not contain either endpoint and are represented as (a, b). Half open intervals are open on one end and closed on the other and are represented as (a, b] or [a, b).

Inverse property of addition – Also known as the additive inverse property, for every real number n, there is a number $-n$ so that $n + (-n) = 0$. For example, $3 + (-3) = 0$.

Inverse property of multiplication - Also known as the multiplicative inverse property, for every real number n, where $n \neq 0$, there is a number $1/n$ such that $n(1/n) = 1$. For example, $7(1/7) = 1$.

Inverse variation – If y varies inversely with x or y is inversely proportional to x, then $y = k/x$ for a non zero constant, k.

Irrational number – A number that cannot be expressed in the form of a ratio or fraction. It is a number that is a non repeating and non terminating decimal. Examples of irrational numbers include $\sqrt{2}$ and π.

Joint variation – The type of variation where one variable varies directly with the product of two or more variables. If y varies jointly with w and x, then $y = kwx$, where k is a non zero constant.

Leading coefficient - The coefficient of the term with the highest exponent. For example, in the polynomial $3x^2 + 5x - 6$, the leading coefficient is 3 since 3 is the coefficient of the leading term $3x^2$.

Lowest common denominator - Also known as least common denominator or LCD, is the smallest denominator in common between two or more rational expressions. We find the lowest common denominator in problems where we need to add or subtract rational expressions with unlike denominators.

Like radicals - Radicals that have the same radicand and same index are like radicals. For example, $\sqrt{2x}$ and $3\sqrt{2x}$ are like radicals as are $\sqrt[4]{5y}$ and $6\sqrt[4]{5y}$ but $\sqrt{3}$ and $\sqrt{8x}$ are not like radicals.

Like terms – Also known as similar terms, are terms that have the same variables raised to the same power. For example $2x$ and $4x$ are like terms, as are $5y^2$ and $-9y^2$, but $13xy$ and $-4x^3$ are not like terms.

Linear equations – Equations that can be written in the form $ax + b = c$, where x is a variable and a,b and c are constants and $a \neq 0$. These equations are represented on a graph by a line.

Mathematical model - The description of a problem using an equation and other mathematical concepts.

Mathematical operation - A calculation by mathematical methods which include addition, subtraction, multiplication, division, raising a number to an exponent and taking absolute value.

Midpoint – The point that lies midway between two other points. If a segment has endpoints (x_1, y_1) and (x_2, y_2), then the midpoint of the segment is $[(x_1 + x_2)/2 , (y_1 + y_2)/2]$.

Mixed number – A whole number and a proper fraction added together. For example, 5 ¼ is a mixed number because it is the sum of the whole number 5 and the proper fraction ¼.

Monomial – A polynomial with one term. Examples of monomials are 2, $4x$, $6x^2$ and $-3x^2y^3z^5$.

Multiplication property of radicals – If $\sqrt[n]{x}$ and $\sqrt[n]{y}$ are real numbers, then $\sqrt[n]{(xy)} = \sqrt[n]{x} \cdot \sqrt[n]{y}$. For example, $\sqrt{100} \cdot \sqrt{4} = 10 \cdot 2 = 20$. Likewise, $\sqrt{(100 \cdot 4)} = \sqrt{400} = 20$.

Natural numbers – The numbers that are used in counting. The set of natural numbers are $\{1, 2, 3, 4, 5, ...\}$.

Negative exponents – If $x \neq 0$ and n is an integer, then $\dfrac{1}{x^{-n}} = x^n$. For example, $x^{-4} = \dfrac{1}{x^4}$.

Negative reciprocals – Two numbers whose product is -1. For example, 2 and -1/2 are negative reciprocals. The slopes of perpendicular lines are negative reciprocals.

Nonlinear function - A function which is not represented graphically by a straight line. Some examples of nonlinear functions are $f(x) = 3x^2$, $f(x) = x^3$ and $f(x) = |x|$.

Numerator - The number, term or expression above the bar in a fraction or rational expression.

Odd root - The expression $\sqrt[n]{x}$, when n is an odd natural number greater than one. For example, $\sqrt[3]{-27} = -3$.

Open interval - An interval with endpoints a and b, which does not contain either endpoint. It is represented as (a, b).

Order of operations – The method in which to evaluate expressions with more than one operation. The order of operations is as follows: Perform all the operations inside the parentheses and other grouping symbols such as brackets and absolute value. Next evaluate exponents. Perform multiplication and division from left to right, then addition and subtraction from left to right.

Ordered pair – The order in which coordinates of a point are listed. The point (4, 6) and (6, 4) are not the same. That is why it is called an ordered pair since the order the points are listed is important. Generally an ordered pair is used to show a position on a rectangular coordinate system.

Origin – The point at which the axes cross on a rectangular coordinate system. This point is represented as the ordered pair (0, 0). On a number line the origin is labeled 0.

Parabola – The graph of the squaring function, $f(x) = x^2$ or any form of the function such as those that are translated vertically or horizontally. For example, $f(x) = (x + 2)^2$ and $f(x) = (x - 4)^2 + 2$ are also parabolas.

Parallel lines – Lines that do not intersect. Parallel lines have the same slope.

Perfect cubes – Numbers which have a cube root that is a whole number. For example, 64 is a perfect cube since the cube root of 64 is 4.

Perfect squares – Numbers which have a square root that is a whole number. For example, 81 is a perfect square since the square root of 81 is 9.

Perfect square trinonmial - A trinomial which is the square of a single factor. For example, $x^2 + 10x + 25$ is a perfect square trinomial because it is the square of $(x + 5)$.

Perpendicular lines – Lines whose intersection forms a right angle. Perpendicular lines have slopes that multiply to -1.

Point-slope form – The equation of the line that passes through the point (x_1, y_1) with slope m is $y - y_1 = m(x - x_1)$. The equation $y - y_1 = m(x - x_1)$ is called the point-slope form of the line.

Polynomial – An algebraic term or many terms added together whose variables have exponents that are whole numbers. A polynomial never has a variable in the denominator.

Power of x – The expression x^n, read as x to the nth power, is known as a power of x.

Power rule – If x and y and n are real numbers and $x = y$, then $x^n = y^n$.

Prime factored form – A number that has been factored into only prime numbers. For example, the prime factored form of 48 is $2 \cdot 2 \cdot 2 \cdot 2 \cdot 3$.

Prime number – A number whose only factors are 1 and itself. For example, 7 is a prime numbers since the only factors of 7 are 1 and 7. But 8 is not a prime number since its factors are 1,2, 4 and 8.

Principal square root – The positive value of the square root. For example, $\sqrt{4} = 2$ and -2, but the principal square root is only 2.

Product rule for exponents – If a and b are integers, then $x^a \cdot x^b = x^{(a+b)}$. For example, $x^5 \cdot x^3 = x^8$.

Proper fraction – A fraction where the numerator is smaller than the denominator.

Proportion – An equation showing that two fractions or ratios are equal. For example, $2/3 = 4/x$ is a proportion.

Quadrant – One of the four regions of the rectangular coordinate system. The quadrants are named with Roman numerals starting with I and increasing counterclockwise to II, III and IV.

Quotient rule for exponents – If x, m and n are integers and $x \neq 0$, then $\dfrac{x^m}{x^n} = x^{(m-n)}$

Radical equation – An equation which contains a radical expression with a variable in the radicand. The radicand is the expression under the radical symbol. Examples of radical equations include $\sqrt{(x+4)} = 10$ and $\sqrt{x} = 121$.

Radical expression - An expression containing a radical. Examples of radical expressions include $\sqrt{(3x+4)}$ and $\sqrt[3]{(4x+9)}$.

Radical function – A function which contains a radical expression. Common radical functions include square root and cube root functions.

Radical symbol – The symbol $\sqrt{}$, which represents the square root of a number or expression. If n is a positive integer greater than 2, then $\sqrt[n]{}$ represents the nth root of a number or expression.

Radicand – The number or expression under the radical symbol. For example, in the radical expression $\sqrt{(5x^2 + 3x)}$, the radicand is $5x^2 + 3x$.

Range – The set of output values of a function. Exactly one value in the range is assigned to each value of the domain.

Rational equation – An equation with one or more rational expressions. Some examples of rational equations are

$$\frac{(x+3)}{4y} + \frac{5}{6} = 0 \quad , \qquad \frac{(3x^2 + 5x + 2)}{2x + 3} + \frac{2x}{3} = \frac{7}{3x} \quad \text{and} \quad \frac{(9x-4)}{12x} = \frac{(4x+3)}{(3-4x)}$$

Rational expression – A ratio of two polynomials. A rational expression is written as a fraction. Some examples of rational expressions are

$$\frac{2x}{3} + \frac{5}{4x}, \qquad \frac{(a-2b+c)}{(a+3c)} \quad \text{and} \quad \frac{(6y^2 - 2y + 5)}{(3y^2 + y - 2)}$$

Rational function – A function whose equation is a rational expression in a single variable and the value of the denominator cannot equal zero. For example,

$$f(x) = \frac{(3x+7)}{(x-2)} \quad \text{is a rational function, where } x \neq 2.$$

Rationalize the denominator – A process by which we remove a radical from the denominator of a radical expression. The radical is replaced by a rational number. For example, if the denominator of a radical expression is $\sqrt{3}$, we rationalize by multiplying the numerator and denominator by $\sqrt{3}$. This will eliminate the radical in the denominator since $\sqrt{3} \cdot \sqrt{3} = 3$.

Rational number – A number that can be expressed as a fraction. Some examples of rational numbers are 14, $\frac{2}{3}$, $\frac{-17}{4}$ and 23.6.

Ratio – The quotient of quantities with the same units. If x and y are numbers, then the ratio of x to y is $\frac{x}{y}$. This ratio can also be represented as $x:y$.

Real number – The set of all rational and irrational numbers are real numbers. All the points on a number line as well as all points on a rectangular coordinate system are real numbers.

Reciprocals – If the product of two numbers is 1, the numbers are said to be reciprocals of each other. For example $2 \cdot \frac{1}{2} = 1$, therefore 2 and $\frac{1}{2}$ are reciprocals of each other.

Rectangular coordinate system – A grid made up of intersecting perpendicular number lines. The grid is used to plot ordered pairs, graph linear equations, nonlinear equations, rational and radical functions. The horizontal axis is generally called the x-axis and the vertical axis is generally known as the y-axis.

Repeating decimal – Decimal values where all the numbers or a set of numbers in the decimal repeat. Some examples of repeating decimals are 0.66666......, 0.454545....., 0.181818..... and 0.222222......

Scientific notation – A method to write very small or very large numbers in a more concise form. If $1 \leq N \leq 10$ and n is an integer, then $N \times 10^n$ represents an integer. Some examples of numbers written in scientific notation are 3×10^4, 6.42×10^{-2} and 8.19×10^2.

Set – The collection of numbers is known as a set. Members of a set are generally written inside braces { } with a comma separating them. An example of a set is {1, 2, 3, 4, 5}.

Slope-intercept form – If an equation of a line displays the slope and y-intercept it is said to be in slope-intercept form. The equation of a line with slope m and y-intercept (0, b) is $y = mx + b$.

Slope – The slope of a line is the amount of slant that a line has. It is often noted as the rate of change. If a line contains the points (x_1, y_1) and (x_2, y_2), then the slope is defined as the rate of change of y divided by the rate of change of x. If m is defined as the slope, then

$$m = \frac{(y_2 - y_1)}{(x_2 - x_1)}$$

The slope is undefined if $x_1 = x_2$.

Square root – The opposite of squaring a number. A number a is the square root of b if $a^2 = b$. The square root of b is noted as $\sqrt{b}$. For example, $4^2 = 16$, therefore the $\sqrt{16} = 4$.

Square root function – A function whose equation contains a square root. The basic square root function is defined as $f(x) = \sqrt{x}$, for $x \geq 0$.

Squaring function – The function defined as $f(x) = x^2$.

Substitution method – A method used to solve a system of linear equations in two variables. An example of the substitution method is shown in the following system

$x + y = 10$
$2x + y = 12$

Solve the first equation for y to get $y = 10 - x$ and substitute $10 - x$ in the second equation to get $2x + (10 - x) = 12$. Therefore $x + 10 = 12$ and $x = 2$.

Substitute 2 back into the first equation for x and solve for y. Therefore, $2 + y = 10$ and $y = 8$.

Sum of two cubes - If x and y are both perfect cubes, then $x^3 + y^3 = (x + y)(x^2 - xy + y^2)$.

Symbols of inequality – Symbols that represent quantities that are not equal. The symbols of inequality are "$<$" for less than, "$>$" for greater than, "$\leq$" for less than or equal to, "$\geq$" for greater than or equal to and $\neq$, for not equal.

System of equations – Two or more equations or inequalities. The solution of a system of two equations with two variables is the point of intersection. The solution of a system of three equations with three variables is the plane of intersection. The solution for a system of inequalities with two or more variables is the area of intersection.

Terminating decimal – A decimal which ends and can be written as a fraction. Therefore, a terminating decimal is a rational number. Some examples of terminating decimals are 3.45, -14.2 and 0.15.

Translation – Shifts that occur in a graph. Translations can be vertical, horizontal or both. For example, the graph of the function $f(x) = x^2 + k$ is the same as the graph of $f(x) = x^2$ except that it is translated k units up. The graph of $f(x) = x^2 - k$ is the same as the graph of $f(x) = x^2$ except that it is translated k units down. The graph of the function $f(x) = (x - h)^2$ is the same as the graph of $f(x) = x^2$ except that it is translated h units to the right. The graph of the function $f(x) = (x + h)^2$ is the same as the graph of $f(x) = x^2$ except that it is translated h units to the left.

Trinomial – A polynomial with three terms. Some examples of trinomials are $5x^2 + 6x - 9$, $-2a^2b^2 + 4ab - b^2$ and $14xyz + 13x^2y^2 + 20z^4$.

Unbounded interval – An interval which extends in either or both directions infinitely. Examples of unbounded intervals include $(3, \infty)$, $[3, \infty)$, $(-\infty, 9)$, $(-\infty, 9]$ and $(-\infty, \infty)$.

Union – The union of two sets are the elements that are in either or both sets. Union is represented by the symbol U. For example, is set $A = \{1, 2,3, 4\}$ and set $B = \{2,4,6,8\}$ then $A \cup B = \{1,2,3,4,6,8\}$.

Variable – A letter representing an unknown quantity.

Vertical line test – A method to determine whether or not a relation is a function. If a vertical line can be drawn that intersects the graph of the relation at more than one point, then the graph does not represent a function.

x- axis - The horizontal number line on the rectangular coordinate system.

x- coordinate – The first number in an ordered pair on a rectangular coordinate system with axes x and y. For example, the x-coordinate in the ordered pair (2, 5) is 2.

x- intercept – The point where the graph intersects the x- axis, represented as $(a, 0)$.

y- axis – The vertical number line on the rectangular coordinate system.

y- coordinate - The second number in an ordered pair on a rectangular coordinate system with axes x and y. For example, the y- coordinate in the ordered pair (3, -1) is -1.

y- intercept – The point where the graph intersects the y- axis, represented as $(0, b)$.

Zero exponent – If $x \neq 0$, the $x^0 = 1$.

Made in the USA
Lexington, KY
10 January 2016